A Radical Lawyer in Victorian England

W. P. Roberts and the struggle for workers' rights

RAYMOND CHALLINOR

I.B. TAURIS & Co Ltd
Publishers
London

Published by
I.B.Tauris & Co Ltd
110 Gloucester Avenue
London NW1 8JA

British Library Cataloguing in Publication Data

Challinor, Raymond
    A radical lawyer in Victorian England : W. P. Roberts
    and the struggle for workers' rights.
    1. England. Law. Roberts, William Prowting, 1806–1871
    I. Title
    344.2′0092′4

ISBN 1 85043 150 7

Typeset by Columns Design & Production Services Ltd, Reading
Printed in Great Britain by Redwood Press Limited, Melksham, Wiltshire

A Radical Lawyer in Victorian England

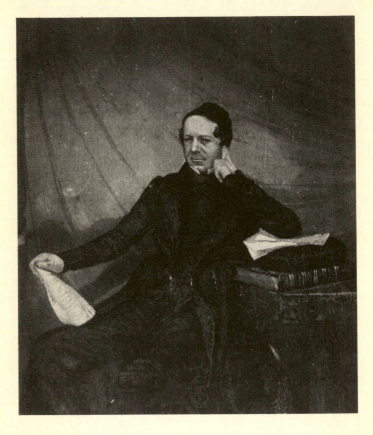

William Prowting Roberts, the miners' attorney, who fought many legal battles in Lancashire. This portrait of him was issued by the *Northern Star*.

Contents

List of Illustrations

Preface

My interest in W. P. Roberts was kindled many years ago. When, in 1966, I was doing the research, along with Brian Ripley, for a book on the history of the Miners' Association, the first pitmen's trade union, it struck me that he was a colourful personality, an individual who had a significant impact on his time which historians have neglected.

I thought a life of W. P. Roberts could also help to supply fresh insights into both Chartism and the rise of trade unionism. In particular, it could deal with the methods used by the state – many of them employed right down to the present day – to defeat, or tame, working-class movements.

My task has been a long and arduous one. It has resembled running an obstacle race, with the painful difference that it has lasted for over twenty years.

The difficulties have been big and numerous. There is virtually a complete absence of personal and legal papers. This has meant that I have had to rely, almost entirely, upon newspaper reports. These, in turn, contain their own hazards. In Victorian times many journalists, like members of the public, did not possess a good knowledge of the law. On occasions, they could make elementary mistakes, writing about a magistrate as if he were a judge or reporting a successful application for bail as if it meant the case had been won by the defence.

Another set of problems arose as a result of official obstructionism. Although the documents relate to events that, in many instances, happened more than 150 years ago, the mandarins of the British state still maintain that national security would be jeopardized if the veil of secrecy were lifted.

It is fascinating to compare government policy on this issue, the jealous way they seek to conceal certain types of information, with the apparent openness expected from the British people. At present, there is a government move to withdraw a person's traditional right to remain silent when in police custody. Why should anybody be reluctant to tell the police they have nothing to hide? But, surely, the same question can be asked in reverse. Unless some highly sinister things have been done by its agents, why should the state remain so coy? Could not glasnost be allowed to reach as far as the Public Records Office?

Mr Douglas Hurd, the former Home Secretary, argued that where a person refuses to answer questions, future courts of law should be permitted to draw whatever inferences they chose from his or her silence. This principle, however, is also capable of wider applicability. In my opinion, historians have a duty to make it clear to their readers that their work has been impoverished through having only a limited and selective access to information. They have been placed in a position very like that of a football commentator who can see only part of the pitch. They should, I think, make it plain exactly where information has been withheld and draw their own conclusions about the reasons for the subterfuge.

Let me start by saying that in the course of my research I found many gaps about state activities in relation to working-class organizations. This especially applied to Chartism in 1839, 1842 and 1848, as well as its response to the Fenians in 1867–8. Applying what I would term the Douglas Hurd principles, I conclude the reason for this is the extent to which *agents provocateurs*, dirty tricks and even downright lying were used. To admit this, may well compromise the state's ability to pose as occupying the moral high ground in similar situations today.

Of course, I may be wrong in my conclusion. I would be only too delighted if all the relevant information were made available to historians to make their independent assessements, even were these to prove me wrong. Until that does happen, I will continue to assert my position.

In my research I have been helped by W. P. Roberts' family. Before he died, Canon Roberts told me his personal recollections of his grandfather. Two other descendants, Rosemary Tucker and Charles Fitzgerald, have also been exceedingly helpful.

Over the years, innumerable people have given me assistance. To list them would almost be like reproducing a telephone directory.

However, I must single out Nick Blake and Bob Simpson, who have provided me with valuable insights into the workings of the law, and Royden Harrison and Dorothy Thompson, who have gone to immense trouble, providing me with their detailed comments. I also thank Bill and Maureen Callcott, Geoffrey Cornwall, Eddie and Ruth Frow, Dorothy Haigh, Alan Heesom, Nick Howard, Norman McCord, Antony McMurtrie, Tom Marshall, R. S. Neale, Stephen Poole, Archie Potts, Bryan Rees, Susan Scott, Bill Turner and the late Geoffrey de N. Clark, of London University, with whom I originally planned to write the biography as a joint venture.

In addition, I would like to thank Judy Mabro and Margaret Cornell for the great kindness and immense care they have shown me in preparing the manuscript for publication.

Above all, I would like to thank my wife, Mabel. Through my long travail, she has been a constant source of help and encouragement. Therefore, I would like to dedicate this biography to her, along with my son and daughter-in-law, Russell and Rebecca. They are fighting injustice in present-day society with all the determination that W. P. Roberts showed in Victorian times.

1 The Making of a Chartist

William Prowting Roberts was one of the most controversial legal figures this country has ever known. The legal battles he fought shed light on the struggles of working people in Victorian Britain to win the right to organize industrially, to secure a political voice in the running of the country, and to have a judicial system that did not operate completely against their interests. Roberts played a leading part in the Chartist movement for constitutional reform, the trade union movement and various civil rights campaigns. He became known as the People's and the Miners' Attorney-General.

W. P. Roberts' life was nothing if not eventful. Infuriated by his radical speeches, Wiltshire farmers and Tories threatened to kill him in 1838. The following year, at the battle of Devizes, after a Chartist attempt to hold a mass demonstration, an attempt on his life almost succeeded. Then came involvement, at least peripherally, with the Newport uprising and a two-year gaol sentence for his fiery public speeches. All this failed to dampen his enthusiasm. A delegate to the 1842 Chartist convention, he helped draft and present the second national petition to the House of Commons. Again, in 1848, the year of revolutions in Europe, at mass demonstrations before the presentation of the third and final Chartist petition, he appealed to the Irish rebels to make common cause with the Chartists against the British government. Even in the tranquil 1850s, he seized upon any pockets of discontent, hoping to use them to inject a little life into Chartism's ageing bones.

Yet, Roberts' enduring significance – and, for that matter, Chartism's – lay in the distinctive conception of democracy it bequeathed to subsequent working-class movements: democracy is not merely vital to their own success and well being, but should pervade the whole of society. In other words, power should reside in the hands of the masses; they should control the rulers rather than be controlled by them. Healthy impulses always arise from below; a political system, like a fish, decays from its head. To further these impulses, Roberts always backed plans that endeavoured to gain for working people greater control over their own destiny – the creation of co-operatives, the formation of friendly societies, or the securing of smallholdings, where the downtrodden town dwellers could gain a new start in life. W. P. Roberts was not only treasurer of the Chartist Land Company; he died in 1871 among his family and friends at Heronsgate, where the O'Connorville company's first settlement had been situated.

But throughout his life, his main battlefield – the arena where his greatest triumphs were recorded – was in industry, fighting for worker against employer. In 1843–5, he fought a crusade against 'the King Coal tyrants' which Frederick Engels described as unparalleled in English history. Soon afterwards he foiled an attempt to use the law to smash the engineering workers' union. An indictment, containing 4,914 counts, faced the hapless officials. His sweetest triumph, however, came almost a quarter of a century later when he succeeded in breaking the Bond, a draconian legally-binding agreement imposed by the coalowners of North East England upon their employees. In the buoyant period after this success the Durham Miners' Association was formed and endures to the present day.

While Roberts always relished the defeat of an opponent, he never believed it was simply the result of his own efforts. More important than the contribution of any one individual was the need to imbue workers with the will to struggle and organize for themselves. Only then could the victory be made secure. Unlike the new breed of moderates who emerged in the 1860s, W. P. Roberts saw no use in union leaders making friends in high places. Alexander MacDonald might dine with Lord Elcho, Scotland's biggest coalowner, and Thomas Burt, MP, might form a mutual admiration society with liberal politicians like Gladstone, but Roberts was sure this would do little to improve the workers' lot. A few months before his death, he wrote a pamphlet criticizing union leaders for welcoming the Trade Union bill then before the House of Commons. They should be less trusting, he argued, for since Parliament passed the Statute of Labourers in 1351 'hardly more than five or six years at a time have passed by without some fresh law of restraint against combinations of working men'. He believed that unity was strength, and that employers and governments had always striven to crush any such unity – and would continue to do so.

W. P. Roberts' lifelong identification with working people is difficult to explain. Born on 11 December 1806, there was little in his background and upbringing to suggest the turbulent life that lay ahead. The family belonged to the professional middle class. His father, Thomas, was vicar of Chelmsford, Essex, and subsequently master of the local grammar school there. For forty-two years, he continued in the post until his death at age seventy-three. In his later years he seems to have been losing his powers, a fact of which some pupils took advantage. Before his replacement was appointed, the parents held a public meeting and advised the governors to select a person who would give scholars an education 'applicable to the purposes of trade and commerce as practised at the present period'.

Thomas Roberts' financial position seems to have been quite modest. He began at Chelmsford Grammar School with an annual salary of £105 which was eventually increased to £210. Out of this he had to pay for the services of an assistant as well as certain school running costs, such as heating and lighting. It could well have been financial necessity that compelled Thomas Roberts to augment his income by giving private tuition and continuing at work until well into old age. He tried to ensure that all his children received a good education and a good start in life. His fifth and final son, William Prowting, arrived when he was fifty years old and was sent to a public school – Charterhouse. After an abortive start in insurance in the City of London, he trained to be a solicitor.[1]

The legal profession, then as now, was divided into two sections, barristers and solicitors. Barristers were the more prestigious, more highly paid; only they could appear on behalf of clients in the high courts. By contrast, solicitors initially saw clients and prepared briefs for the barristers to use. They could, however, appear in the lower courts, presided over by magistrates. It created a situation where solicitors were relatively badly paid – their income was normally between £200 and £300 p.a. Roberts' decision to become a solicitor may have been influenced by his father's financial position. All that was required was to undertake a comparatively inexpensive in-service training under the supervision of a qualified solicitor – W. P. Roberts appears to have done it under a certain Mr Deville – who would then report to the Law Society that a satisfactory level of competence had been attained. Once on the Law Society's register, he was at liberty to practise law. Roberts began his legal career in Bath. His premises were in Westgate Buildings, barely a respectable neighbourhood and close to the notorious Avon Street – home of the denizens of the town's underworld – which could be a further indication of stretched finances.

Even so, Roberts could at least claim to be earning a living. It made him sufficiently confident to contemplate marriage. On 29 August 1828, he wed Mary Moody, the youngest daughter of the Reverend W. Moody, of Bathampton House, Wiltshire, a descendant of Sir Henry Moody of Garsden. She bore him two children – Thomas, born in 1831, and Mary in 1834. His wife died in June 1837. Nothing more is known of the marriage; none of his personal papers from this period survived.

His career apparently started in an orthodox manner, doing ordinary run-of-the-mill cases. In politics he supported the Tories, and it was this that first brought him to the attention of the local press.[2]. One of the most talented middle-class reformers of the age – a barrister named John Arthur Roebuck – stood for Bath at the general election of 1832.[3] W. P. Roberts resolved to attend one of his meetings to fire a salvo of questions at him: What was Mr Roebuck's opinion of the national debt? Did he favour the disestablishment of the Church of England? Did he consider everybody should compulsorily pay for its upkeep? Warming to his task, Roberts attended Roebuck's next election meeting. He returned to the issue of Church tithes, and asked whether Mr Roebuck thought non-believers should be compelled to pay? He was going to inquire about Roebuck's attitude to religious education when some members of the audience, tired of Roberts' monopolizing the meeting, decided to retaliate by quizzing the inquisitor. Was it true Mr Roberts was working for Mr Foster, the Tory agent? Did he belong to Foster's election committee? Were the questions that Roberts asked actually framed by that committee? Angrily, Roberts retorted: 'What is that to you?' But this did not satisfy the audience of nearly 4,000. Amid groans, hisses and other expressions of disapprobation, the young lawyer stormed out of the meeting. The *Bath and Cheltenham Gazette* then carried a report suggesting that Roberts was using political meetings as a way of drawing attention to himself and thus gaining new legal business. Its editorial also accused him of a narrow legalistic approach. It went on to express the hope that Mr Roberts would have the gratification of seeing Mr Roebuck 'crowned with laurels and borne in the triumph of victory'.[4]

In the next few years a remarkable transformation took place in his political views. By 1837, he had emerged as one of the leading figures in the newly formed Bath Working Men's Association and for the rest of his life his allegiance remained firmly fixed to the workers' cause. It must remain largely a matter for conjecture what brought about this personal change. Probably it occurred partly as a result of changes in society, the social tensions generated by industrialization, and partly through the development of politics latent within Roberts' character.

In a study of Chartism in Bath, R. B. Pugh attaches great importance to the nineteenth-century decline of tourism, the consequence of the city's waning popularity as a health spa. This, he argues, resulted in a dwindling number of aristocrats and affluent retired people living there, and also provided fertile soil for Chartism.[5] The economic situation would also, incidentally, have had an important influence on Roberts' career prospects. When he arrived in Bath, he would have found himself competing with already well-established solicitors for a shrinking volume of business from the affluent and elderly. But another historian, Professor R. S. Neale, argues that, far from suffering economic decline, Bath experienced a great growth of wealth and enterprise during the first half of the nineteenth century. This was accompanied by increasing occupational diversity and the emergence of a strong middle class. Many of the *nouveaux riches*, like their new Member of Parliament, J. A. Roebuck, possessed radical inclinations, coupled with a distaste for the traditional Toryism of the county hierarchy. In such circumstances, an ambitious young solicitor would be subjected to push–pull forces: finding it impossible to gain clients among the old established families, he would look to the upwardly mobile, to those replete with fresh enterprise and ideas, as the main source of his livelihood.[6]

Yet, it would be wrong to think W. P. Roberts primarily acted from mercenary motives. Much more influential were the class tensions – and concomitant class injustices – that accompanied economic change. These helped to test the young lawyer's principles, to sharpen his perceptions. In 1830–1, for example, he must have been aware that his own county of Wiltshire was being severely affected by the Captain Swing riots. Agricultural labourers, suffering from seasonal unemployment because of the introduction of threshing machines, demanded an end to their use. When this appeal went unheeded, in their wrath they burnt down barns and hayricks. For a while the landowners, parsons and well-to-do farmers felt threatened. Once law and order had been restored, they unleashed an orgy of retribution upon the poor and hungry. Nationally, a total of nineteen were executed, 505 transported, 644 imprisoned, seven fined and one whipped.[7] Charles Dickens, in *Martin Chuzzlewit*, taunted the perpetrators of this repression: 'oh, magistrates, so rare a country gentleman and brave a squire, had you no duty to society before the ricks were blazing and the mobs were made?'

Another example of the law's inhumanity, its insensitivity to the sufferings of the poor, came soon after. The case of the Tolpuddle Martyrs, the six Dorsetshire agricultural labourers, sentenced in 1834 under the Unlawful Oaths Act (1797) to seven years' transportation, aroused a national outcry. They had been found guilty of administering an illegal oath to a new member of their trade union, a measure taken to preserve secrecy and thereby prevent victimization by farmers. In passing judgement, Mr Baron Williams made it plain that the underlying reason for the prosecution was the need to eradicate trade unionism entirely: 'If the men had been allowed to go on with their wicked plans, they would have ruined their masters, stagnated trade and destroyed property.'[8]

The trial took place at Dorchester, easily within travelling distance of Bath. Whether Roberts went to hear the proceedings or was involved in a professional capacity is not known. But one thing about the famous trial is certain: the treatment of the Tolpuddle Martyrs left the young solicitor with an enduring impression, for he frequently referred to Tolpuddle as the grossest act of injustice.

Undoubtedly, W. P. Roberts' personal qualities played a big role in his evolution. In part, these may have been inherited, along with his Christian names, from his maternal grandfather, William Prowting. A remarkable man who lived eighty-six years, he was revolted by man's inhumanity to man. As governor of one of the country's lunatic asylums, he had introduced a series of measures that lessened the inmates' suffering. In eighteenth century terms, he was a reforming pioneer of these grim institutions. Other factors which may have influenced W. P. Roberts' development are alluded to in Mr. Deville's report to the Law Society. The statement refers to the young man's unswerving religious faith and his firmly held belief in justice.[9] To both of these W. P. Roberts gave an unconventional twist. He believed Christianity should involve deeds, not merely words – to do unto others as one would be done by, to cultivate human fellowship, and to treat all people as God's children were beliefs deeply ingrained in his way of life. In 1647 Colonel Rainsborough declared during the Putney debates that 'even the poorest he hath a life to live.' Like him, Roberts felt passionately that everyone should have adequate food, clothing, and shelter, besides being treated with dignity and respect. As he was to tell the women of Trowbridge in 1838, 'all professing the principles of Chartism and Christianity should really, and in truth, love one another.'[10]

Similarly with the law: Roberts did not believe in mere formal equality but argued that justice should be meted out impartially to all classes in society. In nineteenth century practice, the law was a weapon used by the rich to oppress the poor, and for this reason Roberts was prepared to deploy all his legal skills in the interests of the disadvantaged. It led him along unconventional paths: whereas lawyers were beginning to assert their professionalism and independence, trying to rid themselves of the old image of pettifogging attorneys, he acquired notoriety for his courtroom histrionics. To most lawyers, this was an anathema, a relic of a hopefully bygone age. W. P. Roberts may have been a member of the profession, but he was never fully accepted by his colleagues. They remained vehemently opposed to the methods he used and the causes he espoused.

Yet, in one way, he was like many other Victorians – he was a great believer in self-improvement, particularly through education. But even here there was a significant difference between, say, his position and that put forward by Samuel Smiles in his popular book *Self-Help* (1859). While both were equally convinced of the beneficial effects accruing from the acquisition of knowledge, Roberts regarded it as quite impractical to expect someone working twelve or fourteen hours a day, not having enough to eat and living in an overcrowded slum, to be able to study. First the conditions had to be made right, then the individual and society would be improved. The Reform Bill of 1832, which gave political representation to the middle classes, had been fought for by both middle class and working class radicals. The working class reformers hoped that the next stage would be a further extension of the franchise to at least all adult males. However, beteen 1832 and 1837 they slowly realized that the middle classes and the Whig government were not going to help them.

This led to the rise of the Chartist movement, united around the six points of constitutional reform – manhood suffrage, the ballot, payment of MPs, the abolition of property qualifications for MPs, equal electoral districts, and annual Parliaments. It was an unprecedented expression of the grievances and opinions of usually inarticulate people, which awakened the slumbering talents of many of the working class. W. P. Roberts became impressed by the thirst for knowledge of his West Country compatriots. There were men like Samuel and George Bartlett (shoemakers), who had learnt to reason, state a case, argue cogently and answer critics. Nor were they alone: men like Antony Phillips (plasterer), William Potts (druggist) and William Carrier (hatter) were not over-awed when they came to address large, sometimes hostile, meetings. Most outstanding of all, however, was Henry Vincent, a printworker who, though largely self-taught, acquired an impressive knowledge of history and political thought. He came from Hull, but quickly gained popularity in the West Country. He edited the lively Chartist journal there, the *Western Vindicator*, and wherever he spoke, his fiery oratory drew large crowds. Robert Gammage, a Chartist who later wrote a history of the movement, called him 'the Demosthenes of Chartism'.

The Chartist movement in Bath did not suddenly emerge fully-grown, but developed from the struggles over local issues.[11] Campaigns against inefficiency and extravagance, bribery and corruption – not to mention the burden of regressive taxation in the form of rates – arose from the bitterly felt grievances of both middle and working classes. In the forefront of these protests stood W. P. Roberts, whose loud voice could repeatedly be heard denouncing Bath's leading citizens. In 1834, Radicals had stood in the vestry elections. They wanted to audit accounts, inspect the levying of the church rates and examine the administration of corporation property to discover what skullduggery was being committed. After the passing of the Municipal Reform Act the following year, the local MP, Roebuck, took the initiative to get a common slate of Whig and Radical candidates to fight the impending local elections. W. P. Roberts stood in Bathwick ward, a Tory stronghold, and was defeated. He made it plain that, if elected, he would vote for the abolition of the mayor's salary.[12] Many of the other candidates in the alliance repudiated this suggestion, and Roberts had a strong suspicion that many Whigs in the ward had quietly forgotten the electoral agreement and voted for his opponent.

Whig treachery, however, did not end there: those elected formed a Tory–Whig coalition. Widespread anger greeted the news that the new council proposed to reappoint the discredited old officials. W. P. Roberts chaired a stormy meeting of 800 burgesses on the question. Speakers from the floor denounced the move as a Tory plot, bitterly attacking the newly-elected councillors who had 'ratted'. Others made specific criticisms of particular officers. Still discontented, several hundred people, most of whom were mechanics, formed the Society for the Protection of Municipal & Parliamentary Rights. It unanimously resolved to inform the Home Office that eight out of the twenty individuals nominated as magistrates were unfit for office. They held unconstitutional principles, it was claimed, besides aiding and abetting jobbery in charities and city funds.[13]

The 1836 local elections equally ended in disappointment. A suspicion of corruption surrounded the election of candidates. When most of the old clique were returned, Roberts and Cox, a middle-class radical, held a meeting. It called for a reduction in the mayor's salary, the removal of daytime police, and free access to council meetings. It also agreed to send a memorial, drawn up by Roberts, to the council. This argued that corporation funds were not the property of the town council but of the burgesses, and should be used for the general benefit of all inhabitants of Bath; the salaries of all municipal officials should be related to the value to the community of their services; the council should reduce expenditure, stopping all projects of 'merely a showy or decorative character'.[14]

Roberts backed up these demands with a series of letters in the *Bath Guardian* from 19 November to 3 December 1838. He made a scathing attack on the backsliding Whig councillors, elected on one platform and then implementing another: 'The loudest in their sarcasm of the "lower orders" stood out – drunk in power and mad at the spur – the very men who but for those of the lower orders would have themselves been left in obscurity.' He claimed that experience of all parties, 'Tories, Whigs, Radicals and Trimmers', had shown that 'power Torifies a man.' Roberts' solution, therefore, was that the middle and poorer classes must, in their own interests, extract written pledges from councillors upon which it would be impossible for them to renege. In reply, Whig councillors pointed to the annual local elections as the means whereby the electorate could influence policy. To have to give specific pledges would degrade the council, making its deliberations superfluous. On the question of civic extravagance, they maintained that the office of mayor was essential to the proper and orderly functioning of local democracy.

Throughout 1837 Roberts maintained his interest in borough expenditure. Securing the post of assessor for the Bathwick ward, he went about urging ratepayers to examine the corporation books and report back to public meetings. In particular, he highlighted the exorbitant cost of the mayor's salary, treasurer's stipend, council printing and, above all, the police. He contended that there would be no need to levy a rate if the corporation's business was properly managed.[15] In January 1838, he led a deputation to the council to hand in a report outlining his proposals. The City fathers resolved to let it lie on the table, but W. P. Roberts was not easily thwarted. Two months later he returned to haunt them, having been elected as borough auditor. Fortunately for the grandees of Bath however, a legal technicality was discovered – he had temporarily lost, through an oversight, his burgess qualifications although he was still on the burgesses' roll. It was therefore impossible for him to take up the position. Even so, Roberts continued his opposition to the borough rate, calling it a 'holy cause' on behalf of the poor.

Whatever might be said against him, W. P. Roberts was a man of his word. In June 1838, accompanied by Kissock, another middle-class radical, he disrupted a meeting called to discuss how Bath should celebrate Queen Victoria's forthcoming coronation. Not only did he object to the proposed celebrations for reasons of cost, he also considered it would result in drunkenness and degradation, and thought it would be much better if they organized a day of mourning. As if to underline his contempt for the council, Roberts resolved not to pay his rates and, at the same time, to sue. His case against the City was heard at the quarter sessions in October 1838. In court he argued that property had been unfairly and inequitably assessed for rating purposes; that much of the money collected went to pay for debts incurred before the corporation came into being; and that the council had spent public money in ways not permitted by the Municipal Corporations Act. Dismissing his case, the recorder said his jurisdiction related solely to whether the rate had been properly levied. He advised Roberts to apply for a writ of mandamus at the next quarter sessions if he wished to pursue the matter further.[16]

He had every intention of doing so, but not through the courts. One of the features that characterized W. P. Roberts throughout his entire life was the manner in which he sought to speak through the courtroom window, combining the legal struggle with the struggle in the political arena. Many people in Bath felt a deep sense of anger since they considered Roberts had been denied justice at the quarter sessions by legal chicanery. The setback merely intensified their determination not to let the matter rest. Realizing this, Roberts decided to stand for election in the Lyncombe/Widicombe ward. In his election address he said that since there was no way of obtaining legal redress through the courts, he had no alternative but to fight the council's extravagances and frauds in the ballot box. He pledged that he would drastically reduce the police, the mayor's and treasurer's salaries; remove all pomp, ceremony and trappings of office; and oppose a borough rate of any kind. He added the further pledge that he would resign if asked to do so by a majority of his supporters. Once again he was disqualified, as his burgess qualification had not yet been established.

In his protracted struggle over local affairs, Roberts had touched on issues that affected many people. He gathered around himself a group of like-minded individuals, prepared to denounce what they regarded as the iniquities of the powerful and wealthy. They often harangued the crowd in the Orange Grove, an open space used for meetings, and thus became known as 'The Orange Grove Gang', prominent amongst whom was a person nicknamed 'Black Jack', for the reason explained in this newspaper poem:

The Orange Grove Gang

In Bath there's a man of very great note,
He wears a black neckerchief tied round his throat,
He walks very stiff, and laughs very queer,
And in meetings he loudly cries out 'hear, hear'.
He's feared by the Council, but liked by those who hate,
So often to pay the accursed borough rate.
Now as this said man is known very well,
Who is he our friends may be able to tell.[17]

The battles over local issues, involving as they inevitably did matters of political principle, constituted a good preparation for the rise of Chartism locally. W. P. Roberts was already a member of a group who believed that working people should have a greater influence on the general direction of the country. In August 1837 they formed the Bath Working Men's Association, the city's first specifically working-class organization. It was modelled on its London namesake which had been set up the year before and whose initiative led to the formulation of the Charter.[18] Roberts and his comrades had another advantage: Bath's strong radical tradition. This is exemplified by the influence of J. A. Roebuck. He wrote a letter of support to the inaugural meeting of the Bath Working Men's Association. He also attended the discussions in London that led to the creation of the Charter – some accounts suggest he even wrote the preamble – and he would eventually have presented the petition to Parliament had he not lost his seat in 1837. As one would expect, Roebuck had many radical supporters in Bath. On the city council there were men like Alderman James Crisp, a supporter of the reform movement since the time of 'Orator' Henry Hunt, who had been a Wiltshire farmer and prominent orator from the end of the Napoleonic wars in 1815 until the passing of the Reform Bill in 1832. Other well-known figures included Sir Charles and Colonel William Napier, both retired army officers. Besides individuals like these, affluent and influential, Bath had many radicals who were artisans, small businessmen or self-employed, able to resist the pressures and blandishments of the aristocracy. Such men regarded democracy as an essential cleansing agent for corruption and other malpractices.

From the outset, therefore, Chartism in Bath developed in highly propitious conditions.[19] Consequently, in the movement's initial phase (1838–9), its strategy appears to have been to consolidate the organization there before establishing similar branches in other urban centres, such as Devizes and Trowbridge, and then in the less hospitable, more remote rural regions. As the ground had already been well prepared, achieving the first objective was a relatively easy task. Roberts and Henry Vincent, the printworker from Hull who had become his close friend,[20] attended a succession of small meetings and tea parties held in various parts of Bath. These impressed Vincent, who had never before known a place with so many activists or such a well-developed grassroots organization. The big rallies were still more impressive. In a letter to a friend, he wrote a description of a demonstration in the Guildhall: 'Everything was got up in the most expensive style – in fact, radicalism was never so honoured in any town or city in the nation. The immense number of mechanical, middle class and wealthy ladies that were present perfectly astonished me.'[21]

This kind of well-healed radicalism had a long ancestry. For example, Major John Cartwright, who came from an old Nottinghamshire family, worked for Parliamentary reform from the publication of his pamphlet *Take Your Choice* in 1776 until his death in 1824. In this pamphlet he expounded what was later to become, in essence, the basis of the Chartist programme. It is noteworthy that his reasons for doing so could well have been spoken by W. P. Roberts sixty years on: Cartwright thought they were based on 'the well-known principles of the English constitution . . . the plain maxims of the law of nature and the clearest doctrines of Christianity'. Yet, subtly and imperceptibly with the passing of time, the same words had acquired new meanings. When Major Cartwright talked about universal suffrage, he regarded it as the ultimate goal, not an immediate demand. He wanted to use it as a bargaining weapon to gain a modest extension to the franchise. Similarly, when he called for the abolition of the property qualifications for MPs, it was not because he wanted to see working men elected to Parliament. Rather, he sought to end the overwhelming predominance of landed interests in the legislature and enable business and financial interests to have a voice there. Likewise, Major Cartwright's aim in calling for the payment of MPs was to make members more independent, lessening the influence of ministerial patronage and corruption. He had no conception of a common man entering the Commons. As Professor Albert Goodwin stated, Major Cartwright's demands were originally intended as a draft programme to be adopted by the Whig aristocracy.[22] That it was subsequently transformed into the Chartists' programme, a call for working-class democracy, is one of the ironies of history. Truth is concrete.

It remains essential to analyse precisely who said what, to whom, and under what circumstances. Remarks uttered, almost light-heartedly, to fellow Whig diners at some sumptuous repast of the privileged acquired an entirely different significance when in the 1830s they became the battle-cry of the hungry and dispossessed masses, wanting to transform society, ending the huge discrepancies of power and wealth which prevailed. And yet again, when Parliament agreed to give the vote to working men in 1867, the situation had altered once more. The mental horizons of the masses had shrunk. Instead of toppling the existing system, they were reconciled to supporting one or other of the traditional parties, the Whigs or the Tories. Ironically, as most of the Chartist demands were implemented, piece-meal fashion, far from overthrowing class society, they had helped to integrate the working class into the capitalist system.

In 1838–9, however, Roberts and Vincent rushed around from one venue to another, speaking sometimes to tea parties of young ladies, on other occasions to evening meetings of labourers. Their lives were a long round of engagements. In a letter to his friend John Minikin, Vincent described what this involved. After the Guildhall meeting on Monday, Vincent drove in Roberts' open carriage on Tuesday to a big rally at Trowbridge that ended very late. Several hundred well-wishers accompanied them to the outskirts of the town. Despite arriving back in Bath at 3 a.m., they had to be up early to drive over to Bristol to address a morning meeting.[23] As if this were not enough, they had to be back in Bath at the Guildhall by noon. There they planned to oppose the local Tories' motion that the city send a loyal address to Queen Victoria to commemorate her forthcoming coronation. As Vincent rose to speak, royalists began to yell, disregarding the Lord Mayor's call for 'order'. The meeting had to be abandoned. So the Chartists and their supporters adjourned to the Orange Grove, where Roberts addressed a large crowd on the evils and extravagances of the monarchy.

Once Chartism seemed firmly established in Bath, Bristol and Trowbridge, attention was turned to the rural hinterland, where victimization made things more difficult. Whipping up support involved much public speaking and travelling. Roberts and Vincent bore the brunt of this work. Sometimes, however, Roberts' professional duties prevented him accompanying his friend, especially when engagements were in far-distant places. Even so, he tried to be on hand at the least hint of trouble, as when Vincent, accompanied by someone called Hartwell, was campaigning in neighbouring Dorsetshire. Writing to a friend from the cottage of Thomas Standfield, one of the six Dorsetshire labourers transported from Tolpuddle, Vincent described how the Mayor of Blandford had attempted to prevent the Chartists from putting up posters to advertise their meeting. The mayor, accustomed to having his authority obeyed, could not have anticipated the response he received. Vincent pointed out that His Worship had himself broken the law by issuing a handbill for public circulation which did not contain the names of the publisher and printer. Vincent stated that this was illegal, rendering the mayor liable to a fine of £20. Deflated and annoyed, the mayor sought to prevent the meeting by requesting military intervention, but the commanding officer replied that the military would not become involved unless a breach of the peace occurred. News of the army's unwillingness to take decisive action spread hysteria, and some farmers feared they might be murdered in their sleep. They tried unsuccessfully to prevent their employees from going to the subversive assembly. Somehow, a rumour of Vincent's imminent arrest gained currency and must have reached the ears of W. P. Roberts. To everyone's surprise, he suddenly arrived at Blandford in his open carriage, accompanied by the plasterer and Chartist Anthony Phillips, presumably prepared to help out if there had been any trouble. Once assured that Vincent had not been arrested, Roberts stayed on to address the meeting. A remarkable 7,000 agricultural workers attended, despite the hostile presence of 400 farmers, parsons and landowners, including Lord Portland. According to Vincent's letter, 'Roberts took the chair and made an excellent speech.' To agricultural labourers, usually cowed and submissive, the occasion had been memorable. It showed that it was possible to defy traditional authority and succeed.[24]

By the later part of 1838, Chartism had won mass adherence. Yet, at the moment of its greatest strength, weaknesses began to appear. For the rapid and widespread success had come from a temporary alliance of two mutually antagonistic social forces. The partnership between middle-class and working-class radicalism was beginning to fall apart as their conflicting aims became apparent.

The middle-class radicals wished to improve the existing system, not to wreck it. They advocated the extension of the franchise, a more broadly-based Parliament, as a means of achieving greater political stability – merely a continuation of the process begun by the 1832 Reform Bill. But, as events unfolded, this scenario seemed more and more unrealistic for political life was becoming increasingly polarized. Whig and Tory intransigence was matched by growing Chartist extremism. Workmen mounted public platforms not to demand parliamentary reform for its own sake, but as a means to an end – the redistribution of wealth and power in society. Such a drastic change, suddenly altering the relationship of class forces, would have been as much against the interests of the middle-class radicals as of the Wiltshire landowners and farmers. Not surprisingly, as they felt threatened, their enthusiasm for Chartism waned.

The shift in attitude took many forms. Instead of being

sympathetic to Chartism, Bath City Council showed an unfriendly face. When W. P. Roberts had refused to pay his rates in 1838 and led a deputation calling on the council to reduce the police force by almost half, the council had listened carefully to his case and then cut the police by twenty-three officers. However, once property began to be threatened, the council's attitude dramatically altered – Chartists were seen as adversaries and the preservation of law and order became paramount.[25]

As with the council, likewise with individuals; no longer were the respectable and wealthy to be seen at Chartist meetings. Once they realized that the two principles of democracy and property appeared to be in conflict, they quickly allied themselves with the Tory establishment. There is no better illustration of this political transformation, or the pressures to which old-style radicals were subjected, than the case of the Napier brothers. In September 1838, Colonel William Napier, addressing a meeting in Bath, said he believed that the monarchy, House of Lords and House of Commons should be made to 'feel the controlling power of the people'. He even went on to congratulate the working class for organizing itself and not relying upon other sections of the community to provide its leadership. Taking up this theme, W. P. Roberts then spoke, endowing the idea with entirely different implications. 'This is a glorious day for the working men of this city,' he declared. 'This is a meeting of working men, and gentlemen are only admitted on sufferance.' The cheers had hardly died down before he told them: 'The present is not a struggle of party against party, but of working men against their masters.' Significantly, five months later, in February 1839, Sir Charles Napier took up the appointment of commanding officer of the army in the North of England, whose duty was to suppress any Chartist uprising. Much as the Napiers may have been critical of governmental callousness and indifference to the poor, their over-riding consideration was defence of the social order. Chartist agitation, stirring up unrest in society, could not be allowed to upset the political apple-cart.[26]

2   The Rise of Physical Force Toryism

For some time the defection of middle-class sympathizers did not affect Chartist progress, which had acquired a momentum of its own. Local organizations remained extremely busy, collecting signatures for the petition soon to be presented to Parliament. The forthcoming national Chartist convention aroused intense discussions over policy matters, as well as who should be elected to attend. At the centre of this activity was William Prowting Roberts. 'Black Jack' became a familiar figure on political platforms throughout Wiltshire. He flung himself with frenetic energy into the agitation, 'travelling up to 40 and 60 miles daily ... all at his own expense ... frequently accompanied by his brother agitators ... the consternation occasioned by the breadth and novelty of his doctrines of political freedom drove Wiltshire farmers wild.'[1] Besides the physical effort expended in speaking to large, sometimes raucous, crowds for about two hours each day, the poor condition of the roads often added an extra burden. For example, Roberts complained that on a journey from Bath to Frome, he and his friends had to alight from the carriage and push whenever they came to a hill.

All the Chartist leaders sensed they were on the brink of momentous events. The Whig government had clearly indicated its intention to resist Chartist demands and encouraged people throughout the country to take prudent precautions. In Wiltshire this meant that the Tory landowners and their allies added to their weaponry, improved surveillance and sought to use all means, both legal and illegal, to thwart Chartist aims. In response, Chartists throughout the West Country held a conference on 28 January 1839 to discuss 'the coming struggle'. The consensus appears to have been that the Charter must be won, peacefully if possible, with force if necessary. W. P. Roberts agreed with this conclusion. Stiffened resistance from the enemy camp, he thought, made a peaceful outcome unlikely. Britain's political rulers would not surrender without a fight. Nevertheless, while counselling supporters to prepare for the worst, he thought they should not be despondent. As he told a meeting at Trowbridge, the people possessed the power 'to cut off 50 crowned heads'. His remark gained added menace because some of the audience wore republican emblems while others augmented the cheering by discharging firearms. At Holt, 'Black Jack' displayed a gun, describing it as 'an elegant specimen of physical force workmanship', and advised his audience also to purchase weapons. Although poverty prevented many, some almost certainly did follow Roberts' advice. Trowbridge druggist William Potts, whom the authorities later discovered possessed an arms cache, proudly put bullets in his shop window under the label 'pills for the Tories'.[2]

This bellicose behaviour served to heighten the anxieties of the authorities. A Trowbridge magistrate wrote to the Home Secretary to inform him that the Chartists were not merely armed, they reportedly had weapons to repel cavalry. What made the situation more disturbing, continued Walter Long, who was also an MP, was the absence of reliable intelligence. He did not know whether his own farm-hands and gardeners belonged to these armed bands.[3] Behind the fear, arising from uncertainty about who could be trusted, lurked the most terrifying spectre of all for the Wiltshire hierarchy – the nightmare vision of the poor and discontented in both rural and urban areas combining to make common cause. The heavy punishments meted out to the machine wreckers and hayrick burners in 1830–1 had left an atmosphere of sullen and smouldering resentment in the countryside. Eric Hobsbawm and George Rudé, historians of the Swing riots, say 'there were whole communities that, for a generation, were shaken by the blow,' (i.e. the repression). The opportunity to settle some old scores might easily have been taken.

Equally volatile were the workers, enduring immense hardship and suffering, in the small towns and villages of Wiltshire. Many handloom weavers had worse food and clothing than inmates of workhouses. One newspaper described the plight of the 10,000 clothing workers scattered around the county, labouring from morning till night, forced to leave their children without proper care or attention. Many families, a report to the Chartist convention in 1839 stated, 'suffer so greatly from want, they do not think of tasting any meat from month to month'. In such circumstances, a highly dangerous situation existed.[4]

The Chartists endeavoured to link the struggle in remote rural communities with that in the urban centres. In their speeches, for example, they frequently referred to the grievances of agricultural labourers. Sometimes, at least temporarily, this bore fruit. Even in the normally quiet, conservative area around Warminster, a magistrate became so alarmed about Chartist activity that he wrote to the Home Office. He said there were 8,000 supporters in the neighbourhood. Moreover, at the mining village of Radstock, men had walked out on strike after hearing Chartist speakers.[5]

Events at Radstock were important because they signalled the appearance of a new phenomenon – physical force Toryism, an example of the deliberate use of violence for political ends. As such, it was much more successful than physical force Chartism. What happened at Radstock was that the Chartists George Bartlett and Antony Phillips returned to the village a couple of weeks after the strike. However, a reception committee for them had been organized, the result of spreading the word that free beer would be given to anyone who attacked the agitators. They were quickly captured and a mock trial held. One of them was released once he had foresworn all further political activity in the district. The other escaped and was nearly drowned as he tried to cross a river to evade recapture. Those sponsoring these premeditated acts of anti-Chartist violence, it later turned out, included many local dignataries, such as a colliery manager, a rector, a coalowner, a surgeon, a Poor Law overseer and a churchwarden.[6]

Confronted by creeping anarchy and mounting danger to the established order, Tory landed interests resolved to see whether, by applying 'the Radstock tactic' more extensively, they could stem the tide. Their opportunity came on 22 March 1839, when Henry Vincent, supported by two local speakers, planned to address a rally in Devizes. The primary purpose was to secure signatures from inhabitants of this pleasant market town for the Chartist petition. Almost as soon as Vincent started to speak a crowd of 'drunken farmers, lawyers' clerks and parsons', led by Under-Sheriff Tugwell, broke up the meeting. Vincent and his supporters then retired to the Curriers' Arms, where their meeting was resumed in private. The anti-Chartists, however, did not rest on their success. After a celebratory drink in the Castle Inn, they emerged 'in a state of beastly drunkenness' and marched on the Curriers' Arms, determined to sort out 'those damn Chartists'. Only the arrival of the borough magistrates prevented the situation getting further out of control. They succeeded, with considerable difficulty, in dispersing the crowd, many of whom made it a condition of their departure that the meeting also be ended.[7]

For the Chartists, the encounter was distinctly humiliating. To make amends for this, a mass demonstration in Devizes was arranged for Easter Monday (1 April).[8] A widely circulated handbill announced that Roberts and Vincent would speak and the town would be asked to adopt the Charter. To emphasise their determination to assert the right of freedom of assembly, the Chartists appealed to branches from as far away as Bath and Bristol to send contingents. A leaflet was issued stating that 'the meeting would be held in defiance of the Tory persecutors of the poor.' News of these preparations aroused intense misgivings among the notability of Devizes. Magistrates at Trowbridge and Bradford-on-Avon warned that some of the marchers might be armed. They urged their fellow magistrates in Devizes to inform the Home Office of the potentially dangerous situation, urging that precautionary measures be taken. This appears to have been done. Cavalry and yeomanry were stationed in the town and numerous special constables were sworn in.

On Easter Monday, small processions could be seen converging on Devizes from many towns and villages in Gloucestershire, Somerset and Wiltshire. By early afternoon, they had reached an assembly-point on the outskirts. It was pouring with rain. One reporter, observing the emaciated, wet and bedraggled procession as it set off, considered that 'half of them looked more fit to be the inmates of a hospital than anything else.'[9] Marching five or six abreast, 4,000 demonstrators (according to Vincent), entered Devizes; others estimated half that number. In any case, when they reached the market square, their numbers were swollen by 2,000 local inhabitants.

The Chartists pushed a waggon into a suitable position and the speakers mounted the rostrum. As soon as W. P. Roberts opened the meeting, Under-Sheriff Tugwell, in what must have been a pre-arranged signal, blew his horn. To shouts of 'Corn Law for ever', 'Church and State' and 'no bloody Whigs and radicals', farmers and their allies took the law into their own hands, meting out rough justice with rough implements. In the first salvo of stones, Vincent was knocked off the waggon, unconscious. The demonstrators, most unarmed, seemed unprepared for the fierce onslaught. In the ensuing struggle, the Chartists fought to prevent their nineteen banners from being captured or destroyed. Some changed hands several times. But it was an unequal struggle and after fifteen minutes was all over.

Events then followed very much the same pattern as those of the previous meeting. Again, the Tories repaired to the Castle Inn, where they drank three barrels of beer to celebrate their victory. Again, the battered remnants of the Chartists – those who had not scattered and fled – gathered in the Curriers' Arms. By this time, Henry Vincent had regained consciousness. He counselled them not to resort to arms. This was wise advice, for the Chartists had fewer weapons and further conflict would merely provide a pretext for the military to intervene on the Tories' side.

While W. P. Roberts concurred with Vincent's view, he did not believe they should abjectly surrender, for he had no intention of allowing an ignorant mob to silence him. Asserting the right of free speech, he flung open an upstairs window of the Curriers' Arms and began to resume his speech. Once the Tories in the Castle Inn heard what was happening, they swarmed out, vowing they would burn down the Curriers' Arms and 'the bloody reformers' inside. Whereupon the battle resumed with added intensity, and only the arrival of the high sheriff brought it to a halt. He warned that, unless everybody dispersed, he would call out the yeomanry and lancers quartered in the town. This threat had the desired effect. Fearful of the possible consequences, the demonstrators quietly left. Their leaders, however, were hauled before the authorities and asked to give a written undertaking never to return to Devizes again. A very shaken Vincent complied, but Roberts was made of sterner stuff. He told the authorities that such a document would have no legal validity and, consequently, could not be binding. A prolonged argument followed and eventually it dawned on them that they would never get such a pledge from Roberts. So they decided to escort him to the town boundaries.

News of his departure quickly spread. To the Tories, 'Black Jack' was a most notorious and hated agitator. Soon a large mob was accompanying the small escort party, with the intention of throwing him in the canal. But the magistrates, realizing that Roberts might easily be killed, took him back to the high sheriff. Roberts pleaded to be given a strong escort of lancers, otherwise 'his life would be in jeopardy'; but his entreaties seemed to leave the high sheriff unmoved. Finally, when a semblance of normality had returned, Roberts was escorted out by a back way, across the meadows and on to the road to Bath. Before they left him, he fell – or was pushed – in the town cesspool. Covered in dirt and excrement, he was told never to come to Devizes again.

In his verdict on the Devizes' disturbances, historian R. B. Pugh concludes: 'There seems little doubt that the Devizes Tories (as the anti-Chartists were collectively called) were more willing to break the peace than their opponents.'[10] This seems a fair comment. The Tories went to the demonstration prepared for violence and expecting it. According to the *Bath Journal*, farmers 'scoured the streets like bloodhounds engaging low blackguards. When these hired hooligans committed acts of brutality or assaulted respectable Liberals, who just happened to be passing, they had no need to worry. The law, which the Tories controlled, would look on with benign tolerance, only intervening later to arrest Chartists for sedition and illegal assembly.'

The *Devizes Gazette* sought to justify the conduct of the farmers and their allies. It depicted them as the town's saviours, protecting defenceless inhabitants from a marauding horde: 'Every Chartist was armed; some with pistols; a great many with carving knifes.'[11] But this seems hardly credible. Most Chartists had come for a peaceful demonstration, not a battle. If they had possessed as many weapons as claimed by the *Devizes Gavette*, they would not have been so easily or decisively defeated – nor would the defeat have been so final. Never again did they attempt to hold a mass demonstration in Devizes. The Tories, on the other hand, realized that a tough policy pays. Indeed, from then on, whenever they wanted to threaten Chartists in the West Country, they had only to say: 'remember Devizes'.

Notwithstanding its long-term tranquillizing effect, in the short run 'the battle of Devizes' was unsettling and worsened the unrest. In Trowbridge and Bradford people initially believed a rumour that Roberts and Vincent had been killed, and even when accurate details became available, they still remained incensed. Women boycotted butter brought from Devizes to their local markets. Efforts were made to prevent those individuals known to have fought against the Chartists from entering the towns. At Steeple Arkle, when farmers tried to repeat the Devizes' victory, the crowd joined forces with the Chartists. The farmers got the worst of the exchange, and retreated vowing vengeance. What made the incident more annoying for them was that one of the agricultural labourers, who had remained loyally on their side, returned home to discover his cottage had been demolished in his absence.

The Home Office received grave reports about the situation. They may have been alarmist, even fictitious, yet they were indicative of the disquiet felt in the upper echelons of society. At Trowbridge, it was said, 'the magistracy are completely cowed.' The tradesmen, 'afraid of losing the custom of the unwashed', were equally submissive while 'the town of Bradford is completely in the hands of the operatives.'[12] In the surrounding districts 'bad characters' had been intimidating farmers in a number of places. On 2 May 1839, the *Devizes Gazette* drew a remarkably similar picture. It talked about ricks being burnt; church windows smashed during services; working people withdrawing large sums from benefit societies; women behaving in a particularly violent and outrageous manner; children parading around with banners and, at one school, locking out their master. Respectable citizens were liable to be hooted at in the streets, sometimes pelted with garbage.[13]

Nevertheless, little by little, the authorities were reasserting control. By the summer of 1839, they felt sufficiently confident to go over to the offensive. The police, the law and the military were powerful weapons in their hands. But in most rural areas they could be kept as a last resort. Landowners and farmers gradually regained their dominance: in most villages the threat of ostracism, dismissal and eviction from tied cottages was sufficient to intimidate agricultural labourers. In this hostile environment, the number of Chartist meetings dwindled. At Chalfont, Samuel Harding, a Trowbridge cobbler, managed to speak for only ten minutes – telling his audience not to be afraid of the military – when he had to make an abrupt departure, unsuccessfully trying to avoid arrest by the military. At Westbury, William Potts attempted to speak despite the intimidating presence of magistrates, accompanied by 300 special constables. But he, too, was quickly arrested. When W. P. Roberts tried to act as his solicitor, this led to his arrest as well. Together they were taken, under cavalry escort, to Salisbury. Both were charged and then released.[14] Given the authorities' determination to stamp out all Chartist activities, the big question was whether Roberts and

Potts would, after their arrest at Westbury, risk incurring further official displeasure by speaking at a big rally scheduled to be held at Trowbridge the following evening. Notices had gone out to local associations over a wide area. As seven o'clock approached, a large, excited crowd gathered in Trowbridge market square. The magistrates, acting on instructions from the Home Office, were determined to stop the meeting. They had called upon the hussars from Frome and Bradford-on-Avon to reinforce the two troops of yeomanry already stationed in the town. Potts rose to address the crowd, but was immediately arrested. Whereupon Roberts jumped up to take his place. He uttered a few words before he, too, was taken into custody. Both men were charged and then released. As for the local inhabitants, they were ordered to remain indoors. Troops and police patrolled the streets. Except for an arson attempt and a police shot from an airgun, the town remained quiet.

Still more decisive and spectacular was the display of strength shown by the authorities in Bath on Whit Monday. A big Chartist rally was scheduled to take place and the forces of law and order wished to show that, even in this hot-bed of radicalism, they were now completely in control. All strategic places in the city were occupied. A troop of 200 veteran soldiers from London deployed in the New Market area. Armed police manned the post office. Two troops of hussars, brought from Frome, patrolled the streets, while 600 special constables were kept in reserve in the banqueting hall. The atmosphere of intimidation demoralized many Chartists. At the start of their march, only 300 people were present. Neither Roberts nor Vincent could address the rally for they were being kept under precautionary arrest. Far from being a demonstration of Chartist might in Bath, as Professor Neale comments, the whole exercise 'was a most impressive demonstration of the coercive power of the state.'[15]

Unable to speak to them personally, W. P. Roberts had to resort to expressing himself in writing. On 1 June 1839, the *Western Vindicator* published an open letter he had sent to the Chartists of Trowbridge. It gave them advice on what tactics they should adopt. The intimidation, he told them, had made it impossible to continue with the mass demonstrations. But if they had to forego the general excitement of the past months, the movement's organizational progress could still continue: 'we are calmer, stronger and wiser than we were six months ago.' He recommended them to 'read, mark, learn and inwardly digest' the document recently issued by the Chartist convention. This, based upon a four-point resolution, set out the Chartist attitude to the growing repression: 'that peace, law and order shall continue to be the motto ... but should our enemies substitute war for peace, or attempt to suppress our lawful and orderly agitation by lawless violence, we shall deem it to be the sacred duty of the people, to meet force with force.' In the meantime, to allow no pretext to the authorities to use force, Chartists should give no provocation; all members should behave in a sober, peaceful and orderly manner; marshalls should see to it that demonstrators remained unarmed. In that way it would be clear to everyone, if violence did occur, that the responsibility lay not with the Chartists but with their middle- and upper-class oppressors.

Turning to the situation in the West Country, Roberts' open letter then went on to complain that the law, far from being operated in a just and even-handed manner, had become a weapon to deploy against the Chartists. First, the selective arrests were calculated to behead the movement. Second, the high court costs were designed to deplete their funds. Third, the authorities used all their powers to coerce and intimidate people, frightening them away from Chartism. The eviction of the Trowbridge Chartists from their headquarters and the placing of a squad of the Metropolitan Police there, vividly illustrated the operation of this iniquitous strategy.

> At your first establishment your enemies flagrantly violated the law by breaking into your room and stealing your property – but there was no redress; then they stole the property of your friend, Mr Young – still no redress, no punishment for the thief; again your room has been violated – and again the outrage is unavenged. Unavenged it will be till you avenge it yourselves.[16]

The open letter is significant because it contained the first clear enunciation of Roberts' personal attitude to the law. Identifying himself with working people, he recognized that he would find the complete apparatus of the legal system arraigned against him. As he wrote to the Trowbridge Chartists: 'judges and juries, and all who live by the plunder of the present system will be opposed to us.' Nevertheless, it would be wrong, he contended, to retreat from the legal arena, leaving their opponents in undisputed control. Rather, they should fight court cases, using them as an opportunity to expose the evils of existing society and thereby to advance the Chartist cause. 'I saw Mr Vincent last week in Monmouth Gaol, where in close confinement, he is awaiting trial, convinced that whatever the result it will do good to the cause.'[17]

The adoption of this tactic, Roberts acknowledged, would have personal implications for himself. If Chartists were going to contest the charges brought against them in the courts, they would need sympathetic lawyers, a very scarce breed, and for this reason he proposed to act prudently in the next few months, thereby avoiding arrest. But this, in a sense, was unrealistic. Already in the eighteen months or so that he had been campaigning, Roberts had provided the authorities with many things with which to charge him – and their method was to scatter as many charges as possible about on the principle that some were sure to strike their targets. In July 1839, W. P. Roberts, Henry Vincent and William Carrier were charged at the Wiltshire assizes with attending an illegal meeting the previous September. Once acquitted, they were rearrested and charged again, this time with a string of new offences. These charges were compiled after discussions between local magistrates and the Home Office, which wanted them to be wider and more compehensive than originally planned – thereby providing a greater chance of conviction. Bath JPs had misgivings about this move, for the addition of new charges would provide defendants with an opportunity to traverse and, consequently, to delay proceedings. The magistrates were afraid that defendants would be out on bail – prisons in those times were comparatively few and not large enough to cope with an influx of prisoners – able to continue their agitation and even tamper with witnesses. To prevent this, the magistrates wanted a special commission to deal expeditiously with the matter. However, the Home Office was reluctant to take such an extraordinary measure.

Eventually, it was decided to charge Roberts and his colleagues on seven counts of conspiracy. It was alleged that at Trowbridge, on 19 November 1838, they had 'seditiously and unlawfully assembled' and disturbed the peace 'by the discharge of firearms and the display of weapons of force'. In addition, they were also charged with conspiring to assemble 'with force of arms', at various times between 1 June 1838 and 18 July 1839, 'for purposes of disturbing the peace', as well as advising people to commit acts of arson. The magistrate set bail for Carrier and Vincent at £150 each, both with two sureties of

£50 each. Bail for Roberts was fixed higher: he had to find £500 and three sureties of £250 each.

Roberts protested to the magistrates about the additional charges. He said that he had fifty individuals waiting outside the court, prepared to give evidence. The prosecution's new move would result in delays and extra costs for the defendants. Working men like Carrier and Vincent, poor themselves and without affluent friends, would be unable to secure such large sums of money to obtain bail. It was tantamount to sentencing them to prison for eight months until their trial took place.[18] Even he encountered difficulties: one of his three sureties was to have been John Frost, a prosperous draper and former Mayor of Newport, but the bench refused to accept him on the ground that it did not know him. This was simply magistrates' malice. Frost had become a national figure both through his chairmanship of the Chartist convention and his well-publicized correspondence with Lord Melbourne, the Lord Chancellor, following his removal from the Newport bench. However, it was no use quibbling with the magistrates' decision: a replacement for Frost had to be found. This was done, but he arrived just in time to see all three men being taken, handcuffed, to Salisbury gaol. Once released on bail, W. P. Roberts wrote a letter of complaint to the Secretary of State. While in custody, he claimed, he had been handcuffed, denied newspapers, had his correspondence opened, and been refused a decent bed.

In the midst of the struggle, Roberts surprisingly found time to marry again. His bride was ,Mary Hill Hopkins, whose family were people of substance. The ceremony took place at Combe Down in Somerset, on 24 September 1839. From all accounts, the marriage was exceedingly happy; they had two sons and two daughters and descendants speak of their mutual devotion.[19] The only three of his letters to survive are couched in the most affectionate language. Similarly, her commemorative scrapbook of their visit to the Holy Land a few years before his death, reveals that these feelings were reciprocated. Among her other treasured mementoes was the menu of a banquet at Balliol College, Oxford, on which she had scrawled 'My beloved husband was there.' W. P. Roberts was rarely invited to social events in polite society because of his notoriety, a fact that hurt his wife. Mary Hill Hopkins may never have agreed with, or perhaps did not understand, her husband's politics, although she stood by him throughout his many tribulations. Since she was with him from the time of his arrest and imprisonment, throughout his work for the miners and Fenian martyrs until his death, she played a large part in his life and is known in the family to have been a woman of great strength of character. After his death, she led a concerted attempt by the family to improve his posthumous image, depicting him as just a respectable Victorian lawyer. An example of this is an account of his life, deposited in Manchester Public Library, where they were insistent on deleting all mention of an exceedingly painful episode. Subsequently, however, the librarian, C. W. Sutton, put the record straight, adding a note of his own: arising from the disturbances at Devizes, W. P. Roberts received a two-year sentence for seditious libel. William Potts and William Carrier also received two-year sentences.

The three men appeared before Wiltshire assizes at Salisbury in March 1840.[20] Whereas Carrier and Potts, defending themselves, used the occasion to put forward Chartist propaganda, Roberts was represented by a barrister named Alexander Cockburn, who was later to become Solicitor-General and then Attorney-General, and secured a firm political reputation in 1850 for his defence of Palmerston in the Don Pacifico case. He made a first-rate defence of W. P. Roberts.[21] He started out by questioning the legal principles on which the prosecution was based and argued that his client was simply exercising a constitutional right, trying to influence the legislature. By cross-examination, Cockburn elicited from prosecution witnesses that they had been determined to prevent the Chartist meeting at Devizes, with violence if necessary; and that, having accomplished this objective, they had had no intention of permitting the Chartists to leave the town peacefully. He concluded by addressing the jury for four hours.[22]

Nevertheless, the prosecution successfully rebutted Cockburn's arguments. It dismissed all the talk about exercising a constitutional right in trying to influence the legislature, claiming that, by its very nature, Chartism involved intimidation and violence. Witnesses were produced to support this contention. One of them testified that in a speech at Trowbridge Roberts had told his audience that, as Tory magistrates felt free to take the law into their own hands, banning legitimate meetings, so Chartists should not feel themselves bound by legal restraints. He continued, according to the witness: 'You have found out that Tory constables' windows are made of brittle stuff. I dare say it won't take too long to discover that the Tory magistrates' fine houses have windows made of the same brittle stuff. Mind, I didn't tell you to break windows.' Soon after Roberts made these remarks, the court was told, a farmer called Ingram had his hay-rick burnt down and an agricultural labourer, hostile to Chartism, returned home to find his cottage had been demolished.

Roberts greeted the two-year prison sentence philosophically: 'I see the Wiltshire farmers have determined that I shall go to jail – so be it.' Nevertheless, his imprisonment was an agonizing ordeal. The cramped conditions, poor food, lack of intellectual activity, so unlike what he was accustomed to, all began to take their toll, undermining his health. The prison medical officer expressed his concern about, as well as perplexity at, his rapid decline. There were fears that he might even die in gaol. His frantic wife, Roberts himself and numerous friends bombarded the authorities with letters and petitions. Some newspapers and radical journals reported his plight.

Roberts claimed the prison authorities were deliberately victimizing him. In fact, the opposite was probably true, for a number of concessions appear to have been made. Whereas William Carrier, a worker, was made to do hard labour, W. P. Roberts was excused this punishment. Local justices, paying one of their customary prison visits, commented upon his poor condition, and suggested that it arose from mental causes. They recommended – and it was agreed – that he should be allowed to buy writing materials and to send one letter a week to his family. Then the doctor ordered that his diet should be improved. He was even moved from Salisbury to Fisherton gaol to see if this would result in a change for the better. In a letter to the Home Secretary on 13 June 1840, Roberts repeated his charge of victimization. He argued that the initial cause of his illness was a diet of 'skilly' (bread and gruel); that an improvement had occurred after the doctor ordered a better diet; and that now he was back on the previous regime, which was causing a relapse. He also referred to the harmful effect of the 'silent system', forbidding him to communicate with other prisoners.[23]

One can only speculate about what made the authorities grant him an early release after only five months of his sentence. It could have been the poor state of his health or the public campaign mounted on his behalf. There could possibly have been pressure behind the scenes from Sir Nicholas Tindal, the Lord Chief Justice, who was related to Roberts' mother. In any case, the authorities probably thought that, like so many other middle-class individuals who had flirted with Chartism, he had learnt his lesson and that nothing would be gained from Roberts' further imprisonment. Even so, they seem to have acted with remarkable leniency. He was the first of the movement's imprisoned leaders to secure his freedom.[24]

In another respect W. P. Roberts was also fortunate: he suffered no professional disqualification. The Law Society, formed in 1825, had yet to establish its full authority, surrounding the legal profession with an aura of respectability. The custom gradually emerged of debarring lawyers from continuing in legal practice if they were found guilty of criminal conduct. Had that been the rule in the 1840s and 1850s, then not only Roberts but also two other Chartist leaders, Feargus O'Connor and Ernest Jones, both barristers, would have been unable to continue in the legal profession. They, too, were imprisoned for committing serious crimes.[25]

Roberts' release aroused mixed reactions. Wiltshire Chartists immediately celebrated the return of their hero. Excitement ran high wherever he appeared, the one bright spot in the otherwise general political gloom. But if his return helped to revive Chartist hopes and activities, his enemies were incensed. Two Wiltshire Tory newspapers acidly commented that he looked remarkably fit, and suggested that it might now be appropriate to proceed with the other outstanding charges against him, such as that of seditious and unlawful assembly at Trowbridge on 19 November 1838. Further criticism came from these newspapers when he resumed his work for Chartism: surely, they claimed, this infringed his bail conditions. The Home Office pursued the question. In reply, Roberts wrote a letter to Lord Normanby, dated 9 July 1840, stating that he had not deliberately sought to flout the restrictions; a demonstration he attended at Trowbridge had occurred spontaneously.[26]

What was of lasting significance in W. P. Roberts' life, affecting his entire future development, was that he had come through this testing period with his political beliefs unshaken. In contrast, most middle-class radicals had capitulated. Faced with the emergence of a new working class and heightened class conflict, they understood where their real interests lay. As Edward Thompson put it, they 'were forced to take sides between the two nations'; whatever their reservations, most middle-class radicals eventually made their peace with the established order. He cites W. P. Roberts as one of the few exceptions, individuals 'who preferred to be known as Chartists or Republicans rather than as special constables'.[27]

Far from capitulating, his determination and convictions were reinforced by his prison experiences. To Roberts, politics was an intensely personal matter: he did not believe that other people should be made to endure inhuman and degrading conditions any more than he should. In an open letter to the Trowbridge Female Radical Association, he stated his resolve: 'Tis true, indeed, that the gaol beds in Salisbury are not made of roses; but whether for weal or woe, for victory or death, my mind is made up: come what will and when it will, it is my determination to live and die in the people's cause.'

3   The Road to Newport

Events in the West Country need to be placed in a national context. Chartism contained elements of continuity and discontinuity. On the one hand, many of the attitudes and ideas had been inherited from the great radicals of the past – Major Cartwright, William Cobbett, Tom Paine and John Wilkes – whilst, on the other, they were expressed in a new context by a new configuration of social forces. The industrial revolution had led to the growth of towns and the emergence of a working class, increasingly aware of its own identity and its divergence of interests from other sections of society. Because of the duration of its existence and its impact throughout the whole country, Chartism signalled the arrival of the working class upon the national arena.

Edward Thompson ends his classic work, *The Making of the English Working Class*, with Chartism, indicating that the class had obtained a certain maturity and stability. For Leon Trotsky, Chartism had another significance. He wrote that, 'it affords us an abbreviated and systematic view of practically the entire course of the proletarian struggle – from petitions to Parliament down to armed insurrection. All the fundamental questions of the class movement of the proletariat – the relations between parliamentary and extra-parliamentary activities, the part played by the universal suffrage right, the trade unions and co-operatives, the importance of the general strike and its relation to armed insurrection, even the mutual relation between the proletariat and the peasantry – were not only crystallized in practice in the history of the Chartist mass movement, but found their answer in it as far as principles are concerned.'[1]

Chartism emerged against a background of angry disenchantment with orthodox politicians and the political system. Working people had seen the Tories fight ferociously against parliamentary reform in

1831–2. When the Whigs ultimately came to office, the Reform Bill they passed gave the vote only to the middle class. So far as the vast majority of the population was concerned, the Whig government not only continued to operate with existing unpopular laws (Corn Law, Game Law, etc.), but also introduced measures of its own, such as the Poor Law Amendment Act, that worsened the situation. Add to this the prosecution of the Tolpuddle Martyrs and Glasgow spinners, as well as the fact that from 1837 onwards Britain was slowly slipping into economic depression, and the reasons for the mass explosion of organized protest become clear.

The People's Charter was first published in May 1838. After nine months of agitation and mass meetings, the General Convention of the Industrious Classes had met in London in February of that year. Quite rightly, it was regarded as a unique event: never before had representatives specifically from the working class and coming from all parts of the country, met to discuss their mutual problems. What would the authorities' reaction be to this Labour Parliament? Would they attempt to suppress it? Or would the Labour Parliament gradually gain wider popular acceptance until it superseded the antiquated and unrepresentative Westminster counterpart? Amid the widespread speculation, one thing was certain: the young working-class movement had set sail on hitherto uncharted seas.

Almost from the outset, differences of opinion emerged among the delegates. There were those who believed that it was vital for Chartism to seize the initiative: Britain's rulers would not surrender without a fight; they must be forcibly overthrown. Men like Julian Harney and Dr John Taylor, elected to represent Tyneside, and Dr Peter Murray McDouall from Lancashire, went to the convention to urge immediate action. The enemy, they argued, must not be given time to regroup. Taylor, already a veteran of two continental revolutions, wanted to be involved in a third. He told a Newcastle rally that his ambition was 'to write his epitaph upon the tyrant's brow, in characters of blood, with a pen of steel'.[2] He was described as 'a cross between Byron's Corsair and a gypsy king' and it was said that his speech was 'lava-like eloquence that set on fire all combustible matter in its path'.[3] In some parts of the country, people armed and drilled, mainly secretly at night. Colonel Macerone's military manual, dealing with street and house fighting and purporting to show how irregulars could deal with attacks made by an army of professional soldiers, was republished and read.

Many delegates, however, thought such talk and action was premature. They were believers in moral force, the force of persuasion. Wild speeches and violent gestures, they considered, would antagonize precisely those who might be won over by powerful arguments. Furthermore, there was always the chance that Parliament would agree with the Charter, in which case an uprising would simply involve a senseless, unnecessary waste of life. Others waivered or held intermediate positions. A lot of delegates believed, as most Americans do today, that they had a right to own weapons. Even if they were not used offensively to attain the Charter, weapons could act as a deterrent, curbing the State's misuse of power or preventing a slaughter of unarmed civilians, such as occurred in the 1819 Peterloo massacre. A further variant came from Feargus O'Connor – the threat of violence could lead to the government's capitulation. Ironically, he did not see that the roles could be reversed.

As the convention's debates dragged on, week after week, the government quietly set about taking measures that would permit it to reassert its authority. Sir Charles Napier took up his appointment as army commander in the industrial North of England where unrest was the greatest. He promptly began to regroup his troops, stationing them in three key locations. It was fortunate for the government that Ireland was in a quiescent state; troops could be withdrawn from there to strengthen the mainland garrisons. By June 1839, Napier felt the situation had improved militarily. Intelligence on Chartist activities had increased and, though he had occasional doubts about army loyalty, nevertheless he felt it would survive the crisis. The recruitment of special constables augmented the forces of law and order, as did the formation of associations of armed citizens, gentlemen whose loyalty remained beyond question. All told, he was a much relieved, yet far from happy man. He did not relish the thought of spilt blood, and especially, as he confided in a letter to his brother, the killing of people whose political opinions were 'very much like my own':

> Good God what work! to send grape-shot from our guns into a helpless mass of fellow-citizens, sweeping the streets with fire and charging with cavalry, destroying poor people whose only crime is that they have been ill-governed and reduced to such straits that they seek redress by arms.[4]

Sir Charles Napier had heard it rumoured that the Chartists could put half a million under arms. Indeed, the boast had first appeared in the *Northern Liberator* in an article headed 'The Coming Revolution'.[5] His own estimate, however, was 100,000 and while these might endanger his position, he thought he could cope. What he dearly wanted was to avoid an armed struggle. To this end, he invited some Chartist leaders (probably including Abel Heywood, the Manchester radical publisher) to inspect the most modern military hardware, hoping that this would give them some idea of the dangerous consequences likely to ensue.

But, whatever his personal sympathies for the Chartists, Napier's strengthening of the military position permitted the government to go on the offensive. The Home Secretary issued orders to local magistrates, under the Seditious Meetings and Assemblies Act 1817 (5.7 George III c.19), to suppress unlawful meetings. On 7 May 1839, Lord John Russell extended the remit of the prohibition, telling JPs to suppress all public meetings attended by large numbers of people. In some instances this repression led to disturbances, as Chartists sought to assert their right to freedom of assembly. The worst of these riots happened in the Bull Ring, Birmingham, where, as even historians unsympathetic to Chartism concede, the authorities acted provocatively. Amid the resulting disturbances, a grocer's shop in nearby Market Street was looted and numerous arrests made; at Warwick assizes three men and a boy – one account says four men – were sentenced to death. While the Home Secretary later commuted the sentences to transportation for life, there could be no doubt that the authorities had signalled to the Chartists the introduction of a new tough policy.[6] The Chartist convention's secretary, William Lovett, along with other leading delegates (John Collins, Julian Harney and John Taylor) was also taken into custody. Meanwhile, a petition containing the Chartist demands and with 1,280,000 signatures had been presented to Parliament. On 12 July 1839, the House of Commons decisively rejected it by 235 votes to 46.

Chartism's room for manoeuvre was rapidly vanishing. Besides the blow administered by Parliament, the rigorous enforcement of the bans on meetings, processions, etc., was making it impossible to continue the campaign. The road of peaceful persuasion appeared to be blocked. How it seemed to delegates can be seen from the manifesto issued by the convention the day after Parliament rejected the petition:

The mask of *constitutional liberty* is thrown aside, and the form of *despotism* stands hideously before us. Shall it be said, fellow-countrymen, that four millions of men, capable of bearing arms, and defending their country against every foreign assailant, allowed a few domestic oppressors to enslave and degrade them? . . . If you longer continue as passive slaves, *the fate of unhappy Ireland will soon be yours* . . . We have resolved to obtain our rights, 'peacefully if we may, forcibly if we must'; but woe to those who begin the warfare with the millions, or who forcibly restrain their peaceful agitation for justice – at one signal they will be enlightened to their error, and in one brief moment destroyed. (emphasis in original)[7]

W. P. Roberts undoubtedly endorsed the general sentiments of the manifesto. Though not a delegate, he often visited the convention, participating in informal discussions outside the hall. Even when not present, he would have received full reports of proceedings either from Henry Vincent or John Frost, the ex-Mayor of Newport and the convention's chairman, who was also one of his close friends. Actually, the West Country had close links with South Wales. The *Western Vindicator* sold extensively in the Welsh valleys. The two districts swapped speakers – indeed Vincent was a highly popular platform orator in Wales – and, not surprisingly, the fate of Chartism in the two regions was closely linked.

As the authorities intensified their repression, John Frost, a leading spokesman for the Chartist convention, became a prime target. They scoured his speeches, looking for a suitable excuse for prosecution. One was eventually found in the remarks he had made on 1 January 1839, more than half a year previously. In that address, Frost had castigated the monarchy for its extravagance, which cost taxpayers a colossal £510,000 a year. Turning to a detailed examination of its expenditure, Frost found that Queen Victoria had twelve grooms of her bedchamber, each costing £10,000 annually. Why, he asked, did the young queen require twelve? And what did they do for their money? Queen Victoria's ministers were not amused – Frost was prosecuted for seditious libel.[8]

The true significance of this move was not lost on Frost. The authorities were tightening their grip, using the law to throttle Chartism and arrest its leaders. A Royal Proclamation against Torchlight Meetings had been issued. A few months later, it was followed by another royal proclamation, extending the ban to certain kinds of daytime meetings. The Home Secretary followed this up by writing to magistrates, reminding them that, under common law, meetings became illegal if they 'excite alarm and endanger the public peace', even if nobody carries weapons. Magistrates, almost all of whom were fervently anti-Chartist, could be relied upon to use this advice with enthusiasm, banning all things Chartist. The later action against W. P. Roberts and his colleagues at Devizes was an example of this suppression.[9]

To Chartists all this merely seemed to be a violation of their constitutional rights. In an open letter, 'To the Female Radical Association of Bath', which had written to him expressing its sympathy and support, Frost wrote:

> What is the offence of Mr Roberts and myself? To restore the ancient institutions of our country! To place political power in the hands of those who suffer by the abuse of it! To prevent bribery, drunkenness and violence, which disgrace our elections! To put into the House of Commons better men than now occupy the seats! To prevent the idle and dissolute from living in splendour on the spoils of an oppressed and impoverished people. These are the offences which we have committed.[10]

The letter, at times muddled and incoherent, shows signs of an individual in mental agony, forced to confront an appalling situation not of his making. Already there are clear indications of the genesis of a political stand that was to result in Frost becoming the leader of the Newport uprising. His letter recognized that 'those in authority would not resign without a struggle.' Quoting the convention's manifesto, condemning people content to be passive slaves, he asked: 'Is life, my kind countrywomen, of any value, deprived of liberty?' In an ominous manner, he then stated his personal position, likening himself to Samson, who died through self-destruction, pulling down the pillars of the temple – 'the pillars which sustain our social fabric'.

The dilemma of Frost and the other leaders can easily be understood. Chartism, a movement that signalled the arrival on the national arena of the working class as a significant force, brought

with it new political methods. Never before had there been so many
public meetings. In many a tiny dwelling and street, politics became a
source of daily discussion. Ordinary labourers began to turn to
radical journals in an effort to understand the complexities of society.
Yet, all this agitation, education and organization was placed in
jeopardy. New laws were introduced. Old laws were tightened up.
Suddenly it seemed that Chartism had been left with no space in
which to operate.[11]

The trial of Henry Vincent proved an important turning-point.[12]
He was charged with conspiracy and unlawful assembly arising from
public meetings he held at Newport on 19 April 1839 and several
other occasions. The barrister appearing for the defence was John
Roebuck, MP for Bath, briefed by W. P. Roberts. Roebuck made
great play of the fact that Vincent had repeatedly appealed to his
audiences to remain calm; that the Chartists were holding demonstrations remarkably similar to those of 1831–2 which led to the passing
of the Reform Bill; and that Vincent was merely exercising his
constitutional right of trying to influence the course of legislation.
These arguments held no weight for Judge Alderson who brushed
aside the references to 1831–2 as irrelevant. For him, the crucial
question was whether in 'the opinion of rational and firm men . . .
there was a threat to peace'; Vincent's speeches, he stated, had been
intended to foment class warfare. In passing sentence, Alderson
described the Chartist convention as an illegal assembly, and said the
government might consider instituting legal proceedings at some
future date. From that moment onwards, as the judgement became
case law, the spectre of prison hung over all the convention
delegates, pre-eminently, of course, over its chairman, John Frost.

Matters were made worse by the rumours that Henry Vincent, a
much-loved and respected figure, was being ill-treated in Monmouth
gaol. When the authorities initiated proceedings against Chartist
journals this simply served to increase frustration. How could the
movement continue to function? Its journals acted as its organizers,
bringing people together and giving them a common purpose. All
avenues to peaceful progress appeared to have been barred, and the
Chartists could do little to protect themselves or further their aims.

When Parliament rejected the petition, the convention had
thought of applying economic pressure – through a run on the banks
by supporters, a boycott of pro-government shopkeepers, and, most
important of all, a general strike of a month, to be called a sacred

month. But the Chartists had very little finance and even less industrial muscle. Trade unions were small and weak. Many had leaders unsympathetic to Chartism, unwilling to squander scant resources on a project unlikely to succeed. The authorities, moreover, indicated that they would be taking a tough line. There was the prospect of mass arrests, even of the shooting of unarmed demonstrators. So convention delegates, assessing the situation as reports came in from various parts of the country, vacillated. When, at last, on 12 August 1839, industrial action was taken, the response was patchy and unimpressive – in a word, it was a failure.

The Chartist convention was finally dissolved on 6 September 1839, with all its options save one exhausted. And that one looked increasingly less attractive. In the months since the convention had first met in February, the British state had used the time wisely, prudently strengthening itself until it felt confident it could deal with any eventuality. Had the advice given by delegates like Harney, McDouall and Taylor at the outset of the convention been followed – namely, to seize the initiative and immediately use physical force to obtain the Charter – then possibly the outcome might have been different. Even F. C. Mather, a historian unsympathetic to Chartism who has researched the state's response, admits that, had a Chartist uprising happened prior to 6 May, 'they would in fact have found the government's defences in a parlous state of disorganization – the troops scattered in small detachments, the reinforcements from Ireland not yet arrived, the magistrates inert either from fear or indifference and the propertied inhabitants afraid to come forward as special constables to defend themselves.'[13]

This verdict is largely endorsed by the *Naval and Military Gazette*, the organ of the army officer corps, which was alarmed by the numerous reports of Chartists arming. In March 1839, one officer expressed the view that the army was 'totally inadequate to meet a general outbreak in the North.' Another expressed fears about the situation in Wales, 'a thinly populated and very ignorant part of the kingdom', where he thought Welsh regiments might well mutiny rather than put down a rebellion by compatriots. A third thought the local part-time militias, poorly trained and equipped, would be of little value in a tight spot. In the spring and summer of 1839, the columns of the *Naval and Military Gazette* contained a fascinating discussion of what now would be termed urban guerrilla warfare: cavalry would be of very limited value in small, densely-populated places; by placing mattresses at the windows of captured churches and town halls, the rebels would largely nullify the effect of shrapnel shells; in hand-to-hand fighting, the Chartist pike would probably be more than a match for the bayonet.

Yet, by the summer of 1839 army officers seem to have regained their self-assurance. There was a general consensus that they could now cope with any eventuality. One of its contributors envisaged events taking the following course: sporadic disturbances being dispersed by troops; fires being deliberately started; the capture of a town temporarily and the proclamation·of a republic; more troops being brought in to recapture the town; and irregular warfare continuing for quite some time.[14] Sir Charles Napier held similar views. By being forewarned of the Chartists' moves through military intelligence and by delivering a swift pre-emptive blow, he hoped to defeat and disorganize his opponents before they had time to mobilize their full strength, and to keep casualties to a minimum. This, to a large extent, was what happened.

After the defeat of the Newport uprising on 4 November, 1839, Sir Charles Napier wrote: 'My own opinion is that, had a troop of horse alone been at Newport, the men would have been destroyed or defeated, and a pretty flare up would have run like wild fire to Carlisle.' He added that 'John Frost expected the Newport Uprising to succeed and act as a signal for a nationwide insurrection.'[15]

While information about the Newport uprising remains fragmentary, and conjecture at times is therefore unavoidable, nevertheless recent historical research makes it possible to piece together a fairly accurate account of what happened and why. South Wales was chosen by the Chartists as the venue because of the presence of large numbers of angry, disaffected people. In 1831, there had been Dic Penderyn and the Merthyr uprising. In 1834, colliers turned to what was termed 'Scotch cattle', a violent form of industrial persuasion, where they blew up the mines of coalowners who failed to meet their demands. Most people in that part of Wales were Welsh-speaking whereas most of the employers were English. It was, therefore, exceedingly difficult for the authorities to gain intelligence of conspiracies being hatched. Furthermore, in South Wales the army was relatively weak in numbers. And the date for the uprising was fixed as the night of 3–4 November because the news of it would reach other parts of Britain by 5 November – Guy Fawkes' night, which was then celebrated with much more gusto and abandon than today. Normally on that night the forces of law and order were sorely stretched anyway; on this particular night it was hoped they would have difficulty in distinguishing between fireworks and rifle shots.

The plan may well have been to raise the standard of revolt in Newport before pressing on to liberate Vincent from Monmouth gaol. The first step was to combine the Chartist forces outside Newport before starting the attack at 2 a.m. But the night was exceedingly cold, dark and stormy; some of the marchers lost their way and others returned home. The main contingent, probably around 5,000 strong, arrived outside Newport around dawn. The element of surprise had vanished. The troops in the Westgate Hotel, holding Chartists as prisoners, were prepared for the onslaught. In the ensuing fighting at least twenty Chartists were killed.[16] (Almost certainly, many others were badly injured, some of whom must have died later. It is customary in such circumstances for people to try to remove their dead and wounded; to leave them might give the prying authorities further leads that result in more arrests.) As it was, John Frost, Zephaniah Williams and William Jones, the leaders, along with many others, were detained.

A fraught atmosphere prevailed in the aftermath of the fight. It was estimated that up to 20,000 supporters of Frost remained lurking in the hills around Newport. How would they react to the defeat? Would they realize the futility of armed rebellion or would it make them more determined? Another imponderable was what impact the news would have on the rest of Britain. Thomas Ainge Devyr, a physical force Chartist who fled the country while awaiting trial and later published his memoirs in the United States, movingly describes there how hundreds assembled in the North East (where the military preparations of the Chartists were quite advanced), to await reports from Newport before being 'up and doing' themselves. The first they heard was that Frost had successfully captured Newport, a rumour that quickly spread panic among the Tyneside police. However, when the true facts emerged, the plans for insurrection were immediately abandoned. Similarly, in Lancashire, Yorkshire and the West Country, the failure at Newport led revolutionary spirits to evaporate.[17]

Nevertheless, the authorities had to remain vigilant, investigating any suspicious behaviour or movements. Not surprisingly, therefore, when a wary policeman saw W. P. Roberts at Blackwood, a few miles from Newport, he arrested him and, on investigation, discovered that

the two servants accompanying him were actually Frost's daughters in disguise. He was probably trying to save them from the fate of their brother, Henry, who had been taken into custody. However, it seems the authorities were not actually after them; only Roberts was detained, and this was without being charged, for two days. On being arraigned before the magistrates' court, Roberts repeatedly asked why he had been imprisoned. No explanation was forthcoming. At that time, he was supposed to be acting as Frost's solicitor; his detention had interfered with his work on behalf of his client. But the magistrates refused to comment on this: all they would say was that he was now a free man. To which, Roberts retorted sarcastically: 'Your courtesy is amazing.'[18]

After this event W. P. Roberts withdrew from the case because, almost certainly, it would have occasioned charges of legal impropriety and led to severe family embarrassment. The government had appointed a special commission, a legal device used to deal expeditiously with cases after a serious disorder had occurred. Alongside Mr Justice John Williams, infamous in radical circles for his sentencing of the Tolpuddle Martyrs, sat two other judges, one of whom was the Lord Chief Justice, Sir Nicholas Tindal. Having a close relative playing such a key judicial role, Roberts may have been precluded from direct involvement in the case, but it is possible that he helped his friend Frost behind the scenes. It is not known whether he went to London to engage the services of Fitzroy Kelly and Sir Frederick Pollock, two of the most brilliant lawyers of the day, for the defence, but this was a superb ploy. Such was the calibre of Fitzroy Kelly's advocacy during the trial, that the reputation he acquired in the defence of Frost and his colleagues gave his career an immense boost, leading to his appointment as Attorney-General in 1852.[19]

Facing the charge of high treason, the Chartist leaders had perforce to enter a plea of 'not guilty'. To have pleaded 'guilty' and then argued that there were extenuating circumstances would have been completely futile. The automatic penalty for levying war against Her Majesty, irrespective of the circumstances, was the death sentence. Therefore, Kelly and Pollock sought to belittle the importance of what had happened at the Westgate Hotel, presenting it as a mere riot, not an uprising. Frequently, they were able to expose inaccuracies and inconsistencies in the testimonies of prosecution witnesses, many of whom were dubious characters.

Frost, on the other hand, was a man of high repute, of a peaceful nature, who had given valuable service to the local community as a magistrate.

Nevertheless, all their eloquence and skill would have been of little avail had it not been for the sensational intervention of Sir Nicholas Tindal. Summing up, the Lord Chief Justice gave a careful résumé of all the evidence, witness by witness. He placed great emphasis on the minor concessions the crown had made to the defence's case, making them out to be much more significant than they actually were. Then he reminded the jury that it was not for Frost to prove his innocence; rather the prosecution had to prove its case beyond all reasonable doubt. The law officers of the crown sat and listened aghast. 'To my utter astonishment and dismay, Tindal summed up for an acquittal,' Sir John Campbell, the Attorney-General, explained later. 'What he meant, the Lord only knows. No human being doubted the guilt of the accused, and we have proved it by the clearest evidence. It was of lasting importance to the public tranquillity that there should be a verdict of guilty.'[20]

That night the Attorney-General went to bed a worried man, wondering what the jury would do in the light of the Lord Chief Justice's summing up. He had, however, no need for alarm. The jury of propertied gentlemen only took thirty minutes to arrive at a guilty verdict. Even so, it left the cabinet with an awkward dilemma. Undoubtedly, ministers believed the leaders of the uprising should hang. But in the light of the powerful advocacy of the Lord Chief Justice, together with the court's recommendation of mercy, it became difficult not to deviate from this recommendation. Throughout the country meetings were held and petitions signed calling for clemency. Eventually, the sentences for Frost, Jones and Williams were commuted to transportation for life. By doing this, the government had relieved a highly charged atmosphere. Their decision even received the approval of Sir Charles Napier, the Northern Army commander: 'It is not law but barbarity to slay men for political opinions, in which thousands of honourable men agree with the condemned person! It is not justice, it is vengeance.'[21] Such opinions were certainly widely held, and Chartism would have become a much more bitter movement had Frost and his comrades finished up at the end of a noose. As it was, pleas for their pardon, the right for them to return from Australia, figured for many years in campaigns. These appeals were customarily couched in the language of moderation; a much more extremist line might well have followed public executions.

Naturally, Newport has been, for a long time, a subject of great controversy among historians. While disagreement exists on points of detail, recent research by David Jones, Keith Thomas, Ivor Wilks and others shows beyond doubt that an uprising was intended.[22] The contrary view is well expressed in Professor David Williams' biography of John Frost, basically accepting the defence case put forward in court by Kelly and Pollock. He suggests that it was just a demonstration that went hideously wrong. But if this were true, why were the customary procedures for demonstrations not adopted? Usually there is advanced publicity to ensure maximum attendance, marchers carry banners to persuade members of the general public, the event does not take place when most citizens are asleep, and women and children often participate. In a typical demonstration men do not carry weapons and enough food for several days. Nor do nineteen-year-old youths, like George Shell, killed in the attack on the Westgate Hotel, write letters to their parents before setting out, saying 'should it please God to spare my life, I shall see you soon; but if not, grieve not for me. I shall fall in a noble cause.' Equally, in my opinion, it is difficult to explain how proclamations appeared declaring John Frost to be 'president' of the 'executive government', as reprinted by the *Monmouthshire Merlin*, unless Newport had been intended as a prelude to a nationwide uprising.[23]

In response to the insurrectionary challenge, the Whig government was bloody, bold and resolute. Lord Broughton told his cabinet colleagues that, 'as the object of the Chartists was to knock us on the head and rob us of our property, we might as well arrive at that catastrophe after a struggle as without it; we could only fail and we might succeed.' To which, Lord Melbourne replied 'exactly so'. Recent historical analysis has shown that the government went about this task in a logical, systematic manner. First, it sought to behead Chartism by imprisoning leaders, orators and journalists of national standing. Second, it strove to disorganize rank-and-file Chartism in its strongholds by arresting key figures locally. Third, it put out of harm's way the participants in conspiracies and insurrections. According to the *Northern Liberator*, by the end of 1839 there were 480 Chartists in gaol in England, sixty-three in Wales and one in Scotland, while 221 had been transported to Australia.

Chartism reeled under these blows. As well as those actually imprisoned, many others fled from their homes through fear, sometimes emigrating, to avoid imprisonment. Throughout the country, the 'reign of terror' initiated by the government received able backing and assistance from employers as well as those in minor positions of authority. As a consequence, to be known as a prominent Chartist often led to loss of employment, sometimes eviction from one's dwelling. This, again, forced many to leave home and move to other places, where they kept anonymity by dropping out of political activity. The inevitable consequence of all this repression was a weakening of Chartist organization, already considerably demoralized by the defeat of Newport and the failure of a national uprising to materialize.

W. P. Roberts apparently went on undismayed, as if guided by an inner political compass, helping with the defence of Chartists both in the West Country and elsewhere. The atmosphere in which he had to function, redolent of fear and prejudice, made his task exceedingly difficult. For instance, when he was defending George Bartlett, Anthony Phillips and Thomas Bolwell, the chairman of the Bath magistrates' bench told him 'the proceedings are not to be interrupted by a member of the legal profession, who is here only on sufferance.' The men stood charged with using seditious language. It was alleged that Phillips, in the immediate aftermath of the Newport uprising, had told a Chartist meeting in Bath, gathered to await the news: 'My friends, I suppose you have all heard the reports in the papers about how many were killed. Don't believe it: they don't say how many of the soldiers and special constables are killed. The men had walked 30 or 40 miles, and their ammunition was so wet that they did not make use of it; but they stood their ground like men.' Afterwards he added: 'They are up in the North in full earnest and I hope the West of England will be the same.' In vain, Roberts tried to shake the testimony of prosecution witnesses, questioning their reliability and honesty of character. The prisoners were committed to the next quarter sessions.[24]

In some respects, Feargus O'Connor's trial at York assizes was a more happy occasion.[25] He faced charges of seditious libel for speeches reported in the *Northern Star*. Roberts attended, in his capacity as a solicitor, to give whatever legal advice he could. Since, from the outset, it was clear O'Connor would be convicted, he used the occasion to state and reaffirm his political beliefs. As O'Connor later remarked, 'Every day at York was a Chartist meeting with the judge in the chair'. His courageous stand helped to give fresh heart to the movement's troubled supporters. Shortly after O'Connor received an eighteen-month prison sentence, Roberts' own trial began. He, too, went to prison in good heart, endorsing the famous slogan which O'Connor had coined at the end of his trial: 'Universal suffrage and no surrender'.[26]

4 The Years of Uncertainty

In the period between the Newport trial and his own – in other words from November 1839 to March 1840 – it is impossible to say what role, if any, Roberts played within the Chartist organization. Undoubtedly, he found it prudent to keep a low profile, although he was at the meeting in Bath on 7 November that discussed the post-uprising situation, a meeting that ended with the arrest of Bartlett, Bolwell and Phillips and, as mentioned in the last chapter, their defence by Roberts before the Bath magistrates.[1]

In the absence of any evidence, there is nothing to indicate whether Roberts agreed with the Wiltshire Chartists' response to the changes in the political climate. They had prior knowledge of the plans of the South Wales Chartists, for a prominent West Country leader visited Newport on 1 November. The following day the *Western Vindicator* started a series of articles intended to inform people how they could resist oppression. Sensing something was afoot, the authorities sealed off the town of Trowbridge. Then they investigated a suspicious gathering there; Chartists claimed it was merely a prayer meeting. On 4 November, however, some of the Chartists remained up all night, awaiting the reports from South Wales. When bad news arrived from Newport, it was regarded initially as a battle lost, not the war.

The *Western Vindicator*, of 9 November 1839, declared that Newport was the beginning of the revolution: 'The people, finding moral force useless in effect, are justified in the use of physical . . . Shall the people be content to move *morally* – whilst they are being crushed *physically*?' A ringing call for defiance came from Antony Phillips: 'No peace in the cottage – none in the hall: be there injustice for the poor, vengeance on the rich: be food withheld from the poor by unjust laws, be it taken from the rich by justifiable destruction: be there no security for labour – let there be insecurity of property.'[2]

The *Western Vindicator* also castigated the fainted-hearted waverers, those whose lack of resolution had led to the Newport defeat. In particular, Feargus O'Connor was singled out: 'a traitor to that cause will that man be who, having told people they were oppressed and that they possessed within themselves the power and had the right to remove oppression . . . fails to do his duty, or shrinks from his part in the hour of danger.'[3] O'Connor, aware an uprising was afoot, had sent a representative to South Wales to try to persuade them to call it off and went to Ireland himself so that, whatever happened, he could not be directly implicated. This may help to explain why he lost some of his popularity with the West Country Chartists, as well as Roberts' personal antipathy to him at the time. They may not have accepted the explanation O'Connor subsequently gave for his conduct: 'My opinion, then, with regard to physical force is that a resort to it in the case of legislative oppression and tyranny is a virtue . . . but something like success must be fairly presumed before the experiment is tried.'[4]

The initial effect of Newport was an increase in Chartist support. Those who had never before thought revolt feasible yet harboured feelings of discontent saw, for the first time, that something perhaps could be done to right the wrongs they suffered. The *Bristol Times* claimed the West Country had become the most dangerous part of Britain. Nine-tenths of the labourers in the Bradford-Trowbridge area, it said, had become Chartists since Newport. All troop leave for Christmas had had to be cancelled.[5] Another newspaper reported that soldiers billeted in the West Country, belonging to the same regiment which defended the Westgate Hotel, had been attacked. At Bath, guns had been fired in the night. Wiltshire's Chief Constable informed the Home Office that, if Frost were executed, a general uprising would occur.[6] To prevent better liaison between the Chartists, copies of the *Western Vindicator*, which had been dispatched to South Wales, were confiscated. Its business manager ironically sent a bill to the authorities for copies received and not paid for.[7]

But these feelings of anger soon evaporated once Frost's sentence had been commuted to transportation for life. As people realized the extent of the Newport débâcle, anger was replaced by an attitude of grim resignation: the authorities had the upper hand; they could arrest people, or prohibit meetings, at will. Whatever they wanted to do to Chartism, they could. Under the wave of repression, the hard core of the movement, essential for its efficient functioning, began to buckle and, in some of the smaller places, snap. Victimization by employers, discrimination by poor relief overseers, harassment by the authorities compelled many to abandon their political activity. At best, in many villages Chartists operated in a semi-clandestine manner, holding small, unpublicized meetings, as McDouall recommended, to circumvent 'the farrago of the law'.[8] Almost everyone was in a state of fear, terrified by the thought of incarceration in prisons, an experience that held much more horror than it does today. Definitely, conditions were unpropitious for Chartism: the excitement and enthusiasm of yesterday had vanished; disillusionment and demoralization had replaced them. Not surprisingly, local organizations were reduced to a mere handful of individuals.

In his history of Chartism, Mark Hovell suggests that after Newport the movement went to sleep.[9] This, however, is not strictly true. In a county like Wiltshire, the small number of activists began the slow task of rebuilding from the grassroots upwards. Modest, unspectacular work, not really newsworthy, it meant, however, that the movement had become sufficiently strong to organize a welcome home when W. P. Roberts was released from prison in July 1840. A few months later, the organization being much stronger, a still bigger celebration followed the freeing of George Bartlett and Thomas Bolwell.

Once released, Roberts participated in these humdrum day-to-day activities. Business meetings, education classes, social events were all grist to his mill. He journeyed from Bath to Bradford, Bristol, Melksham, Salisbury, Trowbridge and elsewhere. Operating in a hostile environment, it was essential to either own or rent a meeting-place so as to prevent unfriendly interference. In Bath, they acquired a large assembly-room. In Trowbridge, the Chartists bought some impressive premises. Despite providing financial support to a fund for Chartist prisoners and their families, local enthusiasts were able to raise sufficient money to buy a block of buildings, which were christened 'The Charter House'.[10] Part of the premises was turned into a democratic chapel while the rest became co-operative stores and dwellings. Melksham and Westbury also bought their own rooms. In Bristol, activities including a ball and soirée were held in the Owenite Hall of Science. Guests declared this to be 'the cheapest and most numerous and respectably-attended entertainment they had ever been at', an event that continued from 10 p.m. until early morning.[11]

At a more serious level, Chartists concentrated their efforts on campaigning for 'the Welsh martyrs'. As we have seen, in an effort to persuade the authorities to let Frost and his comrades return from Australia, the general image Chartism tried to project was one of moderation and sweet reason. Roberts, not only a personal friend of John Frost but also closely identified in people's minds with him, figured prominently in this campaign. But it was impossible for him to be at every meeting. In January 1841, a big gathering at Bath petitioned the Queen and Parliament for the release of 'the Welsh martyrs'. Its wording revealed that those present had scant knowledge of either the law or the trial. The petition argued that 'since the judgement of the majority of the judges . . . being in favour of the prisoners, they were fully entitled to acquittal.' Furthermore, it added they had been 'illegally tried and banished from the country'.[12]

Nevertheless, this meeting had a special significance because middle-class supporters – including 'respectable females' according to the *Northern Star* – once more began to attend. And at an April meeting, Bolwell went out of his way to welcome the return of many of the middle class, absent for some time. The wave of political persecutions had landed the organization with large bills, but he was pleased to tell his audience these were now paid (presumably with some help from more affluent backers). He added: 'The democratic spirit largely prevails in Bath; the population was remarkable for their patriotism and love of liberty.'[13]

The underlying reason for the renewed alignment was that, as the Newport uprising receded in people's memories, the day-to-day realities of local politics reasserted themselves. Both the middle and working-class still resented the corruption and inefficiency with which the city of Bath was run. Both found the rate burden unfair and regressive. Both suffered from legislation, such as the Corn Laws. (If the high price of bread meant a smaller residual income was left for the worker, it also meant he had less money in his pocket to purchase commodities from the small shopkeeper.) And, therefore, it was in the interests of both classes to unite to further their common aims.

Only a small proportion of the middle class may have felt

sufficiently enthusiastic to become active Chartist supporters, but all radicals favoured manhood suffrage and allying with the Chartists. This, in 1841, had a practical urgency. A general election was pending. The radicals hoped John Roebuck would regain the seat he had lost in 1837. Their only chance of getting Roebuck returned, however, depended on him securing the votes of those workers on the electoral register as well as their own.

Roebuck showed that he had not altered his fundamental principles. While concerned with distancing himself from violence, nevertheless he made it quite plain that Chartists had been unjustly treated by the legal system: 'Put up a goose and say he was a Chartist and he would by magistrates be given two years' imprisonment.'[14] He still saw the struggle as one where 'aristocracy and democracy will be fairly arraigned against each other; no middle party will exist and no middle course will be pursued.' His definition of 'aristocracy' was 'all who on account of their birth, position or their wealth, believe that they ought to have exclusive and peculiar political privileges.' Obviously Chartists felt obliged to support someone who stood on such a programme.

The problem was that Bath was a two-member constituency. To get elected, Roebuck needed to secure not only the Chartist and radical vote, he also had to persuade some of the Whigs not to use their second vote for the Tory candidate. He succeeded and was again MP for Bath. However, his success was slightly marred by violence on the hustings. Colonel William Napier found the compromise with the Whigs too much to stomach. He punched a Whig supporter in the face. A fight ensued, and Roebuck had to separate them. But Napier was still seething with anger. Along with R. K. Philp and W. P. Roberts, he held a public meeting. He told his audience that he rejoiced at being free from electoral inhibitions; that he would never again stain his soul with hypocrisy, letting himself be 'dragged along at the wheels of the car of Whiggery'. He warned the Chartists that, just as the Whig government (1832–41) had betrayed them, given the opportunity the Whigs would do it again.[15]

Locally, Roebuck's victory, by his biggest-ever majority, remained for Chartists one of the few hopeful signs on an otherwise bleak political horizon. When previously an MP, he had acted as the parliamentary spokesman for the oppressed, voicing a multitude of grievances on behalf of the people. These had ranged from illiterate Irish peasants to London cab drivers, from the writers and publishers who suffered from the act imposing 'a tax on knowledge' (a phrase he coined) to his defence of trade unionists, the victims of anti-working-class legislation. Outstanding was his denunciation of the treatment of the Tolpuddle Martyrs, the political and legal chicanery which lay behind their transportation. Besides all this, Roebuck remained sympathetic to the ends, if not the means, of Chartism.

Members of the Bath Working Men's Association could point to tangible benefits arising from their alliance with Roebuck and the middle-class radicals. When Joseph Sturge formed the Complete Suffrage Union in November 1841, most of them viewed it in a positive light, perhaps as a way of building the type of middle-class–working-class alliance throughout Britain that had worked so well in Bath. When the union held its first national conference in February 1842, Wiltshire was well-represented; Vincent, Philp and Roberts attended, a reflection of the strong support in the county.

But the nature of the Complete Suffrage Union turned out to be rather different from what many Wiltshire Chartists had envisaged. The first conference became bogged down by a seemingly superficial semantic argument. Beneath this, however, lurked a fundamental issue: what kind of organization was the Complete Suffrage Union to be? Formed by a group of millowners and other employers after a meeting of the Anti-Corn Law League, its founders sought to further class harmony, not conflict. They recognized that workers had many legitimate grievances, including the virtual absence of parliamentary representation. In contrast to the generally accepted position of Whigs and Tories, who believed the working class was dangerous and therefore should be excluded from the political process, they thought that to grant manhood suffrage eventually would inject greater stability. Workers would thereby be given a stake, albeit a subordinate stake, in the system. Consequently, conflicts would find expression through harmless constitutional channels; people would not be forced through frustration into extremism or violence.

To achieve this extension of the franchise, however, and not to alienate those as yet unconvinced about the wisdom of the move, leaders of the Complete Suffrage Union considered it imperative for the labouring masses to remain on their best behaviour. Though often described as an attempt to build a middle-class–working-class alliance, Dorothy Thompson correctly says the underlying aim was to prise the moderate and respectable section of the Chartist leadership away from the rest of the movement. She could have added that it was also hoped that Chartism, reeling from this severe blow, would never recover.[16]

Even before the birth of the Complete Suffrage Union, as we have already seen, there were moves in Bath to develop an alliance between Chartists and the middle class. Addressing a public meeting at the Corn Market in August 1841, Vincent denounced the Whigs and Tories, arguing that Chartists should forge an alliance with the middle class against their mutual oppressor, the aristocracy. In an effort to secure unity, Vincent was prepared to jettison things that might offend middle-class susceptibilities, such as the name 'Chartist'. Roberts spoke next and, while making it plain that he wished to attain an alliance with the middle class, stressed that he was not prepared to make the same concessions as Vincent – he was still proud to call himself a Chartist.[17] Moreover, he was suspicious of those middle-class councillors who, while making airy and vague statements of support, did not translate them into action. In particular, he attacked those who still denied Chartists use of the Bath Guildhall.[18] Later, Roberts went on to criticize the 'warily-worded resolutions' of the Complete Suffrage Union, designed to avoid giving offence to individuals of discordant opinions. This running away from statements of political principle would not, in his opinion, assist the cause.

Yet, despite these reservations, Roberts continued to support an alliance. In February 1842, he addressed a big torchlight rally at Beacon Hill, outside Bath, on the subject.[19] The following month influential householders and manufacturers in Bradford-on-Avon organized a meeting for Vincent and himself, when resolutions were passed calling for the repeal of the Corn Laws and in favour of the Charter. In his contributions there and elsewhere, Roberts clearly stated his basic reason for supporting the alliance: many of the grievances of the working class were shared by the middle class. They, too, were under-represented in Parliament. As a result, much of the legislation passed, like the Corn Laws, adversely affected both classes. Both groaned under the heavy weight of taxation, a result of corruption, extravagance and nepotism in high places. The economic policies of the government had produced the current economic crisis – which turned out to be the worst of the century. Universal suffering would, Roberts predicted, create the conditions that led to universal suffrage.[20]

Roberts' forecast proved to be incorrect. Far from forging greater unity, the advent of the Complete Suffrage Union (CSU) had exactly the opposite effect. As David McNulty has stated, the CSU ruptured the Radical–Chartist alliance, weakening both camps: 'The CSU in Bath drew in some Chartists, but more significantly organised the Radicals in an association that for the first time was opposed to the Chartists.'[21] The Chartist defectors included two of their most prominent and valuable leaders, Henry Vincent and R. K. Philp, who had been recently elected a member of the National Charter Association's seven-man executive committee. The division at Bath reflected developments elsewhere in Britain. At a national conference in December 1842, middle-class leaders of the Complete Suffrage Union sought to assert that it was under their absolute control. Without consulting the Chartists or anyone else, they arrived at the gathering with an already printed list of resolutions and declared that, unless these were accepted *in toto*, they would withdraw. Incensed by this high-handed attitude, the rest of the conference rejected the diktat. From that moment onwards, if not before, the Complete Suffrage Union regarded the Chartists as political opponents and sought to poach any of them who might be won to their thoroughly respectable cause.

That Roberts did not succumb to these blandishments may, at first glance, seem surprising. When the CSU was formed, he joined it while maintaining his membership of the National Charter Association. Nevertheless, initially within the Chartist organization, he expressed many of the criticisms made by the middle-class radicals. He attacked what he saw as the personal dictatorship of O'Connor. He also thought that there had been unedifying displays of intolerance. For instance, instead of judging William Lovett's plan to promote educational Chartism on its merits, it had been denounced as an attempt to subvert and destroy the movement.

Notwithstanding these criticisms, Roberts was eventually won back to the cause. When O'Connor made a visit to Bath, the two men struck up a close personal friendship. Roberts took him around, showing the sights and introducing him to people. What apparently clinched matters, however, was experience of the Complete Suffrage Union's actions – or rather lack of them. Since it was not a working-class organization and wanted workers to remain in a docile, passive role, the CSU did not hold any rousing campaigns and demonstrations, which Roberts believed to be an essential ingredient of success. Even more important in his eyes, its quest for respectability made it refuse any assistance when the poor were arrested or imprisoned. The example of Sir John Fife, who belonged to the CSU's Newcastle and Gateshead branch, is illustrative of the gap between Roberts and the Union. He had gained his knighthood when, as Mayor of Newcastle in 1839, he called out the military to crush a Chartist demonstration. The ensuing battle of the Forth (an area behind what today is Newcastle Central Station) left Chartists intensely bitter over Sir John's conduct. Ruefully, they recalled his fiery speeches during the 1831–2 agitation for an extension of the franchise, when he talked about civil disobedience and even an insurrection being necessary.[22] Regarding him as a traitor to the cause, they held Sir John personally responsible for calling out the troops in the summer of 1839 to disperse a Chartist demonstration. With considerable exaggeration, they described the battle of the Forth as the North East's equivalent to the Peterloo massacre.

Nevertheless, Sir John Fife was an individual who favoured the gradual, orderly extension of the franchise. While knowing how to keep the rowdy mob in its place, he simultaneously became a leading supporter of the Complete Suffrage Union. This was in vivid contrast to the stand of W. P. Roberts, who became more firmly anchored in Chartism after the wave of repression. Throughout his whole life, the People's Attorney always identified himself with the victims, not the victimizers.

There was, moreover, another important point, illuminated by analysing the notion of 'alliance with the middle class'. In his research into Bath, Professor R. S. Neale has sought to sharpen definitions of class. He used the term 'middle class' to refer to the petit bourgeoisie, those aspiring professional men, of whom Roberts was one, who did not have a share in the power or privileges of the upper class. From the ranks of these outsiders, remarkably numerous in the city, the recruits to radicalism mainly came. Neale contrasts them with the middle class of industrial and commercial property-owners, and well-established professional men. They tended to be Whig or Tory, combining political orthodoxy with a deferential attitude to the upper class. An examination of Chartist ranks may disclose reasons for accepting Neale's definition as a helpful clarification. Was William Potts, of Trowbridge, with his small chemist shop, to be designated as middle class or working class? And what about the Bartlett brothers, who made a meagre living from their business mending shoes? The fact is that in this period there was frequently little or no difference in income or outlook between the ordinary worker and the small, perhaps minute, capitalist.

It will also be useful, when considering the idea of an 'alliance with the middle class', to further investigate what the actors involved understood by an alliance. Henry Vincent, for instance, was always extremely consistent. Writing from prison, immediately after Newport, the lessons he drew from the débâcle were disarmingly simple: physical force was a dead-end; moral force led nowhere either. All efforts should be concentrated on campaigning for the commuting of the death sentences passed on Frost and his comrades. But how was this to be achieved? As the political influence of Chartism was exceedingly limited – perhaps counter-productive with those wielding state power – the appeals stood a greater chance of success when they came from respectable members of the middle class. Gradually and imperceptibly, therefore, Vincent saw the way forward in terms of winning over the middle class, persuading it to support the desired changes. When Vincent and Philp joined the Complete Suffrage Union, they completely dropped out of all Chartist activity. In some respects, their evolution was like that of many Russian Bolsheviks after 1905: the revolution was defeated and therefore they, demoralized, thought that to maintain a revolutionary organization was futile. They became, to use Lenin's term, liquidationists. Similarly, Vincent was a liquidationist, seeing no further useful role for Chartism after Newport. Working-class strength had been mobilized and found wanting.

A modern analogy can also be made for Roberts' position – that of the united front, where people and organizations of differing political outlooks combine to fight for an immediate common objective. The pre-Second World War anti-fascist campaign or the struggles for nuclear disarmament would be cited as instances of this tactic. Roberts was always prepared to unite on a given issue with those with whom he disagreed, provided he thought it would advance working-class interests. Hence, he was a leading supporter of Roebuck. Dr McNulty even describes him as the pivotal person in the creation of the Chartist–Radical alliance in Bath, and this is correct. But McNulty could well have added that, at times, Roberts had exactly the opposite effect, for his support of Roebuck's philosophical radicalism fell far short of blind adulation. For example, when in 1839 the MP had backed the Poor Law Amendment Act, Roberts was among his foremost critics, denouncing the inhumanity of the new system. He led a group of 120 people, 'chiefly mechanics', who closely questioned their MP and made their own views about the hated workhouses abundantly clear. Also in 1837, when 500 radicals attended the inaugural meeting of the Bath Election and Registration Society, Roberts made it plain from the outset that he thought working people should have a big voice in the new organization. He moved a resolution that a third of the twenty-one places on the executive committee should be kept for workers. This was carried – but at a price. Key middle-class individuals then refused to participate in an organization where the common people figured so prominently. As a result, the new organization, which could have been a vital part in securing Roebuck's re-election, remained still-born. Yet, undaunted by this setback, Roberts proceeded in the same year to help form the Bath Working Men's Association, the first body both entirely run and controlled by working people in the city.

Almost certainly, these notes of discord contributed to Roebuck's defeat in the 1837 general election. Doubtless Roberts regretted this: he wanted to see Roebuck returned as MP for Bath. What had become paramount to him, however, overriding all other considerations, were the interests of working people. Whereas the defeats in the West Country led Vincent to move his political allegiance, they simply served to confirm Robert's general position. He moved geographically, not politically. Wiltshire was now becoming a backwater; the industrialized North of England was emerging as the decisive battlefield for the working class. A general strike of unprecedented dimensions had just occurred there, and that was where Roberts' future lay.

5 The General Strike

The turning-point in Roberts' life came in 1842. From then onwards, he stayed firmly fixed in the camp of labour, a warrior in a class cause. Though playing only a very minor role in the drama of that year, he was deeply and abidingly influenced by the ruthless way in which the judicial juggernaut rode over working people. Obviously, Britain's rulers saw the events in a different light. For them, it was the worst year of the century, fraught with much greater dangers than the existing order had ever encountered. Whereas in 1839 they had faced the challenge of Chartism, its mass meetings and demonstrations – although on a bigger scale than before – were nevertheless a continuation of the radical tradition. In 1842 there was all this and something else as well – mass collective activity, the arrival of the working class as a new, sinister force.

A general strike, unprecedented in any capitalist country, began among the ironworkers and colliers of the Midlands, swept riotously through the Potteries, and then engulfed Lancashire, Yorkshire and parts of Scotland. Almost all the industrialized regions of Britain, except the North East, were affected.

The West Country remained very much a backwater, well away from the storm centres. Even so, it had its troubles. On 14 April 1842, Wiltshire magistrates wrote to the Home Secretary, warning him not to withdraw troops stationed there: 'The spirit of Chartism still exists extensively and public meetings are being held.' They specifically mentioned Roberts' activities, fearful of the consequences these might have among the large number of unemployed. Soon afterwards, as if to confirm their warning, an attempt to levy the burgeoning poor rate led to a riot and tumult. Another communication to the Home Office complained about a Chartist meeting at Trowbridge, where speeches were 'calculated to irritate and exasperate the minds of the people'. Three policemen present had dirt and gravel thrown at them.[1] But this was trivial in comparison to what happened elsewhere.

The general strike has to be considered against the background of a deteriorating economic situation. The down-swing of the business cycle, which had begun in 1837, steadily became worse – workers had been defeated in their attempt to prevent wage cuts – until the trough was reached in 1842, when suffering and deprivation were widespread. A Wolverhampton surgeon reported that many pitmen's families had pawned all their furniture and other possessions to buy food. In North Lancashire people were digging up and eating the carcasses of diseased animals. At Stockport, where unemployment had reached an estimated 75 per cent, the local workhouse was raided and looted for bread.[2]

All this was happening in a society already wracked by the tensions of industrialization. Primary capital accumulation, as Marx declared, was written in the annals of history in letters of blood and fire. In order to introduce the initial capital needed for the industrial revolution, it was necessary to cut the proportion of the national income going to consumption and increase that going to investment. From the low economic starting point, the only way extra resources could be found for building the new factories and machinery was to coerce the labour force into making further sacrifices. To workers, however, accepting that their own labour power created all the wealth, what it meant was a higher rate of exploitation. Longer hours, lower pay and child labour were expressions of this process.

To make matter worse, the growth of urbanization meant people experienced this added hardship while living in towns, usually overcrowded, insanitary and lacking basic amenities. Both the quality and quantity (i.e. expectation) of life appeared to have deteriorated.

In addition to these economic and social grounds for grievances, workers also had political ones. The enclosure acts and game laws made illegal what had been customary practices, such as catching the occasional rabbit and using common land to augment the family diet. The government's fiscal policy, falling disproportionately on the least well-off, included the imposition of taxes upon essentials like bread. It seemed to many people, moreover, that government actions had contributed to – indeed, perhaps, caused – the appalling slump.

The 1842 Chartist convention, where Roberts was one of the twenty-five delegates, resolved to call upon workers everywhere to have a day's stoppage of work to coincide with the presentation of the Charter to Parliament.[3] In that way, it was hoped, the legislators would recognize the strength of feeling which lay behind the petition's 3,317,752 signatures. The public meetings, addressed by prominent Chartists like Roberts in an attempt to win support for the one-day strike, gained only limited support and the Commons rejected the petition by 287 votes to 49. However, perhaps all their efforts helped to lodge in workers' minds the idea of taking industrial action for political ends; an idea which would already be familiar to those who had read, or heard of, William Benbow's pamphlet, published in 1832, advocating a general strike to attain workers' political demands.[4]

The general strike of the summer and early autumn of 1842 was not completely unexpected, for increasingly people were linking economic and political demands, seeing that, by downing tools, they might not only struggle for better conditions but also for the Charter. What was perhaps not anticipated, however, was the result of this mass action, the consequence of so many people learning by doing rather than reading. As people discarded their passive social role and became aware that they could actively mould their own futures, new attitudes and new passions were manifest. The starvelings were actually arising from their slumbers, even though the British state had the force to knock them unconscious again.

Historians, in my opinion, have tended to misinterpret these events. Pages and pages have been written, trying to unravel whether the thrust of workers' demands in 1842 was economic or political, as if everything could be placed into such water-tight compartments. Admittedly, the labourist ideology has always tried to do this. It fails, however, to fit the facts.

The general strike of 1842 can now be considered in the contexts of subsequent general strikes. In 1905, a Russian priest led a march of the Petrograd poor to plead with the Tsar, in the most abject fashion, to help lessen their sufferings. Once the reply came in the form of troops, firing indiscriminately into the crowd, a dramatic transformation took place. From being remarkably servile, from making extraordinarily modest economic demands, suddenly the crowd – indeed, the whole proletariat of Petrograd – began making political demands of the most extreme kind. They set up workers' councils (soviets), starting a revolution that spread throughout the country and threatened the existence of Tsarism itself. Rosa

Luxemburg, whose pamphlet *The Mass Strike, the Political Party and the Trade Unions*, remains one of the most perceptive analyses of the subject, emphasizes the constant interaction of politics and economics: 'In a word, the economic struggle is the factor that advances the movement from one political focal point to another. The political struggle periodically fertilises the ground for the economic struggle. Cause and effect interact every second. Thus we find that the two elements, the economic and the political, do not incline to separate themselves from one another.'[5]

From very differing standpoints, there was considerable agreement on the significance of the 1842 events. Karl Marx, who, it is interesting to note, referred to it as 'the 1842 uprising', observed that 'workers who combine and go on strike very soon find themselves compelled to act in a revolutionary way'.[6] Very much the same conclusion was reached by individuals of a completely different political complexion. On 15 August 1842, Queen Victoria wrote to one of her ministers: 'The character of these riots has assumed a more decidedly political aspect. It is no longer a strike for higher wages, but the delegates, who direct the movement, avow that labour shall not be resumed until the People's Charter be granted.'[7] Likewise Sir James Graham, her Home Secretary, saw the Trades' conference, meeting in Manchester, as 'the directing body: they form the links between the trade unions and the Chartists.' Manchester's chief constable added his support to this view: 'The affair is becoming more and more political.'[8]

From the Chartists' standpoint, the problem was that these links were often tenuous, forged in the midst of struggle and easily broken. The mechanism necessary to direct the struggle, a centralized command structure able to lead the workers to final victory, did not exist. Even had it existed, it remains highly doubtful whether there would have been a successful outcome. Localism, their own pressing personal grievances, limited the mental horizons of most people. Such was the immense suffering and deprivation, the majority had not the resources for a prolonged fight. Once they had achieved their immediate objectives, they returned to work: the withdrawal of the proposed pay reductions, perhaps in some instances even an increase, was sufficient to lure them back to work without any political concessions being granted.

Yet, the first general strike to happen in any capitalist country left the authorities rightly alarmed. It is hardly surprising that Queen

Victoria, as Dr F. C. Mather writes, threw all her considerable influence on the side of energetic repression. Both her crown and her government seemed under threat. Consequently, she wrote to Sir Robert Peel, the Prime Minister, complaining that she was 'surprised at the little (or no) opposition to the dreadful riots in the Potteries ... at the passiveness of the troops ... they ought to act and these meetings ought to be prevented ... everything ought to be done to apprehend Cooper and all the delegates at Manchester.'[9]

The authorities appear to have tried to oblige the royal command. Demonstrators were shot dead in Blackburn, Preston and the Potteries.[10] Mass arrests took place, especially in North Staffordshire, and Chartist leaders were also taken into custody and charged.[11] It was at this stage that Roberts intervened, trying to help those arraigned before the courts. His involvement mainly occurred in North Staffordshire, the area where rioting had been most severe and repression the most intense.

The background to events in the Potteries was similar to those elsewhere. It had been severely hit by the depression; the workhouses were overcrowded, prices high and wage cuts frequent. The spark that set the district alight was struck in early June by W. H. Sparrow, the Longton coalowner, when he disregarded the law and failed to give the statutory fortnight's notice before imposing a hefty pay reduction. The men responded by downing tools. Then they walked around the Potteries, with banners and loaves of bread on poles, demanding money from any wealthy citizen they chanced to see. Also, they vowed vengeance – the killing of Sparrow and his manager.

Early in July, Ridgway, Hanley's leading pottery manufacturer and chairman of the Stoke Board of Guardians, went on a deputation to the Prime Minister. Unless something was quickly done, he warned Peel, 'a struggle will commence, of which no man can foresee the extent and consequences'. His prediction proved to be correct. As other coalowners imposed wage cuts, colliers went on strike. This, in turn, made it impossible for the pottery manufacturers, dependent on plentiful supplies of coal, to continue production.

While a Committee of Operative Colliers strove to co-ordinate resistance, the task was a daunting one. Set up in the heat of battle, it had scant resources, few long-established contacts, and often had to improvise. The arrival of two companies of troops, sent for by the magistrates, gave an indication of the authorities' resolve. The troops might not have been able to protect the widely scattered collieries and potbanks. Nevertheless their intimidatory presence did sap the strikers' morale. Still more crucial in generating a drift back to work was the desperate hunger, the inability to stay out any longer.

By early August, an uneasy peace had returned to the Potteries. Yet, tension remained high. The arrest of three pitmen for begging resulted in an angry crowd, demanding their release, attacking and breaking windows at Burslem Town Hall, as well as the homes of the police superintendent and publican who had been responsible for the arrest. Industrial unrest returned as workers experienced the consequences of lower wages.

Chartism had become strong in the Potteries. A young writer from Leicester, Thomas Cooper, was invited to address a series of public meetings. Speaking from Crown Bank, Hanley, he took the sixth commandment, 'Thou shalt do no murder', as his text, and argued that the existing system was life-denying, or rather life-destroying. In his autobiography, Cooper described how the temper of his audience rose as they heard his speech:

> I showed how kings, in all ages, had enslaved the people, and spilt their blood in wars of conquest, thus violating the precept, 'Thou shalt do no murder'.
> I described our own guilty Colonial rule, and still guiltier rule in Ireland; and asserted that British rulers had most awfully violated the precept, 'Thou shalt do no murder'.
> I asserted that the imposition of the Bread Tax was a violation of the same precept; and that such was the enactment of the Game Laws; that such was the custom of primogeniture and keeping of land in the possession of privileged classes; and that such was the enactment of the infamous new Poor Law . . .
> I asserted that the attempts to lessen the wages of the toilers underground, who were in hourly and momentary danger of their lives, and to disable them from getting the necessary food for themselves and their families, were violations of the precept, 'Thou shalt do no murder'.[12]

As Cooper continued his catalogue of iniquities committed by those in power, his audience grew angrier and angrier. They vowed to take retribution. Twenty-seven years later, he accepted responsibility for causing the disturbances: he wrote that he had 'struck the spark which kindled all into combustion'. But Bob Fyson, who has written the best account of the Potteries in 1842, argues that the decisive factor was the arrival of news from the Trades conference in Manchester, calling for a general strike until the Charter was achieved.[13]

What is not in dispute, however, is the violent sequence of events that followed. This included the enforcement of the general strike at almost every pit and potbank; an attack on Hanley police station, with the release of prisoners and the burning of office files; the wrecking of the home of the collector of poor rates and the office of the Court of Requests. At Stoke, the police station was ransacked, the furniture burnt and cutlasses stolen. Next came the house of Thomas Allen at Fenton, where, after helping themselves to the ample provisions in the larder and wine in the cellar, the climax came when the family deeds were burnt on the lawn. At Longton, the house of the Reverend Dr Benjamin Vale was ransacked and set alight. Some of the looters, who had partaken too freely of the cleric's wines, were so drunk that they were unable to run away when the troops arrived.

The rioters' targets appear to have followed a fairly set pattern. Police stations were raided to free prisoners and acquire weapons; naturally, wealthy coalowners and pottery manufacturers were singled out, as were magistrates, ministers of the Church of England and poor law guardians. Unfortunately for the Rector of Longton, he fell into the last three of these much-hated categories. So detested was he that a Primitive Methodist lay preacher, among those charged with destroying Longton rectory, told the court he was only obeying God's command when he set fire to Dr Vale's house.

The authorities were, at first, quite overwhelmed by the extent and ferocity of the disorders. Under cover of darkness, the magistrates and troops withdrew to Newcastle-under-Lyme. This meant that they had left the Potteries in the hands of the rioters. Destruction continued unabated. The colliery offices of the Earl of Granville, North Staffordshire's biggest coalowner, were set on fire; likewise Albion House, Shelton, the home of William Parker, JP, as well as that of the Reverend R. E. Aitken. A loud explosion announced to the world that Shelton ironworks was no longer in business. It remained out of production for at least two years.[14] But, as the rioting started to subside and the authorities had mobilized superior force, they moved back into the Potteries, restoring order and making mass arrests. They took into custody the largest batch of demonstrators arrested at any disturbance in the nineteenth century. Eventually, 276 people were tried, forty-nine transported and 116 imprisoned.[15]

Regarded as the instigator of the riots, Thomas Cooper not surprisingly found himself under arrest. He was taken to Hanley and from there to Newcastle-under-Lyme, escorted by sixteen soldiers with fixed bayonets, before being consigned to Stafford prison. He was a highly talented, self-educated man. He knew by heart the whole of Milton's *Paradise Lost*, Shakespeare's *Hamlet* and many other works. So, to wile away the long hours of imprisonment, he recited poetry as well as composing some of his own. Suddenly one day his thoughts were unexpectedly interrupted – W. P. Roberts entered the cell. Later, in his autobiography, Cooper recalled his astonishment: 'I felt stunned, as if a person had given me a blow to the head.'

Roberts had come to give him legal advice. In doing this, he was merely continuing to provide the same service he had already given to Vincent at Monmouth in 1839 and O'Connor at York in 1840. In the current case, Cooper was charged with arson, aiding and abetting the burning down of Justice Parker's house. Seventeen others were to be tried for the same offence. From his knowledge of legal procedure, Roberts told Cooper that it was essential he should be tried separately from the other seventeen – otherwise 'you are a lost man.' He then went on to suggest what should be done:

> Mind what I say: you have a chance of a fair trial if you do two things: first, you must demand 'to sever', that is, to be tried alone. If you persist in your demand, you will gain it. Secondly, you must 'challenge the jury', that is, you must ask every juryman, before he is sworn, whether he has served on any trial during this Special Assize – and then object to him if he has so served – for all who have hitherto served are prejudiced men. Refuse to plead either 'guilty' or 'not guilty' before the court grants you leave to sever and to challenge the jury.[16]

Thomas Cooper took Roberts' advice. Despite strong pressure, particularly from Sir William Follett, he insisted on securing both demands. When his separate trial did take place, a formidable number of witnesses gave damning evidence. They had seen him among the demonstrators as they approached Justice Parker's house. Some had even seen him in the bedroom. Others had heard him congratulating the mob as they were returning from burning down the house of Dr Vale: 'My lads, you have done your work well today.' But Cooper denied all this. He said – and brought witnesses to prove it – that he was several miles away when the house of Justice Parker went up in flames. Also, he claimed he had never congratulated the mob that burnt down Dr Vale's home. What he had actually said was 'You have done good work in turning out the hands' – in other words, in making the strike solid. In summing up his defence, Thomas Cooper addressed the jury for two hours. He declared himself to be a Christian, in the fullest sense of the word, an enemy of drunkenness, outrage and killing. Described by the *Northern Star* as a 'most soul-stirring and thrilling defence', almost everybody in the courtroom was overcome by emotion. Even the seasoned Sir Nicholas Tindal, presiding, was said to have been moved by the passionate sincerity of Cooper's oratory:

> The judge, it was observed by Roberts, who was his kinsman and knew him very well, was much affected with my address; and some of the ladies near him shed tears. In summing up, the judge told the jury, most positively, that they could not convict me of the crime of arson; and I certainly was at Burslem, and not at Hanley, during the time Mr Parker's house was on fire. The jury retired; and, after 20 minutes of agonising suspense for myself, gave in their verdict of 'Not Guilty'.

The prisoner left the court triumphant. He told his friends that 'the 10-day trial had made him eager to be tried all over again.' Shortly afterwards, he had his wish granted. As we have already seen, a frequent legal strategem of the authorities was to hold a second set of charges in reserve, to be brought out if the first failed. This time he was charged with conspiracy and seditious libel. All prominent Chartists in the Potteries, including Joseph Capper, William Ellis and John 'Daddy' Richards, were charged with him. Again, Roberts proffered advice, suggesting the case should be adjourned until a later session. Finally, it came before the spring assizes at Stafford in March 1843.[17] Cooper was found guilty, and sent to the Court of Queen's Bench for sentencing. There, in May 1843, he received two years' imprisonment.

By this time, W. P. Roberts' attention had turned to the North East, where at Wingate Grange colliery events were then happening that would result in one of his big cases – the wire-rope controversy. But his experiences in North Staffordshire had an enduring effect upon him. They helped to strengthen even more his links with pitmen and their communities. They also confirmed his view that the judicial system had a built-in bias against working people, especially if they happened to be Chartists. Against them, evidence would not be assessed with anything approaching impartiality. Some years earlier, Lord Brougham had pointed out that the appointment of judges was made on political grounds, a point which he said should have disquaified them from presiding over sensitive political trials. In office at the time of the 1842 general strike, Home Secretary Sir James Graham boasted that all the magistrates he had appointed were Tories. The Jury Act of 1825 imposed property qualifications which, as Professor Pelling states, 'ruled out the great bulk of the working class' from serving. Indeed, where there was a trial by special commission, as in Staffordshire, the position was even worse. To sit on a special jury one had to be a banker, a merchant or to have at least attained the rank of esquire. A relatively recent innovation, special commissions had been introduced because, it was claimed, ordinary juries were often ill-equipped to cope with cases that involved complex commercial issues. They were also, as the Revd J. R. Stephens pointed out at his trial in 1840, handy weapons that the authorities deployed in political trials, tipping the scales of justice still further against the accused.[18]

Severe handicaps like these, obstacles to impartiality, were overlooked by contemporary newspapers and politicians. Those accused of the disturbances in the Potteries were tried before the associated hysteria had died down. Yet, the generally accepted view was that they received fair trials and just punishment. Even with hindsight, historian Bob Fyson thinks those charged in the Potteries were not more severely treated than others arrested in similar disturbances at other times. Professor Radzinowicz goes still further. He believes the authorities showed remarkable wisdom and forbearance; that their aim was not to leave any lasting bitterness; rather to create a climate for reconciliation. He points out that in neither 1839 nor in 1842 did they introduce the Six Gag Acts as in 1817.[19]

It is difficult to reconcile Professor Radzinowicz's view with that generally accepted by ordinary folk of the Potteries at the time. Even the *Staffordshire Examiner* felt constrained to express sympathy with the victims of 'justice': 'He must have a very cold heart who is not deeply moved by the family bereavements which the Special Commission has spread around us ... The accusers of the unhappy convicts, who are now suffering the penalty of their folly, did not come into the courts with clean hands. They should have purged themselves of their own injustice to the poor before executing injustice on despair.'[20] The need to uphold the sanctity of private property appears to have been upmost in the judges' minds and the number of long prison sentences and transportations was greater than those given for any other nineteenth-century riots.[21] For destroying Dr Vale's house, six men were transported for twenty-one years, another for fifteen years and a further five for ten years. On top of these, thirteen more received lesser periods of imprisonment. All told, the total came to 197 years. 'Measured in terms of human suffering,' comments an historian of Methodism, 'the Reverend Doctor Vale had lived in a most costly home.'[22]

In reply, it could be argued, as Radzinowicz does, that nobody was transported only for rioting or for sedition. An analysis of the records reveals that the prisoners had been found guilty of 'demolishing a house', sometimes with 'larceny' or 'cutting and wounding' a policeman in addition.[23] Nevertheless, the punishment of transportation may seem draconian to anyone who turns to the account (in chapter 13) of the ordeals in Australia of John Frost, leader of the Newport uprising. And even the milder sentence of imprisonment in this country could have fatal consequences. Historians of the Radzinowicz school are over-reliant on official sources; almost unquestioningly accepting a Whitehall view of the world, they do not bother to discover how orders from on high are translated into practice by state underlings.

The treatment of Chartist prisoners varied widely. Most of them were rather different from the average inmate – more articulate, better educated, a few of them middle class. There were those prisons where, appreciating the higher quality of prisoner, treatment was exceptionally good. At York, though he complained loudly, O'Connor really had nothing to complain about: he could have guests, a servant and food brought into his cell.[24] Likewise, McDouall in Chester gaol must have had a relatively easy sojourn: he left prison with his future wife, a warder's daughter. The Sunderland Chartist leader, James Williams, went one better and married wealthy Miss Taylor, of Aberdeen, who happened to be staying with the governor of Durham gaol.[25]

But the majority of Chartist prisoners did not receive such favourable treatment. Their gaolers, aware of the hatred and contempt which those in the upper echelons of society had for the Chartists, adopted these feelings in an exaggerated form. They believed they were merely doing their masters' bidding when they inflicted a little extra discomforture, perhaps even pain, on their captives. Years later, Lloyd Jones, whose judgements were usually balanced and who was personally acquainted with some of the victims, wrote: 'The treatment of Chartist prisoners in more than one of the gaols to which they were consigned, however instigated, had as an intention, on the part of those who inflicted it, the death of certain of the prisoners.' He illustrated his point by taking the case of Samuel Holberry, the Sheffield Chartist.[26]

This treatment needs to be set against the fact that all Victorian prisons were hell-holes, places of dirt, disease and death. Ominously, it seems the authorities did not bother to keep records of the death rate in prison, as was done for the country as a whole. Almost immediately after his arrival in Monmouth gaol, Henry Vincent wrote a harrowing letter describing a fellow inmate who had just died of starvation.[27]

W. P. Roberts knew about Vincent's gaol experiences as well as his own. He must also have heard, directly or indirectly, about the experiences of some of the 749 people arrested in the 1842 general strike. Doubtless, it was with this at the back of his mind, wanting to avoid situations which might lead to mass arrests, that he wrote an open letter to all pitmen in the North East cautioning them during the big industrial dispute of 1844 to be ultra-cautious, not to allow themselves to be provoked into violence. He added.

> When one of the POOR are injured very many others necessarily share in his sufferings; you have no pictures, horses or geegaws to divert you: to you, your friends are ALL. It is no exaggeration to say that for one man sentenced as a criminal (and it does not matter whether he is guilty or not – nor whether what he is charged with is a crime or not) ten families are thrown into lasting grief. The evil thus done becomes incalculable.[28]

6   The Victorian Working Class and the Law

By becoming the legal adviser to the Northumberland and Durham miners' county unions in August 1843, Roberts took a historically unprecedented step. Hitherto the law and all its works had been regarded as enemy territory by workers; only when arraigned before a court for punishment did they come into contact with it. To try to alter this situation – systematically using the judicial system both to defend workers and as a vehicle to claim their legal rights – was unheard of before Roberts began his struggle.

There were immense obstacles, inherent in the nature of the class system, that stood in his way. All men might be equal before the law, but some were more equal than others. The poverty and powerlessness of workers, not to mention their lack of literacy and knowledge of the law, were there to thwart his endeavours. The costs of taking a case to the high court could be prohibitive. In their history of lawyers and the courts, Brian Abel-Smith and Robert Stevens describe the position that then prevailed: 'The system of law administered by the superior courts, together with the appeal courts, were concerned with a very small percentage of the population. Only by killing another man was a poor man certain to have any contact with the royal courts.'[1] The prospect of appearing before a magistrates' court was greater but not necessarily more appealing. Giving evidence in 1842 before a Select Committee on the Payment of Wages, Dr McDouall stated that men were reluctant to seek legal redress, even when denied wages which legitimately belonged to them, as they were liable to receive an unsympathetic hearing.[2] Even worse, they might receive no hearing at all: to mention a case cited in a later chapter, a pitman, wanting money he was owed, had his case

71

dismissed by the magistrates at Easington, County Durham, who did not see why they should waste their time bothering about such a paltry sum. Yet, if they had heard the miner's claim, it could well have aroused the coalowner's wrath, having a much worse effect on the hapless man than losing his wages. He might have won back a few shillings at the expense of losing his job and being henceforth blacklisted throughout the industry.

When considering some of Roberts' victories, it needs to be remembered that his successes were often tempered by victimization. In the 1860s, he won two years' back pay for the orphan girl of Blaina (see chapter 14). But he then had to provide her with the money to emigrate, for no employer in South Wales was prepared to engage her. Similarly, in the Preston lock-out of 1853–4, where Roberts represented most of the union leaders arrested, the withdrawal of the charges did not mean that a man like Mortimer Grimshaw (allegedly used by Dickens as the basis for the character of Slackbridge in *Hard Times*) could escape punishment. Out of work, hungry and victimized, he was compelled to resort to begging. Eventually, Ashworth, a compassionate Bolton millowner, realized his plight and befriended him: a pencilled entry, written by Ashworth, in the documents on the Preston lock-out deposited in the Lancashire Records Office, records that he gave Grimshaw enough money to buy his passage to Australia. Even Roberts' triumph over the Bond ended on a sour note: the coalowners refused to open the Thornley colliery until, as happened after the miners' defeat in the 1844 dispute, the men were prepared to accept their interpretation of this document. It was not until 1869 that he finally succeeded in breaking the Bond.

Traditionally, workers were treated legally as non-persons, with no rights and no redress against any arrogant demands made by the authorities or their employers. The plight of the Scottish colliers provides an extreme example of this: under an Act of Parliament in 1606, they were made slaves, a condition that continued to prevail until 1799. The Act empowered masters to force them – as well as any vagabonds and sturdy beggars apprehended – to labour for six days a week indefinitely. Severe punishments were inflicted on anyone attempting to leave work without first obtaining a leaving certificate. In his classic history of the early days of the coal industry, J. U. Nef likens the position of Scottish colliers to that of the slaves on the plantations in the southern states of the USA.[3] Not that other

Scottish workers were given bountiful legal rights. In 1837, twelve Glasgow spinners were arrested, kept in gaol without knowing the reason for their imprisonment, and then never brought to trial. An authority on Scottish law suggests its most distinctive feature has always been, both in tradition and procedure, to emphasize its differences from English law.[4] While injustice was not perhaps as widespread as in Scotland, the English courts sometimes treated workers with the same indifference and disdain. For instance, in 1839 General Sir Charles Napier was being shown round Durham prison, when a man was pointed out to him. The prison inspector told him that the man was being illegally imprisoned for a year: the magistrates had not bothered to hear the case against him; they had merely left it to their clerk to pass sentence. Angrily, Sir Charles commented: 'No wonder we have Chartism' – and, he could have added, trade unionism, too.[5]

Reinforcing the attitude that the law provided employers with an absolute right to do whatever they wanted, was the soothing balm of ignorance. Magistrates, coalowners and others were not in the habit of walking around the streets, bumping into one other because they were so engrossed in reading parliamentary statutes. In other words, more crucial than the actual law was what it was perceived to be: the symbol of the law had more power than its substance. This played a large part in determining behaviour, by giving assurance to those from the upper echelons of society to assert their arrogance, whereas the legislation they cited to justify their conduct did no such thing. Much of W. P. Roberts' job was to prick this bubble of over-weaning self-confidence, based upon unwritten laws that really were not laws at all. The heated courtroom exchanges frequently occurred because he challenged the conception that, far from being impartial, legal authority was simply there to buttress the employers' authority.

Yet, even where laws were nominally impartial as between both sides of industry, capitalist reality still provided a built-in bias. The well-known Combination Acts of 1799 and 1800 illustrate this point.[6] These were supposed to apply equally to combinations of employers as well as to workers. While it is easy to cite innumerable cases where trade unionists were punished, employers were strangely immune from prosecution. Fear of intimidation, victimization and unfair treatment in hostile courts deterred workers from taking the same action against their employers that their employers and the state, with alacrity, took against them. The verdict of posterity on the

Combination Acts simply confirms the widely-held view of the times. One historian refers to them as 'totally selective', quite devoid of any fairness, while another says that they were 'obviously representative of state interference on the side of Capital against Labour rather than true laissez faire.'[7]

By the time Roberts became actively involved with industrial cases, the Combination Acts had been repealed. Their replacement, the 1825 Act, was an ambiguous piece of legislation, leaving trade unions in a limbo between legality and illegality. Section 3 (c) made it illegal to threaten to strike, whereas elsewhere it said that strikes over wages and conditions were legal. To complicate things still further, 'obstruction' and 'molestation', both undefined, broke the law. Then Sir William Erle, one of the foremost legal authorities of the day, construed these terms with a tight harshness. He held that simply to compel a master to raise wages would constitute 'obstruction' and 'molestation', a criminal act violating the 1825 Act section 3(c) as well as the common law. As if this were not bad enough for a trade union wishing to stay on the right side of the law, there were numerous other Acts of Parliament which could be deployed against it whenever it sought to attain its objectives. Among the array of legislation were measures dealing with breach of contract, demonstrating, picketing, oath-taking, etc.

Besides the curbs imposed by statute law, trade unionists also had to contend with another batch of restrictions, this time at the hands of the common law – in other words, the law created by judges. From the standpoint of the class system, the common law was a highly useful weapon because it was continually evolving, dealing with the tensions generated by the industrial revolution as they arose. It was especially vital as an answer to the challenge coming from the lower depths of society, where a newly-emerging working class began to flex its muscles. In countering this challenge, the law of conspiracy proved to be invaluable. It gave legal authority to the view that combinations whose object was to raise wages constituted conspiracies and therefore were illegal. Case law on this point dates back, at least, to the Journeymen Tailors' case of 1721, where it was held that what is quite legal for one to do may be illegal for many. In 1783, delivering a judgement, the great jurist Lord Mansfield elaborated on this principle: 'persons in possession of any articles of trade may sell them at such prices as they individually may please; but if they confederate and agree not to sell them under certain prices, it is conspiracy. So every man may work at what price he pleases, but a combination not to work under certain prices is an indictable offence.' In 1801, another judge explained the law of conspiracy in this way: although nobody has been convicted of hissing at a theatre on his own initiative, yet a joint agreement to hiss at a performance would be an indictable offence.[8]

Clearly, it follows from this that to hiss outside a factory gate – say, on a picket line – was an even more serious indictable offence. Indeed, once the law of conspiracy had been developed, virtually any working-class action *per se* became illegal. For the essence of the position of the working class has always been that as individuals workers were powerless; only through combination could the economic and political position of workers be improved – in other words, as the well-worn slogan put it, 'unity is strength'. So restrictive had the common law become that, as the economist, Nassau Senior, concluded in 1831, there was 'scarcely an act performed by any workman as a member of a trade union which is not an act of conspiracy and a misdemeanour.'[9]

Conspiracy could be used against workers not only when they acted industrially but also politically. A vivid description of what could occur was given by William Dixon, a prominent Lancashire Chartist. In 1846, he bitterly recounted to Lancashire miners how the authorities had violently broken up a Chartist meeting he had addressed at Wigan in August 1842: 'When they met to discuss their grievances, they were told by some upstart Justice, at the head of his mercenaries, that he admitted that the object of their meeting was perfectly legal, but their numbers made it illegal.' Reports written at the time, appearing in newspapers unfriendly to Chartism, nevertheless described the ruthless military repression that ensued. The *Manchester Guardian*, of 24 August 1842, said that Dixon 'had a brother lying seriously wounded, having no fewer than four sabre cuts. They had had a procession at Wigan and all was peaceful. Then the soldiers were ordered out, and they instantly attacked people on all sides.' The *Liverpool Mercury* added that a man, 'who was endeavouring to get out of the way, received a cut on the nose from an officer's sword and two boys were prodded in the thigh by soldiers' bayonets; one poor little fellow bled profusely.'[10]

The law of conspiracy – 'the elastic law of conspiracy' as the Webbs called it – placed tremendous power in the hands of judges and magistrates. Given almost free rein, their own personal quirks and political prejudices naturally came out in their decision-making. The utilitarian philosopher, Bentham, conceded: 'The word conspiracy served the judges as an excuse for inflicting punishment without stint on all persons by whom any act was committed which did not accord with the judge's notion concerning the act in question.' Years later, a left-wing lawyer, D. N. Pritt, added that the law of conspiracy is 'a formidable weapon of the ruling class in times of trouble.'[11]

In addition to all this, the ambiguous wording of much legislation provided judges with ample room for unfriendly interpretation. From the fourteenth century, the Statute of Justices had empowered the authorities to interfere with processions and demonstrations when people uttered 'rash, quarrelsome or unmannerly words'.[12] Where existing Acts of Parliament did not deal with a point, of course the judges could step in, adding to common law. This is what happened as a result of the Fenian cases of 1867–8 in which Roberts was involved: the judge's rulings laid down the principles on which subsequent political murder trials would be run.[13]

The judges' discretion, their ability not merely to be legal arbiters but law-makers as well, meant that immense power was placed in the hands of a few individuals. Who they were – their political attitudes, social position, economic standing – was of considerable importance, for it coloured all their actions. Yet, they were selected from a small, privileged section of the community. Analysis reveals that in the period 1760–1875 'the judiciary was composed primarily of the sons of the upper middle classes of England and increasingly of those from urban origins'.[14] Nine public schools provided a third of the judges appointed; two of them – Eton and Westminster – provided 20 per cent. Only 2.8 per cent came from the working class.[15] The cost of education, followed by legal training and, at the outset, after qualification, only meagre remuneration, placed any prospect of ever becoming a barrister, let alone a judge, far beyond the remotest prospect of the majority of young men. And for that matter it still does: it is a remarkable fact that when the period 1820–75 is compared with the period 1951–68, the percentage of working class judges has dropped by almost 60 per cent. It is now a mere 1.2 per cent of those appointed. So Oliver Goldsmith's adage – 'law grinds the poor, and rich men rule the law' – still holds true today.[16]

It is hardly surprising, in the circumstances, that the judiciary has always remained a bulwark of the established order. In capitalism's initial phase of development, Parliament strengthened the position of judges as guardians of wealth and privilege. It generously extended their powers to impose the supreme penalty: between 1688 and 1820 the number of offences carrying the death sentence increased from fifty to around 200.[17] That it was possible to hang a child for sheep-stealing was indicative of the importance attached to the sanctity of private property. On this, Edward Thompson commented: 'The ideology of the ruling oligarchy, which places a supreme value upon property, finds its visible and natural embodiment above all in the ideology and practice of the law. Tyburn Tree, as William Blake well understood, stood at the heart of this ideology, and its ceremonies were at the heart of popular culture, also.' (Originally, the expression 'to go west' meant to witness a public execution; Tyburn was roughly where Marble Arch is today.)[18]

However outrageous its conduct, the judiciary was able to protect itself from much hostile comment. The law of seditious libel, often used against Chartists, was couched in suitably broad terms, making it perilous for anyone to criticize a judge when he donned the black cap, or ordered the yeomanry, with their swords unsheathed, to charge into an unarmed demonstration. In 1819, at least eight were killed and 600 injured at the Peterloo massacre, and Sir Francis Burdett had the audacity to criticize the authorities for their conduct. As a result, he was sentenced to three months' imprisonment and fined £1,000. Under the law of seditious libel the test is not 'the truth of the language or the innocence with which the statement is published'; rather it is whether its use is liable 'to promote public disorder or physical force or violence in the matter of the State.' To quote the leading authority on seditious libel: 'To slander the sovereign, the administration, the constitution, either House of Parliament, or any judge or magistrate is not only sedition ... the defendant may be fined any amount or sentenced to a term of imprisonment of any length, or both, at the discretion of a judge, as in praemunire.'[19]

Obviously, the context in which criticism was made was always of paramount importance. Not that a few critical remarks uttered in polite society, or published in an expensive publication unlikely to fall into the wrong hands, would be treated in the same way as they would if spoken at a mass demonstration. For instance, in all sections of society, magistrates continued to be unpopular, and it is possible to cite numerous denunciations that did not produce a prosecution.

No action was taken against Edmund Burke when he declared them to be 'the scum of the earth'. Nor was anybody arraigned before the courts when in 1830 they endorsed what Lord Brougham had said, admittedly within the privileged precincts of Parliament, in a six-hour speech about the deficiencies of the judiciary in general and the magistrates' bench in particular. There was, he declared, 'not a worse constituted tribunal on the face of the earth' than the magistracy. Lord Brougham, soon to be appointed to the exalted position of Lord Chancellor – in other words, head of the country's judiciary – went on to say he shuddered 'to see the way in which the magistracy's extensive powers are sometimes exercised'.[20] In July 1841, General Charles Napier was still more scathing about the Newcastle magistracy. He reported: 'Every element of a ferocious civil war is boiling in this district, and if asked what class of men appear most just and most anxious to avoid it, I should say the officers; but of all classes the worst are the magistrates. The Tory magistrates are bold, violent, irritating and uncompromising; the Whig magistrates sneaking and base.'[21]

What made the situation even worse was the magistracy's frequent failure to heed the principles of natural justice. It was an age in which, as Abel-Smith and Stevens observed, 'If, at the central government level, the separation of powers was not yet complete, at the local level the possibility of its existence had scarcely been recognized.' That JPs saw their duties not in terms of judicial impartiality becomes obvious from a cursory inspection of Home Office files: these reveal how magistrates paid an impressive array of spies and informers – Colonel Fletcher, of Bolton, secured national notoriety for his zeal in this respect – resulting in a situation where magistrates could find themselves convicting people on the basis of evidence supplied by themselves. Still more important, their socio-economic circumstances usually prevented them from arriving at a verdict having heard, with open minds, both sides of the case. The magistrates, invariably representatives of the rich and powerful in their localities, had a vested interest in siding with the masters and against the men. Even if they had no direct links with the coal industry, in a county like Durham the fate of Lord Londonderry and other coalowners would have general repercussions on the economy throughout the region. The pull of mutual class interests remained immense and clouded judgement.

Naturally, workers resented the lack of justice in this system of 'justice'; the magistrates, always unpopular, were customarily the first target in a riot. In some instances, wishing to avoid the opprobrium of the mass of the people, individuals refused the invitation to become a JP.[22] W. P. Roberts, aware of their sensibilities, exploited the laxities of court procedure to denounce, and even vilify, magistrates in a manner that would not be permitted today. This, he hoped, would simultaneously have the effect of forcing the magistrates into a more fair-minded approach while strengthening workers' resolve and belief in the rectitude of their cause. Clearly, he had learnt the lessons of Tolpuddle: the six Dorsetshire labourers received a free pardon and passage back to England in March 1836. This happened neither because the law on illegal oaths had been repealed – indeed, it remained on the statute book until Lord Hailsham repealed it in 1981 – nor because suddenly after the 1834 convictions all trade unionists stopped taking illegal oaths. It was rather as a result of the widespread feeling of outrage and disgust: Tolpuddle was not only bringing the law generally into disrepute but also acting as a recruiting agent for the trade unions and other undesirable organizations. In the circumstances, it seemed much better to quietly forget about the act, let it fall into disuse. In a class society, the law has always operated to ensure smooth running of the exploitative system; when legislation actually aggravates the conflict between classes, then it has ceased to perform this function.

Besides expressing his sincere revulsion at the treatment of the working class, Roberts' courtroom histrionics were designed to make laws like the Master and Servant Act inoperable or counter-productive. In his fight, he was helped by the high level of interest Victorian society took in legal proceedings. One indication of this fact was that he regularly published the *Miners' Journal*, later the *Miners' Magazine*, to publicize legal developments relating to the coal industry. He also published verbatim accounts of the Haswell inquest (1845), the trials of the Newton-le-Willows engineers (1846), Dr Peter Murray McDouall (1848) and Janet James, the orphan girl of Blaina (1864). Then there was a pamphlet entitled 'What is a Traveller?', commenting on the changes in the licensing laws in the 1850s. It seems doubtful whether today similar pamphlets would circulate so widely, raising money for the imprisoned man's dependants (McDouall), to provide for a fresh start in Australia (Janet James) or to help continue the legal struggle (Newton-le-Willows). The extent and intensity of working-class interest in matters judicial also manifested itself in the large crowds often struggling for entry to the public gallery when a contentious case was before the court. On one occasion, so great was the crush to gain admittance, a wall fell over, killing a pitman.[23] Nor was the interest all one-sided: sixteen magistrates crammed into a Leeds courtroom to judge a man, defended by Roberts, charged with using threats and intimidation to enforce a closed shop. He told them that what the accused had done was to make a helpful suggestion, hinting to the employer how he could make his workforce more happy![24]

Those watching these legal dramas would quickly become aware that class conflict was re-enacted inside and outside the courtroom, the collision of two worlds with different outlooks and values. As Roberts was later to explain, there were many difficulties with which he had to contend:

> But it is exceedingly difficult to induce those of a class opposed to you to take this view of things. I do not say this sarcastically, but as a fact learnt by long and observant experience. There are indeed men on the bench who are honest enough, and desirous of doing their duty. But all their tendencies and circumstances are against you. They listen to your opponents, not only often but cheerfully – so they know more fully the case against you than in your favour. To you they listen, too – but in a sort of temper of 'Prisoner at the Bar, you are entitled to make any statement you think fit, and the court is bound to hear you; but mind whatever you say,' etc. In the one case you observe the hearty smile of goodwill; in the other the derisive sneer, though sometimes with a ghastly sort of kindliness in it. Then there is the knowledge of your overwhelming power when acting unitedly, and this begets naturally a corresponding desire to resist you at all hazards. And there are hundreds of other considerations – meetings, political councils, intermarriages, hopes from wills, etc. I do not say that all occupants of the bench are this influenced, nor to the same extent; but it certainly is, at best, an uphill game to contend in favour of the working man in a question which admits any doubt against him. It never happened to me to meet a magistrate who considered an agreement among masters not to employ any particular 'troublesome fellow' was an unlawful act; reverse the case, however, and it immediately becomes a formidable

conspiracy, which must be put down by the strong arm of the law.[25]

Reinforcing the armoury of the law, making Roberts' task more difficult, came a further force – the police. Despite public anger and widespread protests, a disciplined, organized body was implanted into urban Victorian society. From its inception, one of the primary purposes was to protect industry 'from the ignorant and unlawful', that is to say, trade unionists. Its duty during industrial disputes was to guard 'the manufacturing prosperity of the country', thwarting those who wished 'to deprive the capitalist of the free choice of agents for the employment of capital', that is to say, free use of blacklegs.[26] To smash a picket line or a workers' demonstration, followed by an appearance before the courts to provide official corroboration for the testimonies of the employer and his agents, became the stock-in-trade of the police. As Engels shrewdly observed: 'Because the English bourgeois finds himself reproduced in his law, as he does in his God, the policeman's truncheon . . . has for him a wonderfully soothing power. But for the workingman quite otherwise!'[27]

Most people objected both to the way the police behaved and to their sweeping powers. The Metropolitan Police Act, 1839 (2 & 3 Vict. c71), became known as 'the breathing act' because, as long as a person was breathing, the police could find some pretext to make an arrest; only once he or she had stopped breathing were they safe![28] Then there was the constant surveillance and spying, an intrusion which working-class communities found most unwelcome. Yet, such tasks were essential for the protection of property. 'Secret societies, working in the gloom of night,' warned one affluent observer, 'may render our homes desolate, and involve country and city in one common ruin.' Edwin Chadwick, the well-known Victorian sanitary reformer, expressed very similar views. He urged that a flying squad be created so that the police could deal with 'picketing and terrorism' anywhere in England. He believed they could strike a useful blow against the 'pot-house conclaves' that ran the trade unions.[29]

W. P. Roberts agreed with the widely accepted view that the new police were 'a plague of blue locusts'. Like rotten boroughs, they needed to be abolished. People, he thought, should have freedom, controlling themselves, not being controlled by outsiders. From his early campaigns in Bath, he had steadfastly held the same opinion. As one of the twenty-five delegates attending the 1842 Chartist convention, he supported the inclusion of a section on the issue in the second petition. Besides endorsing the Charter, those who signed the second petition – almost three million people – declared their opposition to the 'unconstitutional police force, distributed all over the country, at enormous cost, to prevent the due exercise of people's rights'.

Anti-police riots frequently occurred in the years 1839–45. When, gradually, they happened less frequently, a sullen resentment of the police pervaded working-class communities. Small incidents could be easily transformed into physical confrontations. An autobiography of a man who served for forty-two years in the Lancashire constabulary – with the somewhat unfortunate surname of Bent – provides a revealing insight into how commonplace violence was in the county. Admittedly, Inspector Bent probably aggravated some delicate situations. He was far from being the epitome of diplomacy and tact. On his own admission, he thought nothing of approaching a group of miners angrily, with the question: 'You ruffians, are you there again?' Sometimes their response was equally forthright. Inspector Bent suffered several injuries to his face and body. One day, as he rode a police-horse in Rochdale, pitmen saw him and seized the opportunity to use him as an Aunt Sally. More seriously, in the dispute at the Swinton and Pendlebury collieries in 1867, Inspector Bent almost lost his life. The plan to throw him down a mine-shaft was only abandoned because, as their actions were being witnessed by other policemen, some of those responsible would surely hang.[30]

Absence of public support and co-operation handicapped the police force in its early days. A number of other factors weakened its position still further, preventing it from functioning effectively. Low pay and long hours meant it was difficult to attract the type of person the authorities required. Finding that his men easily succumbed to alcoholic temptation, the Chief Constable of Cheshire cautioned members of his constabulary to keep away from any fellow officer who was inebriated, 'so as to avoid the possibility of further offences being committed'. Such tact would have been of no avail in Wigan. Within the first two years of its formation, every member of the Wigan constabulary had been dismissed. Their offences included burgling the Wigan Brewing Company, stealing a watch from a condemned man, hitting one another on the head with truncheons, failing to turn out during a riot in town and 'making water' on the guard-room floor. Finally, it became the turn of the head of Wigan's Keystone Cops: Chief Constable Fegan was sacked because, in a drunken state, he sexually assaulted a prisoner named Martha Seddon. A quarter of the entire Lancashire constabulary was dismissed for disciplinary reasons in the same period.[31] In a letter to the Home Secretary, magistrates from County Durham complained about their policemen's failure to catch criminals. They attributed this to 'a natural dislike on the part of the constables to make exertions for which they receive no adequate remuneration'; the dread of retribution that would be likely to follow these arrests; and, a natural sympathy the constables had for the culprits.[32]

Even in normal circumstances there were problems, but the inadequacy of the thin blue line became glaringly obvious in times of serious trouble, such as the general strike of 1842. The inability of the authorities to cope with the riots in the Potteries prompted the formation of the Staffordshire constabulary, just as the Rural Police Act of 1839, rushed through Parliament as an emergency measure, had been a response to what was perceived as the rising Chartist menace. Yet, far too often, as one historian has pointed out, the police forces created were only sufficient to excite irritation, but not to cope effectively.[33] Those parts of the country which the authorities wanted to subdue were precisely the ones that were the least well policed. The recruitment of special constables presented problems, especially in tightly-knit mining communities, where sympathy for the strike was strongest. In the Black Country, the hard-pressed authorities were even forced to turn to the local sanitary services in their quest for special constables. Much to the amusement of the populace, two men driving the night-soil cart became a symbol of the majesty of the law. More seriously for the authorities, the scarcity of manpower made it impossible to have what would now be termed a graduated response. Consequently, when hungry Lanarkshire pitmen helped themselves to a few potatoes in a field, the sheriff of the county issued a proclamation, threatening to use cavalry, infantry – and artillery![34]

Such prospects filled General Napier with dismay. To order troops to fire on their kith and kin because some petty offence might have been committed would have harmful military consequences. It would, he thought, damage soldiers' morale, lessen their fighting capacity, and might even sow the seeds of subversion within the ranks. While he privately had misgivings about the police methods and control, he strongly urged that civil rather than military forces should normally by employed for law and order duties – to avoid danger to the throne.'[35] And that is what gradually occurred. The police force was strengthened, became more efficient and performed its role of protecting the existing social order with greater confidence. The rising merchant and manufacturing class, represented by politicians like Robert Peel, were determined to see this occur.[36]

In Victorian society, powerful influences were at work to silence dissenting voices. A large scale prison building programme was begun to improve social discipline and control. Pentonville was completed in 1842, and a further fifty-four prisons had been opened by 1848. Jeremy Bentham, the utilitarian philosopher, boasted that these penal establishments he had designed were 'a machine for grinding rogues honest'. To which Josiah Wedgwood, the pottery manufacturer, added that he saw the role of prisons as producing obedient factory fodder, 'making machines of men as cannot err.'[37] As the number of prisons increased, Parliament found it possible to pass the Penal Servitude Acts of 1853 and 1857, replacing transportation with equivalent periods of imprisonment. Besides the gaols, the newly-created workhouses – 'hated Bastilles' – augmented the process of imposing conformity. Their victims were systematically degraded and humiliated, and even denied the company of their spouses and families. Yet, this terrible plight, suffered by thousands, may nevertheless have been preferable to the alternative of starvation through enforced unemployment.

Many examples can be given of how, through the introduction of these various measures, protest actions were sometimes modified, at other times called off. As we have already heard, in 1842 William Dixon, the Lancashire Chartist and miners' leader, experienced a cavalry charge and witnessed his brother being severely injured. Significantly, in the 1848 discussions among Chartist leaders on whether to resort to force once the third petition had been rejected by Parliament, William Dixon was one of the foremost opponents of the use of violence. Similarly, Joseph Linney, a leader of the South Staffordshire colliers in the 1842 strike, six years later told fellow Chartists that he knew what a prison cell was like and did not want to do anything that would put him inside again.[38] In 1810, when the first miners' union in the North East went on strike, arrested pitmen overfilled Durham's Old Gaol and the House of Correction and even had to be accommodated in the Bishop of Durham's stables. But by 1844 the situation had changed. Thanks to the big prison-building programme, ample accommodation existed. In the debates on industrial action, George Charlton, a union leader, counselled caution – otherwise, he warned pitmen, they might all end up in gaol.[39]

By the time Roberts became the Miners' Attorney-General, the nature of social control was changing. The hangman's noose was being replaced by Adam Smith's hidden hand. The number of offences carrying the death penalty was successively reduced from 200 to a mere seven by the mid-1830s. Only an average of about thirty-four public executions a year took place. But if this grisly drama was losing both its frequency and social importance, nevertheless developing capitalism was still keeping the labouring masses firmly in a subordinate position. The manipulation of market forces, of supply and demand for labour, provided potent weapons. Those workers chafing against the system would find themselves out of a job, facing starvation or the humiliating pain of the workhouse. At the same time, the hidden hand received supplementary support from the gaoler's keys as well as the policeman's truncheon, all wrapped up in a parcel labelled 'the law'.

Traditional employers' policy, therefore, started operating in a different context. North-East miners engaged Roberts because the employers throughout Northumberland and Durham all belonged to a mighty association. This annually determined the exact number of tons of coal to be produced and the precise price at which it would be sold at every colliery in the region. It was known as 'the vend'. Alongside this went the Bond, which laid down, in elaborate detail, the pay and conditions of pitmen throughout Durham and Northumberland. To the men, this was a tyranny. Benjamin Embleton, a veteran miner who remembered the 1810 strike over the Bond, wrote in 1843 to Thomas Duncombe, MP, explaining the vicious way in which it operated:

> The coalowners ... have a standing union with regular meetings for combined action. At these meetings they ascertain how many unbound men each of them have in his employ, and five or six weeks before binding, the unbound men are discharged. Of course, they soon have empty pockets and hungry bellies. The consequence was (as the coalowners

expected) that when binding morning came, the unbound men were such as to be close 'clagged' up against the office door and ready to accept whatever terms were offered. They didn't venture to go upon the colliery, among the men; for they felt ashamed of themselves, at the same time they were forced to look about them for a living. It was thus out of the power of pitmen to have a voice in the terms of the Bond. The Bond was concocted in the coal trade office and the coalowners took good care to have the binding all their own way.

When binding morning was come, and the viewer, peeping out of his office window, saw hungry, unbound men coming up the road and clustered round the office door, to compete with the men of the colliery, he saw at once he was going to have his own way, and began his speech by saying, 'We're not going to bind so many this year as last.' Then, the poor hewers pressed still nearer to the door, and cared little what was in the Bond when they heard it read. How should they object, when all objections would be no use? If some hewer, more independent than the rest, dared to object to any regulation of the Bond, the answer was, 'Oh, well, if you do not choose to sign, we don't mind: you can go somewhere else.' This was enough to keep the rest quiet.[40]

The North-East coalowners, through the Bond, could keep the pitmen in servitude. They had virtually unlimited powers. They regulated wages and conditions. They could make a deduction from pay for anything they considered an infraction of industrial discipline. They could have men imprisoned for not working, even when conditions underground were unsafe. And all this could be done thanks to their own 'trade union', an employers' association that was, as much as any workers' organization, a conspiracy. But, as it kept miners in their place, discreetly no one mentioned its illegality until Roberts began his work for the miners' union.

7 The Battle Against the Bond

Newcastle was the headquarters of the national Miners' Association and of the two strongest county unions, for whom Roberts was working. He soon settled down into his offices there, the best he had ever had, and quickly started work. The verdict of a contemporary writer has never been subsequently challenged by historians. In *The Condition of the Working Class in England*, Frederick Engels said that he conducted 'a crusade against despotic Justices of the Peace and truck masters such as had never been known in England . . . the name of Roberts became a terror to the mineowners . . . such was the dread of this 'lightning Attorney-General', who seemed to be everywhere at once.'[1]

The judicial struggles imposed a punishing regimen on the 37-year-old man. Years afterwards, writing to North-East miners, he reminded them what it had entailed: 'During the time I was with you, my day never began later than seven o'clock and seldom closed before midnight. My days – you all know this – were full of work, from morning till night. Once only during the whole time was I absent (except in London or elsewhere on business, and by your direction), and that once was a week only, and in consequence of a death in my family which I was compelled to attend; but during that week I paid another attorney for doing what he could of my work.'[2]

In order to succeed in his efforts Roberts needed more than personal dedication and an iron constitution. Other factors of change were necessary preconditions; for example the slow, inexorable build up of socio-economic tensions, finding expression in the form of legal grievances; some technical prerequisites, the nuts and bolts as it were, with which to underpin his crusade. These included the creation of a quick, cheap postal service – the penny post had been introduced in 1840 – that enabled colliers easily to transmit their grievances to him. Road improvements were equally vital. Had the roads in the industrialized North of England been in the same state as rural Wiltshire, where Roberts had been forced to push his carriage for four of the thirteen miles from Bath to Frome before he could address a Chartist meeting, then he would have been unable to career around the coalfields in his fast-moving gig, handling many cases daily. Even more important were the railways, just developing as a passenger service in the 1840s. Without them, the 'lightning Attorney-General' would have lost much of his lightning, preventing him from making forays into far-distant regions.

Yet, even with the wonders of nineteenth century science and technology, mishaps could still occur. An erratic railway service, prone to breakdowns and delays, in 1846 caused Ernest Jones to take seventeen hours when he came from London to Manchester to stay with Roberts. The uncertainty itself could create further difficulties, as this notice which appeared in a miners' journal revealed:

> Chesterfield – the simple reason why Mr Roberts did not stop there on Thursday night was that he was fast asleep at the time – in fact, he did not wake till asked for his ticket at Derby. It sometimes occurs that Mr Roberts passes four nights out of seven on the railroad and, so far from trying to keep awake, he is glad to get any rest he can.[3]

From the moment of his appointment on 11 August 1843, the coalowners must have realized they were confronting a new, unpleasant phenomenon. They were being systematically challenged, for the first time, in the courts. There was, moreover, a hitherto unknown belligerent assertiveness which entered into legal proceedings. Believing that he represented right against might, Roberts later admitted what his aim had been: 'We resisted every individual act of oppression, even in cases where we were sure of losing.'[4]

One of his early cases related to a collier named Lonsdale, employed at Gameside pit, Durham. He received a wage of only 14 shillings for a fortnight instead of the 26 shillings stipulated under the Bond. J. E. Marshall, for the owners, argued that they had no case to answer – the Bond did not state that each individual should receive a minimum of 26 shillings; what it meant was that the average wage had to be 26 shillings. Roberts retorted that, if Marshall's interpretation were upheld, men could be compelled legally to labour for derisory wages, chained by 'a slave bond to the penalty of starvation'. When the magistrates complained about the inflammatory nature of his comments, 'Mr Roberts replied he had done no more than his duty; and the inflammatory nature of the truth would not prevent him from uttering it.' The bench found against the coalowner.[5]

The same week he defended nine pitmen charged with leaving work without authorization, an offence that could lead to three months' imprisonment. Roberts seized upon a legal technicality, a clerical error that had crept into the wording of the Bond. The owners contended this was a trivial matter, something that should be overlooked. 'Mr Roberts, on the contrary, submitted that, in prosecution under a penal statute, clerical errors were fatal.' The case was dismissed. 'Immediately on this result, the coalowners applied to Roberts for "an amicable conversation to settle it." "No," said Roberts. "You first drag my men here as criminals, seeking to consign them to a felons' dungeon; and then, when foiled in your tyranny, talk of 'settling' it. First learn to treat your workmen as honest men; and, if you must have criminals, seek for them among yourselves."'[6]

A week later Roberts scored another notable victory. Some pitmen, protesting against the arbitrary deductions of a shilling a week being made from their pay, went on strike. Inevitably, since they had thereby broken the Bond, they were summoned. Their employer, John Ramsay, also a magistrate, decided to sit on the bench during the hearing. Roberts vehemently protested, arguing that Ramsay's presence constituted intimidation, and 'his saying he would not act in his case was mere mockery.' Yet, despite failing to secure Ramsay's removal, the strength of Roberts' arguments still won the day. The bench accepted his submission that the coalowner had been the first to violate the Bond, thereby making the document no longer legally valid.[7]

Other successes followed quickly, including the securing of unpaid back wages for the men of Woodhouse colliery, Bishop Auckland. Perhaps the trade union received its greatest satisfaction from the victory at Wingate Grange, where the owners agreed to install a safe rope. Not content to rest on his laurels, Roberts immediately put in a claim for compensation. He wanted the men to be paid for wages lost during the time when the rope was unsafe and they were unable to work. The *Northern Star* commented: 'The usual course was for the men to be beaten; the present course was that the masters went to the wall.' The *Durham Advertiser*, a journal unsympathetic to trade unionism, had to grudgingly concede that Roberts 'was more than a match for all the legal skill the owners could engage, though they had the favourable ear of a biased court.'[8]

Naturally, mining communities took heart from the transformation arising from the victories of their Attorney-General. The union's quarterly national conference, held in September 1843, greeted news of the legal triumphs with jubilation. It congratulated Roberts 'on the able manner in which he has conducted all the pitmen's cases'. When Roberts replied to the resolution, he 'was received with deafening cheers.'[9] Rank-and-file members appear to have been just as enthusiastic as was the union leadership. At an open-air meeting on Scaffold Hill, held the same month, 12,000 North Tyneside colliers are reported to have cheered every sentence he spoke; and he received the same treatment south of the Tyne. On 14 October 1843, Roberts, O'Connor and William Beesley, a prominent North Lancashire Chartist recently appointed as solicitor's clerk, spoke on the same platform. From their vantage point on Sheriff Hill, they witnessed an impressive scene: 'The men could be seen coming up the Hill, headed by bands of music and carrying different devices and mottoes. We counted 67 flags and banners, but we could not ascertain the number of bands.' Once the multitude had assembled, it heard Roberts recount his recent triumphs. Under his guidance, the meeting then passed a resolution resolving 'never to rest satisfied until they had broken down the tyranny of their masters and obtained justice for themselves and their families.'[10]

The coalowners, initially caught off balance by the legal onslaught, planned their counter-attack very carefully. They chose to make it at Thornley colliery, one of the biggest in County Durham. For many years, the pitmen there had been militant and troublesome, a source of deep annoyance to the owners. For the masters to defeat the Thornley men would send shock waves all over the North-East coalfields, damaging morale and lessening union credibility. In any case, in the employers' eyes, the miners of that colliery had got away with outrageous conduct for far too long – it was time to teach them a lesson. Besides being a union stronghold, Thornley had acquired a reputation for political extremism. At the height of the Chartist agitation in 1839, they had commandeered a railway engine and driven off to attend an illegal meeting on Sunderland Town Moor.[11] Then, shortly afterwards, they shut down the colliery, hoping to secure the Charter by industrial action. The fact that four of their number were imprisoned for this illegal strike did not appear to dampen their ardour.[12] Crowded Chartist meetings continued to take place in the village. At the same time, they formed the Thornley Colliery Union, a local organization that, with help from George Binns, took the initiative that led to the creation of strong county unions in the North East.[13] Significantly, at the inaugural meeting of the Durham County Miners' Association at Chester-le-Street, one of the two officials elected came from Thornley; the other, Benjamin Embleton, a veteran of miners' struggles stretching back to the 1810 strike, then worked at Wingate Grange, soon to become the centre of the wire rope controversy.

The events leading to the Thornley trial happened, therefore, against the background of ingrained mutual hatred and distrust. On 13 November 1843, a union deputation went to see the manager. They complained that the machine for weighing coal was inaccurate, resulting in hewers receiving less money than they were entitled to; but Mr Heckles, the manager, refused to do anything about it. To add to their frustration, he deducted a day's pay from those who went on the deputation. This action aroused extensive anger throughout the mine. On 19 November, the men came out on strike. News of this quickly reached Roberts, who immediately jumped into his gig and drove to Thornley, where he held discussions with union officials well into the night. At 6 a.m. the following morning, Roberts addressed a mass meeting at the pithead. He urged the miners to strive for a settlement through negotiation, and proposed that they should resume work while a delegation, led by himself, would visit the colliery viewer. Word of this must have reached Mr Heckles, who was awaiting their arrival on the doorstep of the colliery offices. In reply to the complaint that the weighing machine was unfair, he said he would change it eventually, but at present had better things to do. Roberts suggested that, as the men considered they were not receiving their rights under the Bond, the whole legal arrangement should be scrapped. At this point, Heckles announced his intention not to abandon, but to interpret more strictly, the terms of the Bond.

This was an extremely astute move. It provided management with a strategem for cutting wages while not leaving itself vulnerable to the kind of legal attack made on John Ramsay, the coalowner and magistrate. Far from breaking the rules, Mr Heckles could rightfully claim to be concerned only to see them enforced. The Bond, it should be remembered, had been drawn up by coalowners, and provided ample scope for managerial tyranny. Under it, deductions from wages were made for coal-tubs laid out (i.e., deficient in weight) or set out (i.e., containing slate and stones). Among other things, fines could be imposed for refusal to work, disobeying orders, leaving work before time, hewing improperly, damaging safety lamps, throwing stones at putters, taking coal from side walls and using gunpowder contrary to orders. From 8 April to 18 November 1843, the daily average fine of a Thornley miner varied between three-quarters of a penny and one and a half pence. But once the new regime had been introduced on 20 November 1843, it was a different story: miners could toil hard all day and come out of the pit actually in debt, their fines exceeding their wages. Naturally, the men found this intolerable, and on 24 November they went out on strike. But this, of course, constituted a violation of the Bond. Warrants were issued against sixty-eight pitmen.

It is only possible to speculate what advice Roberts gave the Thornley miners in the pre-strike period. Once he knew that the management intended to enforce the Bond more strictly, did he suggest the colliers should deliberately try to get fined as heavily as possible? Is this how one man collected fines of 22 shillings in two days? And were the miners asked to keep their pay chits as incontrovertible evidence of the scale of deductions imposed? Clearly, in seeking to establish the unjust, oppressive nature of the Bond, the Miners' Attorney-General needed this kind of documentary evidence to show how low was the pay and how high the fines.

Amid great excitement, the Thornley trial began in the Justices' room of Durham County Courts on 7 December 1843.[14] The first batch of the sixty-eight pitmen – Lawrence Smith, George Harwood and John Singlewood – stood in the dock. Many of their fellow workmates, shouting interjections and vowing never to go underground again until their brothers were released, crowded into and around the small courtroom. To the magistrates, all influential and rich, the presence of this unwelcome, unruly mob only served to confirm their suspicions about trade unions in general and W. P. Roberts in particular. It heightened the already tense atmosphere. As the proceedings dragged on for seven days, tempers became frayed and wild scenes occurred. In those days court proceedings were less formal, with greater liberty – or licence – of expression than permitted in present-day courts.

At the outset, however, there was a semblance of order and tranquillity. Opening for the prosecution, J. E. Marshall gave the impression it was an open-and-shut case. He pointed out that the men were bound under an ordinary pit bond, and read out the relevant clauses. He argued that the men freely agreed to these stringent terms; if they now suffered from them, they only had themselves to blame. He could not see what the defence could plead if the men had absented themselves from work; it was no excuse to say the agreement was being too strictly enforced.

Immediately, Roberts applied for the case to be stopped. He did so on the grounds that the weighing machine, not having the official stamp that guaranteed its accuracy, broke the provision of the relevant Act of Parliament and consequently made the Bond illegal. Mr Marshall retorted that the same machine had been used at previous bindings. The chairman rejected Roberts' application, whereupon he asked for the decision to be noted: 'I should like to have that taken down on the notes of the court, as I shall most likely apply to the Court of Queen's Bench.'

The prosecution then called Mr Heckles, the resident viewer of Thornley colliery. He testified that on 13 November he received a letter from the workmen, signed by their secretary, James Bagley. 'The answer I made was: I wondered why they didn't get someone who could write a letter plainer. I sent word to say that if the letter meant anything, they would have to send a deputation. On the evening of the following day, 15 men called upon me, and half of them spoke. The overman, according to instruction, deducted 2s. 6d. fine for the day lost. On the evening of the 23rd, a large body of workmen came up and asked why the 2s. 6d. was deducted. I told them they were asking the road they knew' – in other words, they were aware of usual custom and practice.

Up to that point, Heckles' testimony had been punctuated by occasional comments from the public gallery. They became much louder and more frequent, however, when Heckles said: 'I had instructions from the owners to see the men were fairly treated, and never harshly.' The Miners' Attorney did not understand how he could reconcile this with failing to check that the weighing machine functioned fairly. Under cross-examination, Heckles conceded he did not know if the machine had, as required by Act of Parliament, been stamped. Sometimes he thought it might be incorrect, treating the men too generously. Howls of derision greeted this remark. Amid the noise, the chairman of the bench tried to come to Heckles' assistance. Though it is exceedingly doubtful whether he had ever seen the weighing machine or tested its reliability, the magistrate declared: 'I am clearly of the opinion that the machine was incorrect against the masters and in favour of the men.'

Turning to the question of fines, Heckles said, 'I don't doubt that one man may have been fined 22 shillings for two days. I do know other men have been fined eight, seven, six and five shillings a day.' Hearing this, the chairman commented: 'This is not the ordinary amount of fines. No workman would subject himself to such fines'. Roberts then explained: 'But the men have no other choice.' Still perplexed, the chairman persisted in his attempt to discover the reason for the huge increase in fines: 'The stone was no more liable to fall down then than at any other time.' Heckles agreed that an exceptional number of coal-tubs had been laid out, adding that the stones could not have entered in the ordinary way. In conclusion, Heckles ended his testimony by denying he had ever told Roberts that the men could not earn a living when the Bond was strictly enforced. The prosecution finished presenting its case by giving the factual evidence that the three accused had not worked at Thornley colliery on 24 November 1843.

Opening the defence, W. P. Roberts pleaded with the bench to show mercy:

> He did not wish to be misunderstood. He did not speak of mercy in the ordinary sense of the term because he believed the men guiltless – because he believed that their masters and Mr Heckles ought now to be in the dock and those men now in that place ought to be standing as their accusers. But he asked for their merciful consideration because it was impossible to administer justice, fairly and honestly, unless they weighed all the circumstances of the case ... Let the magistrates consider this – let them look to the advantages which attend the former, when the rich was on one side and the poor man on the other, and he asked them to bring their most merciful consideration to the matter.

Then Roberts contended that, whatever grievances arose, the pitmen were always anxious to reach a settlement.

But the men and the master did not stand on a par. The utmost the men could do was to summon their masters for wages, where perhaps no jurisdiction could be found; but the masters could send men to prison, however gross the fraud committed against them. It was reserved for this country to have a law to give the rich man the power of inflicting imprisonment whilst it did not give the same power to the poor man.

The Miners' Attorney went on to remind the magistrates that, under existing legislation, they could impose a fine, annul the contract, or imprison. In almost every instance, the magistrates had inflicted the severest penalty:

Was it always to be imprisonment – imprisonment – imprisonment, as if the men were all criminals and the masters all angels? The complaint in this case was against the masters and in favour of the men. The masters had proved themselves to be criminal in the eye of the law and, in fact, that if justice was done then, they would find themselves within the walls of the prison to which they were eager to send their fellow men.

And what was the case brought before them by Mr Marshall? Why, it appeared that Mr Heckles had for six months suspected the weighing machine was wrong. True, he suspected it was wrong in favour of the men and against the masters, but when did they find a viewer who supposed anything wrong in favour of the men? Certainly not in Northumberland and Durham. By the wisdom of the law, all the benevolence was to be considered as existing on the one hand and all the fraud on the other. It would be for him to prove, in contradiction to what had been said by the other side, that the law had been complied with by the men, so far as applying to the inspector went. He should be able to prove to them that application had been made for an inspector and that application had been refused. Mr Heckles said he did not know if the machine had been stamped. He would show that it was not stamped, that it was incorrect – and incorrect, too, against the men. So it was in the case of every machine in the coal trade. Here he might say there is no case at all because the Act of Parliament referred to stated that no sale should be valid unless it was by the weighing of a machine properly stamped.

Roberts contended that, as the provisions of the act had not been adhered to, the contract was null and void; the coalowners could not use the Bond selectively.

The Miners' Attorney then turned to his second line of argument: 'The wages guaranteed by the Bond to the men had not been paid in the manner stated in the Bond; and, though he had heard of some very strange decisions, he had yet to hear that service was to be compelled from a man who had not been paid wages he had previously earned.' Making his third and final point, W. P. Roberts broadened the scope of this objection to a discussion of the nature of the Bond itself:

Mr Marshall had said that the law was that the men should be bound by their bond. He did not think that Mr Marshall would say so in his sober senses for, if a man entered into a bond, which it was morally impossible for him to fulfil, which would involve him in utter destitution, he must contend that though, under such a bond, a master had a right to come upon him for damages, yet it had no power to call on the magistrates to send the master to prison. They could not have more solemn evidence of the oppressiveness of the Bond than that. Those men could voluntarily declare – so help them God – that they would not go to work till the men sent to prison had been released.

After a detailed examination of the heavy fines imposed at Thornley, Roberts concluded his address:

He warned the masters that, in the exercise of their authority, they had proceeded too far. Not one of those men would go to work. He would tender them all as witnesses for the purpose of stating their injuries throughout the land – for the purpose of showing the masters exercised their authority in a mischievous manner; and he called upon them to discharge the Bond if he showed, as he was prepared to do, that it was impossible for an honest man to work under it.

He went on to call his first six witnesses. Each gave virtually the same evidence. They quoted from the pay slips, citing the big deductions made, and stated that they could not make a living under the Bond – indeed, would rather go to prison than continue working under it. Since their evidence took a considerable length of time, the chairman of the bench inquired whether Roberts had any evidence of a different complexion to present. The Miners' Attorney replied that, as it was a matter of opinion whether it was possible to work under the Bond, he felt it was his duty to bring as much evidence as possible to corroborate the defence case. Pressed for the implications of his statement, Roberts said that he would be happy if the bench intimated he had proved the point; otherwise he would have to call every hewer to substantiate the claim that they could not make a living under the Bond. He had almost 400 waiting outside the court ready to give evidence.

At this announcement, the magistrates seem to have become somewhat agitated. They faced the prospect of an indefinite future, imprisoned in their own courtroom, listening to the drone of basically the same evidence. It would be the JPs, not the pitmen, who would be denied their freedom. Attempts were made to reach a compromise, whereby the testimonies of almost all the Thornley men would not have to be given in court, but this merely served to heighten the feeling of injustice felt by the pitmen, who considered the bench would not attempt to treat coalowners in a similar manner. The 'compromises' suggested by Roberts as a means of circumventing the need for all the colliers to enter the witness-box involved, in the opinion of the bench, conceding far too much to the defence. Tempers were quickly lost and, in the excitement, unguarded remarks were made. The magistrates stated they would not be bound by any compromise reached; large bodies of men were coming together in open defiance of the law.

By saying 'in open defiance of the law', the magistrates had committed a grave legal error. They could no longer claim to be acting with judicial impartiality, assessing the pros and cons of the case with an open mind. That remark showed that they considered the defendants to be guilty. Without hearing all the evidence – Roberts still had 400 witnesses waiting outside – the magistrates appeared to have already reached their verdict. It provided W. P. Roberts with the type of legal technicality he loved to seize upon, giving him the ground for a successful appeal to a higher court to get an unsatisfactory verdict quashed.

In the slightly calmer atmosphere of the following morning, Roberts rose to remind the bench of the implications of what they had said the previous day. Again, he accused the bench of being biased as they had already pronounced the defendants guilty without hearing a fraction of the evidence. That the Miners' Attorney should seek to recall, indeed emphasize, this indiscretion led each magistrate to deplore his behaviour. Dr J. R. Fenwick said that Roberts had treated the magistrates' bench with the greatest insolence. Another, Mr J. F. Elliott, appealed to the wisdom of the miners: surely they could see the harm being done to their case by their attorney. But neither the miners nor Roberts seemed to be moved by such appeals. Therefore, as no agreement had been reached over procedure, the defence ploughed along the same monotonous furrow. Ten more witnesses were called, all giving basically the same evidence:

> John Stephenson said: No man can make a living under the Bond. The black brass and splint comes down among the coal. In some places the men work by the light of the Davy lamp, but still it is impossible to separate black brass from coal. I have been a hewer for 20 years, and will rather go to gaol till 5th. April, though I have a wife and five children.
>
> William Turner said: He had complained about the scales and applied to Mr Heckles for them to be replaced. In reply, Mr Heckles had told him they ultimately would be replaced, but he had more important things to attend to. No man can get a living as things are. I will go to prison first.

And so it went on and on: every pitman stated his grievances, often gave precise details of his pay and the huge deductions made, and ended up by declaring he would rather go to gaol than continue to endure the slavery of the Bond. The only new evidence came from Newrick Walton and J. J. Bird, who showed that, whilst it was possible for a coalowner to have recourse to the courts to obtain a legal remedy for wrong done, in practice the same did not apply to pitmen. Newrick Walton stated that Easington magistrates had refused to grant his application for the weighing machine to be examined by the mines inspector. J. J. Bird said he had attempted to obtain a summons against his employer for back pay owed him, but had been refused. The magistrate had exclaimed, 'What, for the small sum of three shillings?' Yet, to Bird three shillings represented more than a day's pay.

The magistrates adjourned the case for five days, hoping that in the interval a solution would be found to the procedural impasse. Alas, that was not to be. So, on 13 December 1843, the indefatigable Roberts rose once more to cross-examine witnesses, all of whom gave the well-worn evidence. In an attempt to relieve the tedium, he applied for the weighing machine to be brought into court; he wished to prove the employers were guilty of fraud. But the magistrates, rejecting his application, said they had already ruled that the Act of Parliament he mentioned did not apply in this case. Unperturbed, Roberts wiled away the rest of the day, calling another fifteen witnesses.

On Thursday 14 December, the strain of the seemingly endless procession of pitmen into the witness-box created an atmosphere of tetchiness, where small pinpricks were liable to develop into full-blown incidents. The magistrates could not have been happy when, as miners strode into the witness-box to make the now familiar statement that they preferred prison to working under the Bond, shouts came from the public gallery, 'We'll all gan to gaol.' They suspected that Roberts, with strong ulterior motives, had orchestrated the whole thing, and they hinted as much. This led Roberts to inquire from his fourth witness of the day whether he had heard anything to justify the imputation of the bench that he had tried to widen the breach between masters and men. The chairman objected to the question, saying he was not aware the imputation had been made. Roberts retorted it had – 'by those who ought to be ashamed of themselves'. Mr Elliott rejoined that Roberts was probably alluding to a remark he had made during a disorderly scene that had occurred earlier. He was surprised and sorry to see a man professing to have a liberal education behave in this manner, and added that Roberts' conduct could only be characterized as indecent. He asked him to apologize. But, far from making a retraction, the Miners' Attorney sought to justify his attacks with a further diatribe against the magistrates, ending up by saying: 'Some people can only be lashed into justice, and I have applied the lash.'

Finding this last intemperate utterance too much to endure, the magistrates decided to retire. In their opinion, W. P. Roberts' remarks could no long be taken as jibes, directed at individual magistrates; they constituted contempt of court. When the magistrates returned, the clerk of the court, Mr Hays, read the following resolution:–

The Bench is of the opinion that a gross contempt of Court has been committed by Mr Roberts in the observations just addressed by him to the Bench, which, in a superior court of justice, would have led to immediate commitment, and the magistrates are willing to hope that another mode of proceedings which is open to the Court may be rendered unnecessary by a proper apology.

This threat seems to have had its intended effect. Roberts apologized. In the more mellow mood then prevailing it was possible to reach a compromise over the pitmen still waiting to give evidence. After some hesitation, the bench agreed to a rather irregular procedure: it consented, as all the men's testimonies would have been basically the same, to take them as sworn. Clearly, all participants in the trial had long since reached the point of exhaustion. The facts of the case had been amply stated. Neither the prosecution nor the defence saw any benefits from further prolonging the proceedings.

Therefore, W. P. Roberts and J. E. Marshall made their final submissions. The Miners' Attorney summed up the case for the defence, stressing that only minor concessions would have kept the men at work. Marshall, however, pointed out that, even if this were true, the pitmen had still committed a breach of the law. Personally, he thought that they had nothing genuine to complain about. If they returned to work, they would be subject to the same scale of fines that operated at other collieries in the northern coalfields. He read to the court a declaration of the company, stating that it had no desire to victimize any employee. Roberts thanked him for making this offer, but said the men would not return to work until their grievances were settled.

Giving their verdict, the chairman of the magistrates pronounced the three miners guilty as charged. They were each sentenced to six weeks imprisonment. A request from Roberts for the judgement to be deferred was refused, and the three men were removed to Durham prison. Immediately the Miners' Attorney sought a writ of habeus corpus, successfully arguing that their imprisonment had not followed the due process of law. The case was then referred to the Court of Queen's Bench where, on a legal technicality, Roberts gained their acquittal.

The three freed miners, accompanied by their attorney, returned from London in triumph. People lined the streets for miles, cheering the victors as they passed by. At Thornley itself, Roberts and the others were carried by an ecstatic crowd around the village. In every colliery community throughout the northern coalfields, the Miners' Attorney had suddenly become a great hero, the man who had fought the King Coal tyrants – and won. In a letter written towards the end of his life, Roberts recalled the occasion, one of the highlights of his entire career: 'Thousands, as I drove along, came out to bless me: the homage was more than agreeable – it was intoxicative; and though I was in constant dread of violence, I was never so happy and never should be so again.'[15]

Notwithstanding the general jubilation, Thornley was far from being the complete victory it at first appeared. Durham coalowners had no intention of permitting pitmen to work other than under the Bond; to do so would be a shining beacon of incitement to other pitmen to smash the Bond elsewhere. Consequently, their powerful employers' organization invoked a clause in their private agreement which allowed them to indemnify a coalowner suffering loss through an industrial action. Thornley stayed idle, therefore, its men a debilitating drain on union funds.

In addition, a further difficulty arose. Coalowners, feeling that they were being denied their legitimate rights under the Bond, were equally determined to stop miners securing their rights. This was soon revealed by a case heard at North Shields. The background to the dispute was that a fire broke out at the north-west heading of Seaton Delaval colliery on 6 November 1843. Two days later, colliery officials pronounced the pit safe to resume work. Men went down at 2 a.m., but many quickly left because of the smoke and the gas. Despite pleadings, management refused to make a second inspection. Instead the overman simply cursed and swore at the men, the 'damned, lazy toads'. When it became plain that this pressure would not make miners descend again, the management eventually called upon two viewers to visit the workings. They declared them to be safe and the colliery management announced that, under the Bond, they would fine every man 2s 6d who refused to work. Following this threat, some miners went underground, only to return because of the conditions they encountered. Again, on 9 and 10 November, viewers stated the colliery to be quite safe. On 14 November, a deputation of pitmen told the management that miners were prepared to work anywhere in the colliery, except the north-west heading. Later the same day, miners went to the colliery offices as usual to collect their pay, pointing out that, under the Bond, they were guaranteed a stipulated wage every fortnight. But the management refused to make any payments whatsoever.

The union's actions against the colliery for payment of back wages was heard by North Shields magistrates on 21 January 1844. Presenting the case, W. P. Roberts emphasized that the miners were prepared to work anywhere that was safe and yet were being denied wages to which they were legally entitled. The masters had no right, he contended, to expect men recklessly to endanger their lives. He stressed the importance of safety and proper ventilation; disregard for them had resulted in the loss of hundreds of lives at nearby Wallsend only five years before. Roberts' powerful pleas fell on magisterial deaf ears – the case was dismissed – but his setback, according to the union journal, left their members undismayed:

> Mr Roberts thanked the magistrates and said he would get justice in any court but North Shields. The men returned home in high spirits, although they had lost their trial, and resolved not to risk their lives until the pit was made safe. For they were sure, if they went to work under such circumstances and lost their lives, the agents would not be husband to the bereft widows, a father to the fatherless children, nor a comfort to the parents who had lost their affectionate sons, but, on the contrary, would have been ready to turn them out of doors after a few weeks.[16]

The last remark is a reference to the fact that many colliers lived in tied cottages, where employment by the colliery remained the chief condition of tenancy. In a sense, it was a partial victory for the union: a few months earlier before the Miners' Attorney had begun his campaign, a stoppage of work was likely to lead the owners to seek redress through imprisonment and evictions. Now they had become more cautious.

Besides the back-breaking volume of work from the northern coalfields, Roberts somehow found time to make expeditions to other coalfields. The North East remained his priority area, but, if other districts of the Miners' Association wanted his services, they had to pay the Durham and Northumberland unions (his employers) an appropriate portion of his salary.

In the week before the Seaton Delaval case, for example, Roberts had travelled to Staffordshire to secure the release of three pitmen imprisoned by Bilston magistrates. The men had refused to work on a coal-face which threatened to cave in and which had, indeed, done so before work was resumed. At the Court of Queen's Bench, Judge Williams granted Roberts a writ of habeus corpus, freeing the three men. In Lancashire, the Miners' Attorney operated in much the same manner. Four pitmen had been imprisoned at Preston, but the news of his arrival in the town was enough to secure their release. Then he was called to Manchester, where seven colliers employed by Lancaster & Company at Patricroft colliery, Eccles, had been gaoled for breaking their contracts. They had gone on strike without giving the requisite month's notice. Before sentencing them to two months imprisonment, Mr Maude, the magistrate, had offered to allow them to reconsider their conduct, stating they would not be punished if they returned to work. However, they all remained unrepentant and as none earned more than sixpence a day, prison held few horrors. Again, Roberts took the case to the Court of Queen's Bench and had their sentences quashed. At Prescot, nine miners were in gaol, accused of creating a disturbance in St Helens; again, the mere arrival of the much-feared Roberts led the magistrates to free them. This was followed by a notable triumph in South Yorkshire, where Roberts and the pitmen released from prison headed a triumphant procession through Barnsley. Colliers and their families 'came in their thousands, with flags and music, to meet their advocate.'[17]

Over the years, magistrates had become accustomed to a happy informality, doing very much as they wanted to do, without strict adherence to legal procedures. Almost invariably, workers did not have legal representatives nor did they know the law. Roberts' arrival, however, created an unpleasant new situation for the magistrates. For instance, he found that at Chesterfield they had dispensed with the time-consuming procedure of hearing both sides before deciding in favour of the employer. They 'had sent four men to Derby jail without suffering them to speak for themselves.' This violation of the rules of natural justice provided Roberts with grounds for a successful appeal. A very similar case in Leicester had the same outcome.[18]

One of Roberts' main targets was the truck system. Repeatedly, in many districts, he secured the miners their legal entitlement to be paid in coin of the realm. The tommy shops, selling 'tommy-rot' (that is, inferior goods at high prices) had to close down once tokens had been replaced by real money. In Derbyshire Roberts' arrival aroused such panic that a Belper coalowner immediately issued a declaration renouncing the truck system:

Pentrich Colliery

Messrs. Haslam think it right (to prevent mistake) to give notice that all men employed at their colliery will receive their wages wholly in money, and be at liberty to spend it where they like. If they buy at Messrs. Haslam's, they will be supplied (as heretofore) at wholesale prices; but they will not be expected to buy there, and will have the same work and wages whether they go to that shop or any other.[19]

This notice serves to confirm the prediction made by the Derbyshire Miners' Association in a letter to Newcastle, pleading with North-East pitmen to release Roberts for legal work in its county: 'His very presence would make the tyrants tremble . . . Sir, the very name of Roberts strikes terror in their souls.' Actually, very much the same language was used by Frederick Engels: 'The name Roberts began to be a terror to the mineowner.' In his book, *The Condition of the Working Class in England*, he made seven references to Roberts, every one of them favourable. Engels included as a twelve-page appendix an account of Roberts' legal tussle with Messrs Pauling & Henfrey, an epic struggle in Lancashire, which boosted working-class morale there, and had an effect akin to the Thornley case in the northern coalfields. Not surprisingly, Karl Marx and Frederick Engels used W. P. Roberts as their English solicitor.[20]

The opinions of the authors of *The Communist Manifesto* received endorsement in many forms and many places. In a period when there was an influx into trade unions, when there was a rising tide of militancy and when the labouring masses were beginning to question as never before the laws that controlled them, W. P. Roberts became the man of the moment. To them, he was a great hero, a man of superhuman qualities; indeed, sometimes his feats were exaggerated or misunderstood. To workers accustomed to seeing legal action against them following the inevitable pattern of arrest, trial, imprisonment, for the Miners' Attorney even to secure the release of a prisoner on bail could be seen as a great triumph. In their ignorance of the law, some may not have understood that bail might only mean a temporary respite from the prison cell. Whatever the precise legal position, in their eyes one thing was incontestably true: for the first time, they had a representative who would stand up to the masters and say what so many had wanted to say for so long.

Of course his critics, particularly those unsympathetic to the pitmen's cause, regarded his courtroom histrionics as demeaning the law, an example of unprofessional conduct. In his treatment of magistrates and prosecution witnesses, he appeared to be the reincarnation of Mr Jaggers from Dickens' *Great Expectations*: 'If anybody of whatsoever degree, said a word that he didn't approve of, he instantly required to have it "taken down". If anybody wouldn't make an admission, he said, "I'll have it out of you!" and if anybody made an admission, he said, "Now I've got you". The magistrates shivered under the single bite of his finger.'[21]

Besides expressing his pent-up emotions, W. P. Roberts's courtroom conduct served another useful function; he needed well-publicized dramatic events to shake the bench and the masters out of the errors of their ways. Though he sought to obtain strict observance of the law when it was in his clients' interests, he was well aware of the shortcomings of much of the legislation. Yet, he was also aware that labour laws possessed a unique characteristic: they changed with fluctuating class fortunes.[22] This provided him with a second aim: to transform them from being an instrument with which to beat the workers, into one they could use for their own protection. As an initial step to this objective, he first had to help organize the pitmen into a mighty union, a force that judiciary and legislators alike would have to take into consideration.

The triumphs of the Miners' Attorney imbued pitmen with a new self-confidence, a feeling that they need not always remain submissive. Thanks to W. P. Roberts, they had acquired a new assertiveness. They rewarded him by building up the union and lavishing him with praise which at times verged on idolatry. One newspaper, for example, reported: 'Among the pitmen of this neighbourhood are many of the religious sects termed Ranters and Latter-day Saints, and these men, it is stated, believe – poor, deluded creatures – that Mr Roberts, the Pitmen's Attorney-General, is a second Moses sent for their deliverance.' A less extreme but more widespread indication of the high regard in which he was held was the large number of folk songs written about him. These became very familiar, a source of inspiration and solidarity during the great strike of 1844 and later struggles. Elizabeth Gair, a pitman's wife, wrote a song called 'The Colliery Union', which contains the lines:

> Success to your commander
> And Roberts is his name,
> Since he has prov'd so loyal,
> We'll spread about his fame.

Another verse praised his clerk, 'young Beesley', 'a man of wit possessed', and there was a rousing chorus:

> So stick unto your Union,
> And mind what Roberts say.
> If you be guided by his word,
> You'll surely win the day.

Two ballads recount the triumph of the Thornley trial. One entitled 'Mr Roberts, The Pitmen's Friend', says:

As their oppression was so great, they could not with it stand,
Which made them join in heart and voice, likewise in hand in hand,
And meetings rose in different parts their rights for to unfold,
Then O'Connor thought of Roberts and his name unto them told.

It goes on to relate how, after the Queen's Bench acquittal, Roberts took the three released men for a celebration dinner with O'Connor, and 'he treated them far better than the noblest in the land.' The twelfth and final verse presses home the lesson:

Now here's to Mr Roberts, for he's the Pitman's friend,
He's worthy of his salary to make the tyrant bend,
Now may he live in unity and his men unto him cling
For to take all tyranny from them out of them the sting.

The second poem about Thornley has the chorus:

> Cheer up, my lads, for Roberts's bold;
> And well defends our cause,
> For such a drubbing he's gi'en them
> With their own class-made laws.

A careful reading of some of these songs reveals a popular
perception of Roberts not as an employee of the union, taking orders
from its executive committee, but rather as its unelected leader.
Perhaps, this is understandable: of all its spokesmen, he had the
highest profile and became known to the biggest number of its rank-
and-file members. Most of the leaders would only be well known in
their own coalfield, or might have been performing essential
administrative functions at the Newcastle headquarters. Whatever
their role, they were unlikely either to come into contact with so
many miners, or to be involved on such dramatic and memorable
occasions.

Certainly, as the Miners' Association grew, he came to be regarded
in the North East as the person who had taken on the mantle of
Tommy Hepburn, the leader of the earlier union of 1830–2. A
popular song entitled 'the Pitmen's Union' had been the battle-hymn
during those previous struggles. In its original version, it had the final
lines:

> Long, long may Hepburn live;
> Long may our Union last.

By the 1840s, Roberts' name had been substituted for that of
Hepburn. He could receive no bigger compliment.[23]

8   On the Eve of Battle

Whatever their political complexion, the press and politicians alike held W. P. Roberts primarily responsible for the massive industrial dispute that erupted in the North-East coalfields in 1844. In doing so, they followed a time-honoured tradition. It has always been – and still is – easy to blame sinister outside agitators for industrial strife. This procedure absolves employers from inquiring whether genuine and justified grievances actually exist, and, consequently, if the poor pay and bad conditions they provide might not be responsible. Only two years before the 1844 dispute, the mines inspector reported on the women who worked at the Earl of Balcarres' Wigan pits. They dragged coal out of the mine. Chained round the waist and with a belt between the legs – a most uncomfortable experience for anyone, and particularly for those who were pregnant – they earned a penny for every three tons they brought to the surface. Yet, if Inspector Tremenheere is to be believed, they were quite happy and content. Then, alas, Chartists came along, stirred up trouble, and the women went out on strike.[1]

Similarly, in the North-East coalfields, the same type of simplistic explanation was used, blaming Chartism – or, rather, a single wicked Chartist – for all society's ills. To apostles of accepted orthodoxy, W. P. Roberts was public enemy number one. By their reaction, Chartist and radical journals unwittingly gave credence to this view because, in response to the vilification of him, they clamoured to defend him, making him their great hero and overstating the role he played. Even Engels verges on idolatry when he describes how 'Roberts himself organised with incomparable perseverance both the strike and agitation.'[2]

In fact, they all exaggerated: he was the catalyst, not the cause. Not a person known for his undue modesty, Roberts pointed out the limited nature of his intervention. His function had merely been to articulate the anger which prevailed among the mass of miners. Injustice and tyranny, he argued, created the underlying reasons for revolt; look to the coalowners, not him, to find the culprits. Yet, this view needs qualification: it overlooks the fact that Roberts' advocacy of the pitmen's cause, through its forceful coherence and clarity, imbued colliery communities with greater confidence, greater militancy. Without the fiery eloquence of the Miners' Attorney, there could well have been a strike; it seems unlikely that it would have been so prolonged or severe.

An analysis of his speeches and writings reveals that, even when he argued for the same demands as others, his language tended to be more intemperate, making it less easy to reach a compromise. The concept of 'fair wage', for example, is open to numerous interpretations; customarily it allows for the idea of a 'fair profit'. When it is linked to what is tantamount to the labour theory of value it becomes exceedingly difficult to make such an interpretation – and Roberts expounded a doctrine very close to this theory. In his *Miners' Journal,* he wrote that he was 'convinced a working miner is of more value than all the Coal Pit Kings in Christendom.' He went on to affirm:

> They shall now be taught, to the utmost of our humble abilities, that labour is more value than gold; and that without labour Mankind could not exist and the splendid carriages in which are drawn the bodies of their owners; the magnificent palaces that are built in our green fields and in our fertile plains; the superb furniture with which they are adorned; the garden and pleasure grounds by which they are surrounded, and in which steel traps and spring guns are laid; the greenhouses and the ponds – have all been filched from the earnings of the working miners.[3]

Many pitmen in the North East, remembering how the Hepburn union of 1831–2 was crushed by strike action, wanted to avoid making the same mistake again. Roberts agreed with this, although he gave the argument a different twist. He regarded the avoidance of strikes as a temporary expedient, a necessity until the union had fully built up its strength. To stop work at a single colliery or in an isolated coalfield, he claimed, usually ended in failure, depleting the coffers and producing demoralization among the membership. Instead of frittering away resources in small disputes, he argued that the miners should garner their strength, organizing pitmen throughout all the coalfields in Britain and, once this had been completed, bring the entire industry to a standstill. In his magazine, Roberts affirmed: 'We are in favour of a strike, A GENERAL AND UNIVERSAL ONE: a general cessation of work in the pits in order that by universal combination, the coal hewers may obtain a fair price for their labour.' The article continues by advising readers to start laying in supplies for the great battle ahead: 'Rely upon it that the time of your emancipation is not very distant; it may be nearer than the most sanguine expect.'[4]

Roberts' writings led Tremenheere, the mines commissioner, to express concern in his annual report, contrasting them with the more level-headed approach of official union publications. Tremenheere took particular exception to the way the *Miners' Journal* published:

> accusations of cruelty and oppression practised by the masters, and the abuse of the men promoted to offices of trust; encouragement to use violence to those who refused to join the union; extracts from works calculated to give a false impression of the general conduct of the upper classes towards the lower; complaints relative to grievances; and recommendations to prepare for a general strike of all coal-miners in the kingdom.

On the other hand, he welcomed the union's official organ, the *Miners' Advocate*, many of whose articles were 'in all respects unobjectionable, display excellent feeling and a sincere desire to promote the improvement of the colliers in every point of view.'[5] While not actually cited by the mines inspector, an open letter to clergymen, magistrates and shopkeepers, which appeared in an early issue of the *Miners Advocate*, was undoubtedly what he had in mind. Designed to reassure everybody, it stated: 'Our Association is based upon truth and justice ... it is intended to take no power from honest and upright employers.'[6]

The problem for Roberts was that he rarely came into contact with any 'honest and upright employers'. To him, those he did daily battle with in court were robbers, who could only be stopped in their infamy by adopting a highly aggressive attitude. As he later explained:

> When I was acting for the Colliers' Union in the North, we resisted every act of oppression, even in cases where we were sure of losing; and the result was that in a short time there was no oppression to resist. For it is to be observed that oppression like that we are speaking of – which after all is merely a more genteel and cowardly mode of thieving – shrinks from a determined and decided opposition.[7]

Despite the characteristic overstatement on Roberts' part – obviously oppression was not eliminated as he claimed – nevertheless, it is certainly true that pitmen gained improvements as a result of his efforts. Quite naturally, it threw up in pitmen's minds the vital question of the way forward: should they back conciliation or confrontation?

It is important to remember that this debate was happening in a period when trade unionism was still in its early phase. Nowadays, after two centuries of industrial experience, it is usual for most unions to have their moderates and militants, the gist of whose speeches can be fairly accurately predicted in advance. In the era of the Miners' Association, however, the situation was far more fluid. People might quickly move from a position where they supported strikes to one where they opposed them. Local experiences, where pitmen could become embroiled in disputes not necessarily of their choosing, often caused them to change their minds, dependent on how their organization had emerged from the encounter. Indeed, the state of local organization and pressing local problems, which varied widely from one part of the country to another, made it exceedingly difficult for the national leaders of the Miners' Association to preserve the unity and coherence needed to function as a single collective unit. In their headquarters in Newcastle, they seemed remote, of little consequence, to many members. Theirs was an age in which strong centralized national leadership of trade unions had not emerged on the scene. Yet, with a farcically inadequate back-up and staff – working from a public house near the River Tyne where he was the landlord – Martin Jude, a prominent colliers' leader from the late 1830s to late 1850s, and his handful of fellow union officers faced the impossible task of keeping this unwieldy coalition of pitmen together. And to complicate matters still further, as well as a membership that almost reached 100,000 at its peak, they had W. P. Roberts to contend with.[8]

The Miners' Attorney-General and the union leaders tended to experience events differently. He rushed around the coalfields. His was a stormy life of legal battles with the coalowners, hearing angry colliers expressing deeply felt grievances, and addressing emotional mass meetings, where he was lionized. To many pitmen, he was the union; they remained indifferent to what the union leaders said and did. In their daily activity, however, these officials saw how weak the union was in some coalfields, the reluctance of pitmen in many local unions to send subscriptions to the centre and the consequent financial inability of the association to sustain a prolonged strike. In the circumstances, it is hardly surprising that they counselled caution while Roberts favoured a more robust approach.

Initially Roberts' differences with the executive appeared to be of emphasis and tone rather than substance. Union policy was supposed to be formulated at quarterly delegate conferences. The first he attended was at Newcastle in September 1843. Though 200 delegates attended, membership in many coalfields remained small. Roberts endorsed the generally accepted resolution that 'a strike under existing circumstances would be partial and inimical to the best interests of the Society; and that it would be injudicious to adopt such a measure until the country is properly organised.'[9] He did not attend the next quarterly delegate conference, held at Manchester in January 1844, because of illness. Yet, almost certainly, he endorsed Martin Jude's words of caution, which delegates approved. Rather than seek confrontation, it was agreed to enter into negotiations with the employers.

What the prolonged debate at Manchester made apparent, however, was the difficulty of formulating, let alone implementing, an industrial strategy on a nationwide basis. Each coalfield had its own specific problems, so pressing that it was loath to subordinate them to national considerations. If the local situation seemed propitious, pitmen saw no reason why they should not obtain wage increases, striking if necessary to win them. By the same token, coalowners felt no obligation whatsoever to obey the union injunction to avoid partial disputes. Why should they idly sit back and watch the colliers' organization building up its resources until it could hold a successful general strike? Far better, if the opportunity presented itself, to go on the offensive and nip the local organization in the bud. Not surprisingly, therefore, the union found itself, despite the resolution passed by the Newcastle conference in September 1843, involved in serious conflicts in Lancashire and South Staffordshire.[10]

W. P. Roberts, too, found that reality wrenched apart his theory and practice on this issue. He believed, as we have already seen, that pitmen should not fritter away their gunpowder on making small bangs; what was necessary was a big explosion that would dislodge King Coal Tyrant. He had another reason for favouring a general strike instead of a partial one:

> It frequently occurs that the masters possess several collieries: a strike therefore at one merely leaves him to supply his trade from the others. He grins! evil devil that he is. More work is given to those who continue at their employ. The process which is starving a portion of his slaves has no effect at all upon him, save enabling him to get rid of a stock that was fast mouldering away. He calculates that the strikers will now 'come to' and he calculates rightly; for he has nothing to 'come to' for. he grins again! His wife chuckles, poor soul, the 'partner of his bosom', and little Susan has a new pair of dancing shoes.[11]

However, quite inconsistently, in some instances Roberts backed partial strikes: where he considered the employers were violating the law – for example, using the truck system – or not making adequate safety provisions, then he believed colliers were entitled to withdraw their labour. He appears to have been unaware that the scenario he described in the above quotation, suggesting that partial strikes damaged the pitmen but not the owners, applied on a coalfield basis throughout the North East. The mighty employers' organization had secretly created arrangements whereby any coalowner who suffered as a consequence of industrial action would be indemnified by his colleagues. In other words, a stoppage at a colliery would result in the master receiving full compensation for losses incurred, whereas the men received only a few niggardly shillings in strike pay – if they were lucky.

This information casts fresh light on Roberts' victories at Thornley and Wingate Grange. Determined to allow collieries in the North East only to operate under the conditions stipulated by the masters in the Bond, the coalowners' association was prepared to allow the collieries to remain closed indefinitely. Obviously, Roberts could not advise the men to return under the old terms. Having fought a tremendous legal battle to win the men the right to resist, he could not now recommend what was tantamount to a complete capitulation. Moreover, in the eyes of the Thornley pitmen, he was a great hero. They were accustomed to seeing miners hauled before the courts, prosecuted and imprisoned: now Roberts had shown them that this process did not have the grim inevitability they had hitherto thought. Yet, the rank-and-file enthusiasm for the Miners' Attorney-General was not necessarily entirely shared by the union's national leaders. The Miners' Association's financial resources were precariously meagre. Were they to be drained away, by paying men stoppage-money in disputes like Thornley and Wingate Grange, where no end seemed in sight?

In February 1844, the simmering discontent with Roberts in the upper echelons suddenly boiled over. A leaflet was published addressed to the miners of Durham and Northumberland. Written under the nom-de-plume of 'An unsophisticated unionist and hater of humbug', its author was Antony Stoves, a Newcastle pitman and close associate of the executive. It was published by T. Dodd, who printed the *Miners' Advocate* and all the rest of the union material. To give it an almost semi-official stamp of approval, the executive circulated it, along with official union literature, to miners' lodges not only in the North East but also elsewhere. The leaflet attacked Roberts and went on to declare that the legal department's 'days are numbered unless it be placed in the position it was first intended and be made subservient to the rules of the Society instead of the rules being laid aside by that establishment.' It went on to accuse Roberts of actively encouraging strikes at single collieries, a contravention of Rule 11 of the constitution. It questioned the high cost of the legal department, particularly the appointment of William Beesley as articled clerk at an annual salary of £140. He had already shown himself unsuitable for the post by being drunk in South Shields when he should have been at Jarrow colliery. The inebriated Beesley, it was alleged, 'then drove his pony with such violence as to precipitate the pony, carriage, his companions and himself over a wall, the consequence being much injury both to the carriage and his own bones.'

This titbit of scandal may well be an invention. Beesley had the reputation of being staunchly anti-alcohol. He had even edited a Chartist journal with the fascinating title of the *North Lancashire and Teetotal Letter-bag.*[11] At the 1842 Chartist convention, Feargus O'Connor had proposed that delegates abstain from alcoholic drinks for the duration of the proceedings. But Beesley thought this motion did not go far enough. He argued that if it was wrong to drink during the proceedings, then it was wrong to drink at any time. Roberts had tried to smooth over the disagreements, saying he knew teetotallers and men who drink who were equally good men. He thought the matter should be left to the personal judgement of each individual.

Whether Beesley had changed his way of life when he came to Newcastle, through contact with hard-drinking miners, it is impossible to say. What was clear, however, was that the leaflet's intention was to blacken Roberts and all closely associated with him. Most of the accusations were levelled at the Miners' Attorney himself.

The leaflet came as a shock to Roberts, who had just returned from London on union business. Immediately he dashed off a letter and asked for it to be circulated, along with the leaflet, to all collieries in Northumberland and Durham:

> Mr Roberts wishes the Secretary to whom this letter is directed, IMMEDIATELY to call a meeting of all hewers, etc., in his colliery – to read the enclosed handbill slowly and distinctly – and to invite the most full and complete comment on each charge. So that the delegate at the district meeting, to be held at Durham on Friday next, may be able correctly to represent the feelings of the pitmen who have elected him.
>
> Mr Roberts wishes the men at each colliery to come to a vote on the subject – that is to say – whether Mr Roberts is guilty of the charges or not?

Lodge after lodge in the region quickly jumped to Roberts' defence. The Durham delegate meeting unanimously supported him and, for good measure, authorized the publication of a statement to refute the charges against him. It also passed a resolution that called for the resignation of all the national executive committee for circulating Antony Stoves' original leaflet. The *Northern Star* added to the leadership's discomforture, describing members of the executive as 'too idle to work and too poor to live without work'. The paper went on to suggest they were in league with the coalowners. At a mass meeting, Roberts endorsed this opinion: he even described drunken evenings the executive had happily spent with the masters.[12]

The fact that both sides resorted to lies and counter-lies is indicative of the strength of feeling and the crucial issues that were at stake. Undoubtedly, John Hall, for the executive, was right to brush aside the slur that its members were in league with the coalowners, referring to their distinguished records in working-class movements, past and present. Nevertheless, the executive's case had fatal weaknesses. Most important of these was that W. P. Roberts was not employed by the union nationally, but by Durham and Northumberland, whose pitmen were incensed that it should dabble in matters that did not directly concern it. Moreover, as the sweeping vote of confidence obtained by Roberts from the pitmen of Durham and Northumberland proved, the executive's principal charge was false. It was not correct to say that 'a great portion of the members felt dissatisfied at the conducting of, and the enormous expense of, the law establishment.' Had that been the case, the executive would have been praised for its actions, not – as it complained – 'examined, cross-examined, and teased, taunted and grossly insulted' by delegates, even after it had apologized for what it had done.

Behind the quarrel lay vital questions of strategy and tactics. The North East had the biggest coalfields and the most pitmen. There the union was strongest. Should their financial strength be used to assist other coalfields to reach their degree of organization, creating a truly strong national union, or should it be used to finance the law department? When Roberts was engaged, it had been hoped that his employment would help to eliminate industrial disputes, that disagreements with the masters would be settled in court rather than on the picket line. But far from creating tranquillity, the court appearances of the Miners' Attorney usually aroused further discord, widening differences with the coalowners. Not only did Roberts' conduct threaten the authority of the union leadership, making it more difficult to give coherence and stability to the organization throughout the country, there was also a danger that it might drag the Miners' Association into a general strike that could destroy it.

In March 1844, Roberts started publishing his own journal, the *Miners' Magazine*. This was tantamount to appealing to the rank and file over the heads of the executive committee. In it, he openly declared: 'We are in favour of a strike, A GENERAL AND UNIVERSAL ONE: a general cessation of work in the pits in order that by a universal combination, the coal hewers may obtain a fair price for their labour.' He admitted that to achieve this goal would involve an immense struggle, and advised them, therefore, to make preparations: 'large sacrifices will be required from pitmen; they must live hardy, both at the time and previously; they must buy a stock of eatables and drinkables to support them while their masters are awakening from their slumbers of luxury.' The glittering prize to be won, Roberts believed, was not some slight marginal adjustment: he told them 'the time of your emancipation is not very far distant.'

While the overwhelming majority of North-East pitmen accepted that they should campaign for a general strike, astutely Roberts laid down contingency plans in the event that the national union delegate conference did not back this call. The March issue of the *Miners' Magazine* contained proposed amendments to the Bond, which would completely transform it from an instrument of discipline used by the coalowners, into one that would protect the workers. These counter-proposals sought to compel coalowners to make a legal commitment to introduce improvements, including payment by weight; payment for all coal hewed; stone or splint not to disqualify a whole tub; 10 shillings a week sick ('smart') pay; and five shillings a week plus house and free coals for widows during the first year of bereavement. Besides enshrining their rights, miners wanted the new-style Bond to curtail and lay down precisely the owners' opportunities to make deductions from wages. This article, a summary of the Durham and Northumberland men's negotiating stance, drawn up by their legal adviser, was submitted to the coal trade for its consideration.

The North-East pitmen arrived at the national conference in Glasgow on 25 March 1844, panting for action. All other business should be swept aside – delegates should immediately begin discussing the resolution on the proposed general strike. After this had been agreed, the conference divided largely on a coalfield by coalfield basis. Lack of organization made the strike impractical in some areas; counties like Staffordshire and Lancashire had been exhausted already by recent strikes. A lot of delegates feared that, as a large amount of coal had been stockpiled, the time was inopportune; while others seemed too preoccupied by local problems to become involved in nationwide action. When it was put to the vote, the North-East resolution was defeated by 28,042 votes to 23,357, a majority of 4,685.

At this point, the specific problems of the North East intruded. Normally, the Bond ran from April to April. Since the coalowners' terms for the forthcoming Bond were unknown, it would obviously be wrong for the pitmen to make a prior commitment to labour without first knowing the pay, hours or working conditions. To facilitate progress, Roberts had drawn up for the union those conditions that the pitmen would like included in the Bond and this had been submitted to the coal trade as a basis for possible negotiations. All the North East asked of other coalfields was that, if unfortunately no agreement with the masters was reached, pitmen from other collieries should not act as blacklegs. Christopher Haswell of Tyneside, who successfully moved the resolution, also appealed to pitmen in other parts of the country to restrict coal output where practical.

In fact, the passing of the resolution amounted to conference sanctioning a strike of the North-East pitmen. There was never the remotest chance of the coalowners agreeing to the concessions which the union wanted over the Bond. Far from intending to make it easier for the men, the employers' plan was to increase its severity. What made the proposition even less palatable from the masters' standpoint was that, under the proposals drawn up by Roberts, the Bond would run from April to October, not the customary year. In other words, they were expected to go through long and difficult discussions with the miners over an agreement that would last a mere six months – knowing that, at the end of that period, the union's membership would almost certainly be higher and that, with the onset of winter and higher demand for coal, its bargaining strength would be greater. The coalowners were quite aware that the colliers would then demand the Bond's abolition. Class instinct as well as common sense urged them to fight, not to fall into this trap.

Some historians, in my opinion, have not understood Roberts' role in this struggle. Dr Robert Colls, for example, has misread the significance of what Roberts said at the Glasgow conference, taking at face value his remarks urging restraint and attacking strikes. It is much more likely that this was a tactical move, made when it became clear that the general strike resolution would be lost.[13] Roberts wanted conference to leave the North East free to pursue its legitimate demands, with industrial action available as one of its options. Union leaders, however militant, have never wanted strikes for the joy of striking. If they can obtain their end without a stoppage, then they will do so. This was equally true of A. J. Cook in 1926 and Arthur Scargill in 1984. Had the coalowners in 1926 withdrawn their demand for a wage cut and an increase in the working day, then nobody would have called for a stoppage. Similarly, in 1984, had the Coal Board not insisted on colliery closures, there would have been no strike. Similarly, if it had been possible to smash the Bond without encountering any resistance, Roberts would have been delighted. The draft proposals he drew up performed three functions: first, they codified the miners' demands; second, they made it tactically much easier to get national conference to back any action contemplated by the North-East pitmen; and third, in the eyes of the general public, the pitmen would appear more reasonable *vis-à-vis* the owners since they had displayed their willingness to negotiate. Roberts, however, was under no illusion that the objective could be attained without an industrial battle. In the *Miners' Magazine*, he wrote that he had always known that 'the owners will not easily yield the power which wealth, union, community of interest and consolidation of thought have given them.' Yet, despite the enormous resistance they expected to meet, both he and the pitmen were determined to end the Bond – 'to be free' by 5 October 1844.[14]

Of course the coalowners had other plans. Faced with a deteriorating economic position, they did not wish to end the Bond but to increase its onerous conditions. They had to tackle the problem of declining productivity, a natural consequence of the exhaustion of easily-won seams, situated near the surface. The need to go deeper and deeper resulted in dramatic increases in on-cost expenditure (on haulage, maintenance of underground roadways, and so on). In 1831–2, there had been 12,696 men employed underground in the northern coalfields, a figure swollen to 22,749 by 1844 – an increase of 79 per cent. One handbill issued by the coalowners' supporters just before the 1844 dispute, suggested that 6,800 men were surplus to requirements.[15]

To compound its difficulties, the coal industry was suffering from a classic crisis of over-production. Slack demand left collieries working at well below full capacity, yet the owners had to bear the cost of irrigation, ventilation, and so on as though they were working flat out. In the mid and late 1830s, an unprecedented amount of speculative capital entered the industry, opening up mines in hitherto unexploited areas. The number of collieries rose from fifty-nine in 1830 to 129 by 1844.[16] Under the impact of new workings, the normal instrument for regulating output and price – the Vend – was beginning to break down. Its existence had depended upon the region's isolation and quasi-monopoly position, which gave the northern coalfields virtually all the London market. But the advent of railways was enabling other coalfields to compete and a national market for coal was beginning to emerge. Instead of being able to maintain artificially high prices, the North-East owners had to brace themselves for cut-throat competition. Even earlier, Lord London-derry, County Durham's largest coalowner, had claimed that in the previous four years the profits he had made would not buy him a pair of boots. In addition, his financial plight had been aggravated by over-extending himself in the construction of Seaham harbour.[17] His Lordship belonged to an endangered species. With the exception of the Lambtons, the Londonderrys were the only remaining aristocratic family in County Durham and Tyneside to retain their mining interests. The rest had abandoned the industry, mainly through force of economic pressures. They had been replaced by a new breed of entrepreneurs, industrial adventurers out to make a fast buck – or, rather, sovereign.

It would be wrong, however, to think that it was simply economic forces which pushed the owners in the direction of confrontation. Far more important, in their view, was the political threat which the Miners' Association constituted. The owners believed they had a right to use and dispose of *their* property as they chose, without any outside interference. It was not merely that the union wanted to meddle in the methods and amounts of production, it was also destroying the paternalistic relations they had traditionally enjoyed with their men. So long as there were mass meetings, where evil agitators and attorneys sought to stir up trouble between masters and men, peace would not return to the coalfields. They found it quite intolerable that these mischievous individuals 'could haul you before the magistrates whenever they please.'[18] Therefore, in order to reassert what they saw as their rightful power over their collieries and communities, the masters were determined to smash the union. They had no intention whatsoever of entering into negotiations – Roberts and the rest would have to be sent packing.

The coalowners compiled their battle plans with care. Large stocks of coal were accumulated and tentative steps taken to arrange for the importation of strike-breakers if that should become necessary. Both the owners and the police kept all union activities under surveillance. From almost the first day of his appointment as the Miners' Attorney-General, Home Office files contain reports about meetings addressed by Roberts.[19] A police spy infiltrated the Glasgow delegate conference in March 1844.[20] When he heard that the next delegate conference was to be held at Burslem, the Chief Constable of Staffordshire wrote to the Home Secretary to ask whether he should endeavour to secure information about the proceedings. Obviously he did, since a further report made it clear that W. P. Roberts was no longer the legal adviser to the North-East miners; he had been officially appointed the Attorney-General for the entire union in July 1844.[21] In the meantime, the army also made preparations. General Thomas Arbuthnot was placed in charge of all military personnel. The authorities feared – and rightly, too – that the troubles might spread to other coalfields. Consequently, they created an organization that played a similar role, in many respects, to that of the Police Reporting Centre in the 1984–5 miners' strike. When all these moves are put together, it is clear that the coalowners and the authorities were determined to resist, and defeat, the miners' union.

9 The Big Strike

The 1844 dispute began in almost a festive mood. Throughout Northumberland and Durham, pitmen held huge meetings. The brilliant sunshine of 6 April helped to dispel any gloom: everybody present seemed quietly confident, happy that the coalowners' tyranny would soon be vanquished. Nearly all the 33,000 men and boys had heeded the union's call. What was more, the rock-solid support remained as the weeks went by. After almost eight weeks Lord Londonderry reported to the Home Secretary that 'not a man is to be seen, not an engine in operation, not a curl of smoke from any pit.'[1]

Unable to understand the depth of the miners' commitment to their union, the coalowners had expected a quick collapse. They had believed it would be easy to rid themselves of the accursed union, and had not anticipated the discipline and order that would be shown. Pitmen and their families revealed themselves prepared to endure extreme hardships for their cause.

W. P. Roberts had advised everybody to remain peaceful. It was vital, he said, not to provide the owners with a pretext to resort to massive repression. Troops on hand would drown the union in a bath of blood. Generally, his appeal was heeded by pitmen. A handful of newspapers, avowedly anti-union yet nevertheless fair-minded, praised the pitmen for their conduct. The *Gateshead Observer* thought:

It is as satisfactory as it is creditable to the sense of the men to know that nothing like a desire to violate the peace has been manifested to an extent likely to excite apprehension. Such disturbances as have occurred have been comparatively trivial in their character and seem to have originated in the ill-restrained zeal of the women and children rather than in any bad intentions on the part of the men.

The *Newcastle Courant* concurred, saying that nothing had happened to justify serious or general alarm: 'In fact, it would be unjust to the great body of men not to state distinctly that their general demeanour is remarkably peaceful; hardships they appear to expect, but their determination to hold out stands unshaken.'[2]

Many newspapers, however, combined a complete laziness in collecting facts with a prodigious energy in distorting them. Aware that they themselves would be unwilling to make the same sacrifices as the pitmen were making, these gentlemen of the press concluded that solidarity shown by the colliery communities required the cement of secret intimidation. The absence of any evidence did not prevent them from asserting that the Miners' Association was terrorizing the pitmen. The alarmist *Durham Chronicle* predicted that 'a second part of the Newport tragedy' would be enacted; before the drama ended, it argued, some strikers 'may have to wear the adornment of the hempen necklace'. The Tory *Newcastle Chronicle* considered the union leaders had caused all the trouble by 'operating a system of compulsion, discipline, espionage, terror, social restraint, incendiary threats and dread of deadly violence'. The *Newcastle Journal* sought to link the industrial dispute with workers' struggles for the franchise: Chartism has 'brought to the surface of society a great deal of scum that usually putrifies in obscurity below'.[3] Others concurred: the Home Secretary, who saw the drama as a repeat of the 1842 disturbances, thought the pitmen were under the 'persistent guidance of the Chartists'; while Lord Londonderry noted that the two organizations were so intertwined that the Chartists held their county meeting at Pittingham immediately after a union delegate meeting and invited everybody to remain.[4]

The chief architect of evil, in the eyes of the *Newcastle Journal* (and most of the press), clearly had to be W. P. Roberts. Wrongly claiming him to be a relative of John Frost, it said that he moved north after Chartism's defeat in 1842, and at once set about infecting 'miners with the virus of his malignant notions'. Again inaccurately, it stated he had received £1,000 plus expenses in six months; after which, it claimed, he passed his days in the following way. He 'mounts the office stool, and plods through foolscap sheets the live long day, except only such brief portions as lawyers usually devote to tooth picking, digit brushing and mahogany hewing. There being, in truth, but little to do for Mr Roberts and his Man Friday, it was a most gross imposition on the gullibility of poor men.' The Man Friday mentioned was William Beesley, appointed by Roberts as his solicitor's clerk. In fact, if the newspaper is to be believed, 'Beesley thrust himself upon the pitmen, who employed him as a runner among the various collieries for a few shillings per week. That was certainly better than starving.'[5]

The coalowners and their media supporters used what would now be termed black propaganda. Deliberately telling lies and half truths, with the occasional true statement thrown in to confuse things further, helped to distract public attention from the main issue – namely, the Bond and how it operated – and concentrate attention on minor, peripheral issues, such as Roberts' life-style. He was always depicted as living in the lap of luxury, although significantly his standard of living was never compared with that of others in the same occupation. It was alleged that whenever he went to a union meeting it would be held in the taproom of Martin Jude's pub, amidst ample supplies of beer and tobacco. If he was not living it up in the North East, the Miners' Attorney was portrayed as deserting his post, guilty of a dereliction of duty, abandoning the union ship as it sank.

A moment's critical reflection leads one to doubt many of the newspaper accusations. Admittedly, Roberts had his much-publicized carriages and fast-trotting horses, but these were necessary if he were to complete his punishing schedule of legal work. Likewise his journeys from the North East on occasions during the strike: while newspapers drew attention to his absences from the region, they never bothered to find out where he had gone. Invariably, Roberts was in other parts of the country, addressing meetings and trying to raise money for the strike fund. Sometimes in their haste to blacken his character, newspapers indulged in inexplicable inconsistencies: the *Durham Chronicle*, for instance, completely changed its tune. A few months after describing Roberts' legal victories and saying he 'was more than a match for all the legal skill of the owners', it dealt again with the same cases but now concluded that it saw Roberts 'in a light but little more favourable than that of a common swindler, who choused his clients of the money by the most ludicrous and grossly fraudulent devices.'[6] Similarly, it is difficult to reconcile the

Newcastle Journal's depiction of Roberts as a grasping, Shylock kind of figure in 1843–4 – battening on to the pitmen merely for what he could make out of them – with the gleeful way it described his impoverished situation a year later, when the union had collapsed and Roberts was working for the miners virtually for nothing. Was this what they would expect of an avaricious lawyer?

But, in any case, had there been any truth in the accusations made by these Tory and Whig newspapers, it seems likely that the coalowners and their supporters in the Press would have wanted to suppress the information. For if Roberts was squandering large amounts of union money, had been negligent about his duties and culpably absent at crucial times, would this not operate in the employers' interests? Out to smash the Miners' Association, surely the coalowners stood to benefit if the trade union used its funds imprudently rather than wisely, employed officials of poor rather than high quality, or had a lawyer who was unreliable and away from his post when most needed?

The private correspondence of various magistrates and coalowners makes quite clear their real opinion about the Miners' Attorney-General. In a quaint epistle to the Home Secretary, the Bishop of Durham warned him that an exceedingly dangerous situation had arisen. He explained to Sir James Graham that the country was 'teeming with a numerous and ignorant population, under the influence of Chartists and other artful men, and were easily stimulated by liquor'. As many magistrates were also coalowners, 'the pitmen cannot believe that they are before an impartial tribunal when disputes arise between them and their masters – and these jealousies are furthered by the acts of a man named Roberts, who has unfortunately gained the confidence of the pitmen.'[7] Lord Londonderry also believed his pitmen had become 'the deluded and obstinate victims of designing men and crafty Attorneys'. In a letter to the Home Secretary, His Lordship made it plain that he regarded Roberts as the main obstacle to a return to tranquillity. Another letter from Lord Londonderry to the Home Secretary, dated 21 July 1844, urged the Government to prosecute Roberts: 'It now evidently appears to me that, whatever influence individual coalowners may have over their own people, so long as these assemblages and meetings are permitted every second or third day, so long will the power of Mr Roberts and his leaders prevail.' In further correspondence, His Lordship told the Home Secretary that, even if they overcame the present problems, they would soon emerge again because pitmen could expect their dissatisfaction with the Bond to be voiced by Roberts: 'Mr Roberts might order another strike in October, and the coalowners would again be in dismay.'[8]

Adopting another tack, the masters approached the miners' leaders and hinted that they might be more conciliatory if the union sacked Roberts. Without even debating the issue, the union replied that, as long as the conditions existed which had led to Roberts' appointment, his dismissal would not be contemplated. A mass meeting, attended by 20,000 on Shadon Hill, cheered Thomas Pratt when he declared that it was they, the coalowners, who were responsible for Roberts' employment in the first place: if the owners acted honestly towards their workmen they would cease to need the services of an attorney.[9]

Foiled in their attempts to persuade either the government or union to rid them of Roberts, the coalowners met on 24 July to discuss the question of doing the job themselves. At first, it seemed to them a mere formality, involving recourse to the criminal law. Five days later, Lord Londonderry informed the Home Secretary of their determination to go ahead with the matter, especially as there was no sign of the miners surrendering. But when they sought legal advice, W. H. Watson, the barrister approached, counselled caution. He expressed the opinion that some of Roberts' publications were libellous and there were reasonable grounds for thinking a jury would convict. Even so, he doubted whether it would be expedient to proceed. There was a possibility it might fail – 'an acquittal might be highly injurious' – and the case could not be heard till the spring assizes. By then, he thought, given Roberts' character, he could be expected to come out with even stronger utterances, statements that would leave the outcome of a court case beyond doubt.[10]

In the light of this legal advice, the Coal Trade Committee decided to leave the prosecution on the table. If further offence was given, the committee resolved to proceed with all possible charges.[11] However, this resolution was overtaken by events – after twenty weeks of struggle, the pitmen's resistance collapsed. This primarily occurred for two reasons: first, the masters imported strike-breakers on a large scale; and, second, the length of the dispute had driven strikers and their families to destitution and hunger.

In the latter stages of the dispute, Lord Londonderry brought in a continual stream of agricultural labourers from his Irish estates.

Other masters acquired strike-breakers from Cornwall and Wales. The customary procedure was for the blacklegs to replace the strikers both in the employment and the home. Arrangements were therefore made for mass evictions, a procedure that usually followed a set pattern. Police, and sometimes soldiers, accompanied the resident viewer to the pitman's cottage. Before touching the furniture, they would ask, 'Will you go to work?' When told 'No!', orders would be given. All furniture and belongings would be thrown out, often deliberately broken in the process. The same rough treatment, a lack of humanity, was also shown to some individuals. A woman was dragged from her home at West Moor and pulled 80 yards along the waggon-way till she fainted. Because their son was a local union leader, Lord Londonderry had no compunction about evicting 79-year-old Henry Barrass and his wife. 'I was bound to act up to my word,' His Lordship explained in a letter, placarded around Durham villages. 'Bound by duty to my property, my family and my station.' In this way he hoped to persuade his pitmen – 'the deluded and obstinate victims of designing men and crafty Attorneys' – to foresake the union. Feeling he needed to be cruel to be kind, Lord Londonderry personally supervised the evictions at his collieries and ended his open letter to the miners, where he outlined his plans: 'I am, your sincere friend, Vane Londonderry.'

The spate of evictions led Roberts to reiterate his earlier advice. The owners, he said, were deliberately being provocative, trying to goad men into committing acts of violence. To succumb to temptation would be disastrous for the union. It would provide the authorities with a pretext to resort to massive repression, slaughtering some and transporting others. Perhaps with thoughts of what happened at North Staffordshire in 1842 at the back of his mind, he went on to give miners the following advice:

> Stay in the house, your families around, lock the door (as against an ordinary housebreaker), sit down or go to bed, firmly and quietly state your disinclination to leave the spot; and you may add (but only in joke, mind) that you have read in a book that 'an Englishmen's home is his castle'. Beyond that, offer no resistance. Let them *carry* you out.[12]

In his appeal to the pitmen, Roberts had written: 'You have

Pitmen encamped (*Illustrated London News* 1844)

trusted me as perhaps you never trusted a man before.' Evidence supporting his view came from the manner in which they all obeyed his recommendation. Unlike the 1831–2 dispute, the 1844 stoppage produced few violent evictions. It did, however, take the authorities longer and, for their personnel, created greater stress. The physical task of manhandling miners, sometimes whole families, with the children crying, would not have been a very pleasant task, particularly as often the job had to be done to the accompaniment of barracking from an angry crowd.

Soon whole villages sprung up by the roadside. Chests of drawers, desks and tables formed the walls; the roofs were supplied by canvas and bedclothes. Sometimes sods of grass and earth were used. Richard Fynes, a participant in the 1844 struggle, recalled that in adversity morale in the roadside encampments remained remarkably high: 'Here and there, fiddles might be heard; whilst the men grouped together, smoking, singing, or chatting about the great battle, but never wavering in their confidence or in their determination to fight the battle to the bitter end.' People gave their precious possessions, including wedding-rings. These were sold and used to buy food, shared equally among all families.[13]

The army, even high-ranking officers, had reservations about the policy the coalowners were pursuing. Lieutenant-Colonel J. Bradshaw, commander-in-chief in County Durham, reported that all ejections had been carried out peacefully. Nevertheless, he still felt the owners' move was misguided. It would strengthen the pitmen's resolution, prolong the strike and leave a legacy of lasting bitterness. In vain, he tried to get further evictions postponed. As he explained to General Arbuthnot, the overall commander, he considered a little kindness and good temper from the owners, coupled with a few concessions, would result in a resumption of work. Given a more conciliatory attitude from the owners, he believed that the pitmen could be persuaded to cast aside leaders like Roberts and Beesley, 'whose real aim, I fairly believe, is to induce them to become Chartists'. In his reply, General Arbuthnot agreed with Bradshaw's analysis, and urged him to continue the dialogue with influential coalowners. Nevertheless, he felt obliged to remind Bradshaw of his legal responsibilities: whatever his personal reservations, his duty remained to provide military assistance to the civil powers to preserve the queen's peace.[14]

Yet, in view of the rivalries and mutual hostility of those supposed to maintain law and order, the queen's peace was a very fragile commodity. A drunken brawl in Newcastle between soldiers and police escalated. On hearing about the disturbance, troops swarmed out of Fenham barracks to help their comrades. A report to the Home Office stated, 'The town was for several hours kept in a state of great alarm and discord.'[15] What worsened the situation was that, in the government's eyes, it appeared doubtful whether, in some towns, even the mayor and the magistracy could be guaranteed to keep the queen's peace. Unsure whether the Mayor of Gateshead and his colleagues could be relied upon to behave in a restrained and responsible manner, an instruction was sent from Whitehall ordering them to return immediately the 100 swords, 100 pistols and 3,000 cartridges on loan. After consulting the local magistracy, the mayor simply disregarded the order.[16] While the government feared that local notables might become too hawkish, with the worst scenario being the staging of a second Peterloo massacre, another fear was, paradoxically, that the special constables might not be violent enough! They had to police the areas where they lived and rather than endure lasting unpopularity, they might have shrunk from doing their duty. The Chief Constable of Durham declared: 'Having been asked by a magistrate if I have any confidence in the special constables, I had to state in reply that I have none, that they have none in themselves, nor have the miners who desire to work.'[17] Plans to augment the regular police force ran into resistance. Rural areas, unaffected by the strike, resented being asked to pay huge sums for a service not intended to benefit them. Eventually, a sort of compromise was worked out. To meet the immediate situation, Metropolitan police were brought in. To cope with special needs, though the legality of this seems dubious, individual coalowners could pay and equip policemen, whose activities would concentrate on their particular collieries.[18] Even so, the overall position, especially in County Durham, remained highly unsatisfactory until the end of the dispute.

Lord Londonderry, Lord-Lieutenant of County Durham, foremost coalowner and landlord, was at the epicentre of an industrial whirlwind that scooped up and destroyed all that lay in its path. Initially, he had gained from the dispute. Panic buying in the first few weeks pushed up the price of coal and thus he could profitably dispose of his stockpiles. Then, thinking a few union agitators at each colliery were responsible for all the trouble, he believed that if they were removed everything would return to normal. However, when the evictions only stiffened resistance, he imported more and more strike-breakers. Yet, he did this with misgivings, highly conscious of the dangers he was running. With the newcomers living in the miners' cottages while their former occupants huddled in the cold outside, an explosive mixture of anger and hate was being generated. Moreover, the newcomers were not as good as the old hands at doing the job. They did not possess the knowledge and skills which pitmen take many years to acquire. On 24 July, Lord Londonderry wrote to the Home Secretary that the colliers were not capitulating and 'I am almost fearful of bringing over more Irishmen.'[19] Although at the beginning of the dispute he had been the foremost advocate of continuing the struggle until unconditional surrender had been secured, Lord Londonderry changed his mind during the summer. He now wanted his fellow coalowners to enter into negotiation with the pitmen's representatives over the terms of the Bond. But the rest of the coal trade, quite rightly from their standpoint, stayed firm in their determination to continue the fight to a finish.

From the outset, the executive of the Miners' Association had realized the gravity of the situation. It was a dispute, as they made clear to the Glasgow conference, which they did not want to fight. The very existence of their organization had been brought into question. In a circular sent out to all coalfields at the beginning of the strike, the executive warned that, 'from what we can learn, the masters built themselves up so that, if they can succeed, it will go a great way towards annihilating the entire Association.' As no money was coming in from the northern coalfields (more than a third of the total membership), the executive appealed to other members to pay an extra twopence a week besides contributing to a fund to help the strikers. However, inspired by the example set by the coalowners of the North East, the masters in most other coalfields had gone on the offensive, determined to rid themselves of trade unionism. As a result, preoccupied with the struggle in their own areas, pitmen elsewhere sent little or no money to their brothers in the North East.[20]

Well before the dispute ended, both union funds and personal savings had been exhausted. The authorities did everything within their power to curb poaching and scavenging, harassing pitmen as well to make their lives additionally unpleasant. Pressure was brought to bear on shopkeepers not to extend credit. The courts added to the misery: to steal a turnip could result in a heavy fine or imprisonment. One of the road-side dwellers – William Young of Castle Eden – was sent to Durham gaol because he scared one of Lord Londonderry's horses as it passed by. According to Roberts, all this amounted to 'cruelty unexampled, I believe, in the annals of British history.' Again, he reiterated his message that it was vital to maintain solidarity and avoid reacting to provocation: 'Peace for the next fortnight – and the cause of the Northumberland and Durham colliers is won.'[21]

Unfortunately this was not to be. In a deliberate attempt to sap strikers' morale, the owners had daily been bringing in a trickle of blacklegs. In response, each day a few more pitmen returned to work. Then the drift back on Tees and Wear became more pronounced. Nevertheless, hardcore support still remained solid and union activists believed they could stop the flow. Their efforts were defeated when the news spread that some pitmen, wanting to return to work, had discovered that blacklegs had taken all their jobs.

Desperately, they trekked across the Tyne, looking for new work. For Northumbrian pitmen to see their brothers from Durham – good trade unionists who had endured the deprivations of almost twenty weeks – taking their own jobs was the final blow. The union realized the strike was collapsing and ordered, where possible, an orderly return to work. On 17 August 1844, Robert Gill, secretary of the Coal Trade Committee, reported that all collieries were again operating normally, the men having accepted the terms offered by the committee on 6 April 1844.

Now the pitmen had to taste the bitter fruits of defeat, a realization that all their sacrifices had been in vain. A labour surplus, the consequence of the mass importation of strike-breakers, gave employers even greater power than before. They could pick and choose who they engaged, victimizing anyone with a reputation for union activity or guilty of the slightest infringement of the Bond. What made things still harder was that, as cold winter winds started blowing, some families continued to live in makeshift roadside encampments, without a wage since April. According to one report, some men through lack of nourishment could not even stand up.

The owners' vindictiveness was matched by the colliers' desire for vengeance. Regarding the blacklegs as the cause of the current calamities, they vowed to make them suffer. Tokens were taken from their tubs, thereby depriving them of wages for coal they had hewn. Stones would deliberately be thrown into their coal, leading them to be heavily fined under the Bond. Besides working hard and ending up with no payment, thanks to other tricks played by Geordie pitmen, the blacklegs could find that all their gear, picks and drills had been stolen and thrown down disused workings. Sometimes all their clothes – pitmen often worked naked on the hot coal-face – mysteriously vanished. This would mean the nude strike-breakers making a humiliating journey home, accompanied by a crowd of women, banging pans and shouting ribald comments.

In addition to all this, much more dangerous practices could occur. One of these was to hang a rope across the main roadway at neck-height. In a drift mine, driven into a hillside and entered on foot, not by a shaft, it was customary for the putters to push the heavily-laden tubs out of the pit and then rush down at great speed for the next load. For strike-breakers at Seghill colliery, this could have fatal consequences, as the well-known miners' ballad grimly recounts.

Oh don't go down the Seghill mine;
Across the mainway's hung a line
To catch the throat and break the spine
Of the dirty blackleg miner.

So join the union while you may;
Don't wait until your dying day
For that may not be far away,
You dirty blackleg miner.

In normal times comradeship and friendship characterize the mining community, born out of facing the same hazards and understanding that your life might depend on a neighbour's actions. But this prerequisite did not exist after the prolonged struggle of 1844. Moreover, many of the blacklegs were new to the coal industry, unacquainted with the inherent dangers. To make matters worse, owners tended to appoint such individuals to positions of responsibility because they regarded the criterion of loyalty as more important than those of experience or technical knowledge. These personal inadequacies were more serious given the state of the collieries, the months of idleness, when explosive gases had been allowed to accumulate. It was not surprising, therefore, that in the six months immediately after the strike, four major colliery disasters happened.

On 28 September 1844, an explosion took place at Haswell colliery in Durham, killing ninety-five men and boys. Roberts, assisted by Jude and a pitman called Clough, appeared at the inquest on behalf of the union. He sought to prove the explosion had occurred as a result of bad management. Had the colliery been properly run and ventilated, the foul air would not have been allowed to accumulate. Roberts accused George Forster, the colliery viewer, of negligence, and argued that the owners were equally culpable since they placed inexperienced persons in positions of trust, having to perform potentially lethal tasks: 'One of these three men was a stonemason, another was a watchmaker; none of them were ever pitmen before the strike last April.'

From the outset, Roberts encountered obstruction in his attempt to establish that the coalowners were guilty of criminal negligence. The coroner, aided by J. E. Marshall, solicitor for the owners, constantly interrupted him. Extraordinarily, when George Forster, the viewer, objected to another person testifying because the evidence might contradict his own version of events, the coroner ruled in his favour. An outraged Roberts immediately shouted 'Apply this doctrine to the Old Bailey, and how many cells at Newgate will be occupied?' This did not stop the coroner calling a succession of witnesses, supplied by the owners. Each of them expressed confidence in the colliery management and declared that ventilation in the pit was exemplary. As the dreary repetition of the same story continued, Roberts remarked that he had no desire to hear any more; but the coroner replied that it was his duty to continue hearing the evidence. It would be more helpful, Roberts suggested, if some independent expert, such as the distinguished mining engineer Matthias Dunn, was asked to investigate and produce his findings. However, J. E. Marshall, for the owners, would have none of it. An angry scene ensued. Above the noise, the loud voice of the Miners' Attorney could be heard: 'Justice would not be done, the ends of fair inquiry would not be answered, if the owners refused to allow Mr Dunn to examine the pits.'

Another obstacle to judicial impartiality was the composition of the jury. As Roberts was later to observe: 'They were all farmers or shopkeepers – some directly, and many of them indirectly – under the influence of the owners. One of them, at the close of the first day, remarked "he could not see the use of examining any more; it was clear that it was all an accident".'[22]

The Haswell disaster was soon followed by another at Coxlodge colliery, near Newcastle. Here, mindful of the disorderly scenes at the previous inquest, the coroner began by making it clear he intended to give Roberts no latitude. Sternly, he remarked: 'No attorney shall come here to interfere with me.' At this, Roberts turned to his assistant and told him: 'Take that down.' But the coroner said he would run the inquest in the manner he deemed proper: he had decided to assert his authority by denying others the right to take notes of proceedings. Roberts just disregarded this. Within a short time, proceedings got out of control. Into the heated argument entered Mr Ruan, a mining engineer, who thought it an excellent opportunity to expound his own pet theory of colliery ventilation. To add to the confusion and disorder, Martin Jude and Thomas Horn – a person with no relevant experience who kept a music shop in Newcastle – entered the fray. When stripped of extraneous matter, the respective submissions closely resembled those heard at the Haswell inquest a few weeks before. Again, the Miners' Attorney claimed that the colliery had been badly managed and badly ventilated; the direct cause of the disaster had been a man named Brown, a former agricultural labourer, who only went into mining after the strike started. The explosion had happened after he entered gaseous old workings with a naked flame – a reckless step which no experienced collier would take. Mr Liddell, for the owners, did not attempt to defend Brown's conduct. Nevertheless, he went to considerable length to assert that the management was excellent and the ventilation was as good as possible. In concluding, the coroner agreed with Mr Liddell. Bringing in a verdict of accidental death, he declared that he was certain the ventilation was always as good as possible.

Hopelessness and dismay spread in pit communities at the apparent official indifference to the loss of lives. As mining operations went deeper, the possibility of explosions increased. At one blow, all the menfolk of a village could be wiped out. Usually their dependants ranged over three generations: old people as well as children would rely upon the breadwinner. Yet, the coalowner would not be liable to pay compensation. Under the principle of 'common employment', first propounded by Baron Abinger in 1837, it was claimed it would be 'an absurdity'. It would mean that 'the footman, who rides behind the carriage, may take action against his master for drunkenness, neglect, or want of skill in the coachman.'[23] Every attempt, whether before a coroner or judge, to prove culpability of the coalowner was frustrated. As the *Miners' Advocate* bitterly commented: 'Truly, coroner's inquests, as at present conducted, are a farce.' Little ground for optimism seemed to exist.

Nevertheless, though not appreciated at the time, significant changes of attitude were occurring – changes that drastically altered the whole approach to the question of mine safety. To this, W. P. Roberts' pamphlet, *The Haswell Colliery Explosion*, made an important contribution. Well documented and well researched, it exposed the inquest, showing its primary function to be the protection of the coalowner, not the discovery of truth. It helped to fuel public disquiet, making it imperative for the government to act. At Roberts' request, the prime minister, Robert Peel, granted him an audience. Roberts journeyed down to Brighton for the meeting. Partly arising from their discussion, the government appointed two eminent scientists, Professors Lyell and Faraday, to investigate. While they refused to join the chorus of condemnation of the Haswell colliery management – a fact that caused Roberts to visit the prime minister again and express his dissatisfaction – the Lyell–Faraday reports set a vital precedent. They showed that science could be an invaluable tool in helping to prevent accidents in mining which, up till then, had been regarded as an essentially practical matter. Other outsiders, such as James Mather and the South Shields committee for the investigation of accidents, through their patient and painstaking work, also helped to promote a more enlightened approach. Among the progressive moves was the appointment of Matthias Dunn as an official government mines' inspector for the North East.

For the miners' union in Northumberland and Durham, however, this news was at best a crumb of comfort, for everything else was bad. Quite ruthlessly, Lord Londonderry and his colleagues pursued a policy of victimization. Prominent union members were not merely denied employment – it was made plain they would never work down the pits again. Consequently union organization was virtually smashed. Insofar as it did continue to exist, a few members here and there held secret meetings. They exerted little or no influence. What a few months previously had been a thriving, strong organization was now reduced to an empty shell.

Obviously, Roberts' own position did not remain unaffected by the change of fortunes. At the Glasgow conference in March 1844, it had been decided to postpone taking a decision on his place within the organization until the next quarterly meeting. This took place at the Temperance Hall, Burslem, on 15–19 July 1844. Since this was in the middle of the strike, when the coffers of Durham and Northumberland were empty, no struggle was put up by the North-East pitmen to keep him exclusively in their employ. Instead, it was agreed that he should be appointed as the legal adviser to the whole association. Each member was to pay half a penny a week to the law fund. Every quarterly conference was to audit the accounts of the legal department for the previous quarter.[24]

These arrangements, it would appear, remained largely on paper. In reality, Roberts received hardly any salary. In most coalfields membership drastically dropped and, where money was collected, it was immediately allocated to alleviate the sufferings of strikers and their families. Indeed, Roberts himself recognized their needs as paramount. Far from taking money from the union, Roberts planned to hand over some of his own. During the big strike, he went to

London 'and proposed to raise £1,000 on his own security' for association funds. But Feargus O'Connor persuaded him it would be a futile gesture. It would, O'Connor argued, paralyse other collections taking place; provide the enemy with ammunition, allowing them falsely to depict Roberts as affluent; and, furthermore, it was unlikely ever to be repaid.[25]

After the strike ended, Roberts remained in the North East. For more than six months, as he was later to remind the pitmen of Northumberland and Durham, he stayed among them, 'doing the same work, attending inquests, meetings, disputes before magistrates, etc., the same as before with this difference, however, that I was not paid, not even out of pocket expenses'.[26] That he made considerable sacrifices, living in poverty, was certainly true. Six months after the strike ended, the *Gateshead Observer* reported: 'Roberts is still lurking about the district, so miserably clad and dirty in person, that he might be taken for a hewer in his second best.'[27] In April 1845, the *Newcastle Journal* was able happily to announce his imminent departure from the region. In his valedictory address to the Northumberland miners, Roberts told them that the income of the legal department had hardly reached 30 shillings a week. As a consequence, he had been compelled to pay almost £1,000 out of his own pocket and had almost been reduced to penury. His financial discomforture led this jubilant Tory paper to inquire: 'What is to become of the fast-trotting ponies?'[28]

In the streets, handbills mysteriously appeared to celebrate his departure. A new era, one of co-operation between masters and men, would now be inaugurated. An anonymously-written poem expressed the hope that pitmen would become more enlightened:

> Also, O Lord! give men to see
> That strikes and kick ups wanna dee
> But best when men an' maisters 'gree
>   Upon each place
> To bargain for his sell, be free,
>   Each knows his case.
> So farewell Union and farewell Roberts
> And farewell Beesley and all sick loberts.

A song drew the same conclusions, albeit in more abusive language. Its chorus went:

> Hokee, pokee, wankee fum,
> Roberts and Beesley, England's scum,
> The curse of all, the fear of some,
> This rogue of a pitman's attorney.

Because of defeat and demoralization, such sentiments gained a resonance within some sections of the mining communities. But Roberts believed this would be only a temporary phenomenon. Actually, in staying in the North East after the strike ended, he had taken a calculated gamble, believing a revival was just around the corner. Although he conceded the 'union has sustained a heavy blow', yet he was prepared, even in March 1845, to wager five to two that there would again be mass meetings of 20,000 pitmen in County Durham within three months. Only slowly did he begin to accept the scope and magnitude of the disaster, and then he still maintained: 'A large experiment has been tried – and it has failed. It was an experiment, however, which colliers were perfectly justified in making.' Still he believed in trade unionism: 'Every working man in the kingdom might be employed at double his present rate of wages if they were united,' he claimed. But industrial action, to be effective, needed the resources to sustain it. Therefore, he now favoured small localized strikes, which the rest of the membership could sustain indefinitely. Another modification of his opinions was that he now considered general unions, encompassing workers from many sectors of the economy, could be a more effective weapon than unions confined to a single industry.[29]

Leaders of the Miners' Association were probably uneasy about some of Roberts' new ideas. They were more cautious, more concerned to avoid strikes wherever possible and more prone to organizational conservatism. They did not back him when he favoured general unions as against industrial unions, as this would deny the Miners' Association its *raison d'être*. Yet, they still valued his services highly. He had stood steadfastly by them throughout their great ordeal, sharing in their sufferings. In November 1844, the quarterly delegate conference at Wakefield unanimously expressed its appreciation. Later, when Roberts announced his intention to close the *Miners' Magazine*, it was agreed to offer him space to write a regular column in the union's official journal.

His reply to this invitation is both intriguing and mysterious. Rejecting the offer, he began by giving minor technical reasons, such as dislike of the format of the *Miners' Advocate*. Then he went on to refer to his individualism: 'My mode of thought has now become habitual to me; it does not always harmonize with such as cannot understand it. Such as it is, however, I like to stand alone.' Finally, he made a proposal that is difficult to reconcile with the determination to stand alone, free from encumbrances: he suggested that the Miners' Association should close down the *Miners' Advocate*, start a new journal, and appoint him editor. He would be prepared to work, he stated, for an annual salary of £50 plus an extra £10 for every 1,000 copies sold after the first thousand. His readiness to take on this new commitment cannot be reconciled with his grounds for discontinuing the *Miners' Magazine*, namely, the time and energy it absorbed.

The explanation for the apparent contradiction may lie in Roberts' personality. His own paper achieved a respectable circulation, fluctuating between 3,000 and 5,000 copies an issue, but he begrudged the effort it entailed because it failed to put him at the centre of the union stage. Likewise, simply to write a regular column would leave him marginalized. If, however, he edited the union paper, as well as running its legal department, he would have achieved incomparable power and influence. But Roberts' problem may well have been that, while he sought personal power, he was not prepared to accept the controls that often accompany it. In trade unions, officials are usually expected to fit into a structure, to work as one of a team; Roberts tended to be too erratic and idiosyncratic.

Though nobody seems to have realized it at the time, failure to reach agreement over his proposal to issue a new paper for pitmen marked the end of a phase in Roberts' life. Henceforth he would never play such a leading role in any single union. While he continued to work for various miners' unions, almost till his death, they never monopolized his time again. Also, the North East was no longer his main stomping ground. Instead, from the summer of 1845, he moved to industrial Lancashire, where fresh challenges awaited him as the legal adviser of the Lancashire Miners' Association.

10 Uncle Bobby in Lancashire

Moving to Lancashire must have been like moving to another world. In the North East, the Miners' Association had virtually ceased to exist whereas in Lancashire, despite the tough battles of 1844, it continued to thrive. Their contrasting bargaining positions were reflected in the miners' fortunes: declining pay and conditions in the North East, steadily improving pay and conditions in Lancashire. In Lancashire, moreover, the union operated in a context of optimistic expansion, where other groups of workers were becoming organized and accruing benefits therefrom. Behind all this lay the rapid development of the county's economy, a period of prodigious growth in the textile industry, with King Cotton selling goods all over the world. This did not merely bring considerable wealth back to Lancashire, it helped as well to stimulate the growth of other industries, particularly engineering and coal. Textile machinery and fuels were essentially part of the same success story. The Manchester area had accumulated the greatest concentration of steampower in the world.

Roberts quickly settled down there. As a result of his legal battles, Lancashire pitmen already knew him well. Almost a year before, a mass meeting of 10,000 held on Amberswood Common, near Wigan, met to celebrate his many courtroom victories and to appeal to him to become their legal adviser.[1] Only existing arrangements with Durham and Northumberland, coupled with the decision of the Glasgow national conference (March 1844), prevented this from happening. Now, however, nothing stood in the way. He acquired offices at 8, Princess Street, convenient for the centre of Manchester, and a residence at Seedley House, Pendleton, on the outskirts, quite close to a working-class district.

In many respects, his work was the same as it had been in

140

Newcastle, representing pitmen arraigned before petty sessions and sometimes journeying to London, hopefully to secure the release of those imprisoned. His complete dedication to the cause, furious energy and numerous triumphs quickly won him enormous popularity. One of the Lancashire leaders, William Dixon, stated the generally-accepted view before he asked Roberts to address a large strike meeting at Bolton: 'If a warrant were taken out against a man, he said, "Oh, never mind, Uncle Bobby will defend me", and even if sent to prison, "Uncle Bobby will get me out again". If it were not for the legal talents of Mr Roberts, there was not a prison in Lancashire but would be full of colliers.'[2]

It is difficult to describe the exhilaration that swept through mining communities, generating greater conviction and self-confidence, as he won victory after victory over a hostile judiciary. A typical instance occurred in Rochdale when he secured the release of an imprisoned miner. This led to an unprecedented event – a downing of tools in order to hold a wild celebration, as a participant described in a letter to the *Northern Star*:

> O Sir! It was glorious news, and right gloriously was it demonstrated. The glad tidings flew like lightning through the country. Every pick was thrown aside; every old man appeared to have cast off his age; the cripple threw away his crutch; and every man was proud to be a miner on that day. Never did the eyes behold such a spectacle.[3]

The long procession wended its way through Rochdale. As it reached the bank owned by Mr Harvey, who had been the presiding magistrate, the band ironically played 'See the conquering hero comes'. On another occasion – 27 September 1845 – the pitmen of Central Lancashire took a day off to celebrate Roberts' legal victories. Uncle Bobby, as he had affectionately become known, was described as 'not only the General Gaol Deliverer but Purifier of the Bench!'

By 1847, Uncle Bobby's exploits were considered even greater than those of a few years before in the North East:

> What a man this Mr Roberts is! – how his power grows! In Northumberland he destroyed the appetite of many a justice –

some to our knowledge brought up their breakfasts and lost all desire for dinner. In Durham there were similar distressing results, and, on the release of the Thornley men, two of the most courageous of these administrators of the law promised to commit suicide; but, alas, they forgot to do it.[4]

The liberation of two men from prison occasioned this outburst. A celebratory procession, waving flags, cheering and singing 'For he's a jolly good fellow', marched through Warrington. It was led by two fat old women dressed up as 'Thomas' and 'Billy', the gaoling magistrates, Thomas Lloyd and William Stubbs.

Naturally, Lancashire employers sought to counter the new threat. When cases came before court, their legal representatives often asked for the bench to imprison rather than fine. They pointed out that a fine would be no punishment; the wealthy colliers' union could easily pay. But to have a lot of men serving short prison terms might create difficulties for the union. Faced with so many in gaol, they thought Roberts could well find his resources stretched, making him unable to take each case to a higher court. Moreover, they believed that if the prisoner had only a short sentence to serve, recourse to such action would probably not be considered worth the time and trouble involved.

A second strategem was to speed up the process of litigation. As a result, pitmen were sometimes charged and sentenced before Roberts could arrive. This nearly happened to six workers employed by J. B. Edelston, of Warrington, charged with leaving their employment without due notice. Roberts only heard about this as he was eating his breakfast. Immediately, he set off for the railway station, but there was no train running before 11 a.m. So he hired a post-chaise, paying the driver double fees to go as fast as he could. He arrived at Warrington after one of the defendants had already been sentenced to three months imprisonment with hard labour. The magistrates had not been prepared to accept the defence submission that a long bout of illness had left the accused with no money; one of his children had died and he had not the wherewithal to pay for the burial; and therefore he had been compelled to absent himself from work to visit relatives and friends to raise the requisite cash. J. B. Edelston had offered to advance him the money, but only on condition that he sign a contract to remain in his employment for the next five years. When the worker refused, the prosecution and conviction ensued.

On arrival, Roberts applied for an adjournment on the grounds that there had been insufficient time to prepare the defence. In the short period allowed him, he discovered the accused did not know what they were accused of. They were, like many others in Victorian England, illiterate and consequently required the charges to be read out. Yet, this had not been done. In the case of one of the defendants, a man named Dobson, it could not be done for his charge-sheet had been lost! At once, Roberts asked for Dobson to be released since he had no case to answer. But the magistrates' clerk casually replied: 'Oh, no, we can make another.' This was done and Dobson was tried and convicted. The magistrates told the six workers that they would receive three months hard labour unless they agreed to return to Edelston's employment.

Outraged by this and similar cases, Roberts wrote an open letter to Thomas Duncombe, MP, on 29 January 1847.[5] He pointed out that two fundamental principles of English justice had been violated. Citing the relevant Acts of Parliament, he stated that accused persons should not be denied the benefit of an advocate by summary jurisdiction and that it was absolutely essential in law for them to receive information about the charges levelled against them.[6] But in Lancashire, Roberts continued, the bad habit had developed of trying people soon after they had been taken into custody. The shortage of time not only prevented the accused from obtaining legal advice, but also from enquiring as to witnesses, and so on.

The Edelston case highlighted a further abuse. Where an employer could combine these autocratic legal powers with those arising from public office, then the workmen would be still more at the master's mercy. J. B. Edelston belonged to the local Board of Guardians. He threatened Thomas Wyke, one of the six accused, that unless he worked harder his mother would lose her weekly parish allowance. She was a woman with two small children. When Thomas Wyke, doing a fifteen-hour day, responded to this threat by stopping work, Edelston prosecuted him under the Master and Servant Act.

In his open letter, Roberts supplied other examples of abuse of the legal system. A Rochdale worker, arrested under the Intimidation Act, was tried within an hour and sentenced to three months imprisonment. Still worse, children at Ashton 'were summoned in the morning, and kept at work until the magistrates were ready to try them the same afternoon – and they were in jail before night.' In conclusion, Roberts stated that he intended to draw public attention to the magistrates' abuse of powers by initiating a campaign and petitioning Parliament.

Thomas Duncombe raised the cases mentioned by the Miners' Attorney in the House of Commons on 23 February 1847. He kept up the pressure by presenting six petitions, and a spokesman for the government stated the matter would be given due consideration. On 2 March 1847, Sir George Grey announced: 'The result of that consideration was that the government considered that the convictions were illegal.'

Roberts had gained a limited victory, one which would affect all workers irrespective of occupation. Indeed, one of the interesting aspects of his open letter is the indication that he was extending his sphere of concern beyond pitmen, including such as mill-girls in Ashton and factory workers in Warrington. From being the Miners' Attorney, he was becoming the People's Attorney. The diversified character of the Lancashire economy was primarily what prompted this change. In the same community, there were frequently people belonging to many occupational groups. Through close contact, a tradition of mutual co-operation grew up, of helping each other in times of trouble. Unlike the North East, where most pitmen lived in colliery villages, a single occupational group dominating an entire community, Lancashire pitmen were usually interspersed, living in communities where they constituted a small proportion of the total population. Not only the outlook, but also the number of Lancashire miners was pushing him in the same direction: whereas there were 33,000 miners working in the North East, only 16,000 worked in the North West. To keep himself busy, therefore, as well as to earn sufficient to live on, he needed to look outside the Lancashire coal industry. With the national union organization declining, diminishing membership and finance, it was clear that a change was needed – which, incidentally, fitted in with Roberts' own belief that the maximum working-class unity should be the overriding aim.

As he was already aware, political action often had the effect of bringing together people from diverse occupational groups, encouraging them to sink their differences in order to gain some legislative objective beneficial to all. This was what had happened in 1844, when Parliament had before it a new Master and Servant Bill, and it seemed to be happening again in 1847. From his experiences on the earlier occasion, Roberts realized the vital necessity of mobilizing support and sustaining it by an ongoing campaign.

Initially, the proposed measure would have extended workers' rights, giving them the opportunity to appeal to a magistrates' court when defrauded of wages. In the committee stage, however, a clause was inserted giving sweeping powers to any master or his agent. A single magistrate would be empowered to send to prison for two months workers who were found guilty of any 'misbehaviour concerning such service or employment' or who absented themselves before completing their contracts.

In organizing opposition to the new clause, Roberts had first sought to persuade the Miners' Association delegate conference in Glasgow (March 1844) to print leaflets and dispatch them to other working-class organizations. At the same time, the Miners' Association, on behalf of its 60,000 members, passed a resolution deploring the proposed extension of the arbitary powers of magistrates and informed Thomas Duncombe, MP, of the fact. He succeeded in obstructing the bill's parliamentary progress until after the Easter recess. Meanwhile, up and down the country, mass meetings were being held. People had hoped for reforms – Parliament had the Ten Hours' Bill before it – not more repressive legislation. Understandably, they expressed their anger by sending Parliament 200 petitions containing more than 2,000,000 signatures. It gave doubters fresh courage to back Duncombe and W. B. Ferrand, the only two MPs who had vigorously opposed the bill from the start. With mounting pressure, both in Parliament and outside, the bill was defeated.[7]

Such a volume of trade union activity aimed at influencing the legislative process, had rarely, if ever, been seen. Success in this venture persuaded some people that the strategy had further possibilities. In a wide range of occupations, trade unionists wanted restrictions imposed on the hours of labour, including the passing of the Ten Hours' Bill, the tightening of the provisions of the Truck Acts to stop evasions, and the repealing of the punitive provisions of the existing Master and Servant law. On these, all were agreed – so why not speak with one voice? Even where demands specific to a given industry were being advanced, it might be helpful to have them channelled through a central organization, possessing the necessary skill and expertise. Such a body might make more effective the miners' campaign for legislation on safety and ventilation, the seamen's concern for amendments to the Merchant Seamen's Act, and the woolcombers' struggle to end insanitary working conditions.

Thinking along these lines, coupled with the feeling that it was time to organize the unskilled workers, led to the formation of the National Association of United Trades in March 1845.[8] Delegates to the inaugural conference came from many geographical areas and occupations. A groundswell of support existed in many industrial regions and prominent middle-class radicals gave their support. Most famous of these was Thomas Slingsby Duncombe, still basking in the glory of his victory over the 1844 Master and Servant Bill. The *Northern Star* reported that London trade unionists as a testimonial to 'the ability displayed by that gentleman in resisting aggressive lesiglation and his zealous, untiring advocacy of the right of labour' held a celebration in his honour. Engels concurred: 'Thomas Duncombe, the representative of the working men in the House of Commons, was the great man of the session.' Appropriately, he was appointed president of the National Association of United Trades.[9]

Naturally, W. P. Roberts and Feargus O'Connor fervently supported the new venture. Besides coinciding with their own views on what was required on the trade union front, it also filled what otherwise would have been an embarrassing gap in activity. Chartism was slumbering, doing nothing and of no consequence. Only thirteen delegates, the lowest number ever, attended the 1845 Chartist convention. Its proceedings were described by the *Northern Star* as 'a mockery to the cause'. Perhaps an association with the burgeoning trade unions would help to revive Chartism. In any case, whether it did so or not, to improve the industrial strength of the working class would be, in itself, beneficial. O'Connor told workers: 'No political change that the mind could devise – not even the People's Charter itself – could relieve your condition.' To do this, greater industrial muscle was required, an ending of the fragmentation and internecine strife of the existing puny unions which only benefited the enemy. 'Your disunity constitutes their strength,' he added.[10]

High hopes rested on the National Association's endeavours. Its annual conferences were described as 'labour Parliaments' and it was seen as providing 'trade unionism for the millions'. In the early euphoria, nothing seemed beyond its attainment. Besides helping to organize the unorganized, the largely unskilled who represented a threat to the pay and conditions of others, many believed that the National Association would be able to apply the motto of 'unity is strength' to other spheres. Let the National Association, since it encompassed a wider variety of workers than any other body, formulate and give coherence to working-class demands on legislative proposals, helping labour to speak to Parliament with a single united voice. To do this, however, it had to know what various groups of workers thought, and many envisaged it acting as a kind of TUC. In addition to all this, the National Association of United Trades had a sister organization, formed at the same time – the National Association of United Trades for the Employment of Labour – with the aim of creating jobs by co-operative enterprise for the unemployed and those made idle by industrial dispute. So with the slenderest of means went the most grandiose of schemes – a general union and a trades union congress combined, with a co-operative society thrown in for good measure.

In the honeymoon period, before cold reality dashed the dreams, the Miners' Association adopted a mildly favourable attitude to the new organization. Admittedly, it did not send a delegate to the inaugural conference, diplomatically pleading poverty as the reason. But it made friendly noises and passed resolutions of encouragement. Pitmen thought they might benefit from closer ties with other workers. It would be excellent if their campaigns for improved mining legislation gained extra weight through the National Association's backing. Even so, the miners' union remained distinctly less enthusiastic than Roberts. He wanted it to submerge itself, lose its identity by joining the new body. An industrial union like the Miners' Association, however, had much greater bargaining power than a general union like the National Association, trying to organize the unskilled and poorly paid. Therefore, whatever Roberts might say, the miners remained adamant that they had nothing to gain from a merger.

Anyway, staying independent, the Lancashire miners continued to make remarkable progress. Why throw away the organization that was winning victory after victory? By 1846, pay was 50 per cent above what it had been two years previously. Before the 1848 slump, in some places it had almost doubled. At strike meetings, speakers boasted of their new affluence: children had clogs on their feet and buttercakes to eat while their fathers wore good jackets and trousers.[11] All this had been achieved through the use of the Lancashire strike tactic, a traditional practice in the county, dating back to at least 1818. It involved securing wage increases in a piecemeal fashion, one locality coming out and receiving financial support from the rest. Once victory had been won, it was the turn of the pitmen in another area to press their claim. Lancashire coalowners were specially vulnerable to this type of attack. Unlike those in the North East, they were not organized among themselves, and could be picked off one at a time. Moreover, again unlike the North East, the majority of collieries were small, with scant financial resources, and could not sustain a prolonged stoppage. In this period, therefore, it is not surprising that one comes across repeated references to the power and affluence of the Lancashire miners' union.

So wealthy was the Lancashire union, it possessed sufficient funds to purchase a colliery and eighteen acres of land near Oldham. At the ceremonial opening, W. P. Roberts was invited to dig the first bucket of coal. In his address, he spoke of what he saw as the project's significance:

> Under ordinary circumstances – with a lord or a lord's tool for an owner – more than three-quarters of the money produced by the coal would find its way to London, or perhaps to the Continent, ministering probably to the pleasures of a French dancing woman, or laying in a stock of paint for the decoration of her ladyship's pale-faced daughter. Now the whole produce will be expended in Oldham and its immediate neighbourhood.

An additional advantage was that, if necessary, the colliery could provide jobs for the pitmen at Messrs Swire and Lees, near Oldham, where there had been a dispute for sixteen weeks.[12]

Local miners' unions in other coalfields were generally less fortunate and could not, therefore, so easily insulate themselves from predators. In the opinion of many, the Miners' Association itself bore responsibility for the post-1844 setbacks; perhaps a different union, with different leaders, would have acted more prudently. By contrast, the National Association, new and undefeated, had a beguiling appeal. Since financial resources were slender, the two unions were seen more as competitors than as complementary. A worker joined one or the other, not both. After the 1844 débâcle, the Miners' Association cast aside all pretensions to establish a highly centralized structure – which merely served to heighten rivalry. Both organizations, having loose, federal structures and operating in a very similar way, were striving to secure the support of the same workers.

Leaders of the National Association of United Trades argued that general unions were, in principle, superior to industrial – they used the term 'sectional' – unions. This was because they embodied a greater degree of unity and therefore potentially more power. In his address to the National Association's inaugural conference, Thomas Duncombe made exactly this point. He alluded to the sad experiences of the Durham and Northumberland pitmen in 1844:

> Through the legal acumen, perseverance and steady watchful-ness of the miners' legal adviser, Mr Roberts, that large body of men were able to continue what I call the most justifiable and extensive strike in history. That strike failed, not because it was capriciously entered into, but because there was wanting a proper plan of national organisation to ensure success.[13]

More bluntly, Feargus O'Connor denounced those leaders of sectional unions, selfishly clinging to their independence, placing their own interests above the general good of workers: 'Shame upon such vermin!'[14] In the wake of O'Connor's vituperation, officials of the National Association accused their counterparts in the miners' union of maladministration and financial malpractices.[15]

Uncomfortable as it was, Roberts could not avoid becoming embroiled in the row. The conflicting forces pulled him in opposite directions. On the one hand, he was the Lancashire miners' attorney, the union's most prominent spokesman. On the other, he was a member of the National Association's nine-man executive. While resisting pressure to align himself with one or the other camp, he did not conceal the fact that his own opinion straddled both positions: he favoured general as against sectional unions (making him pro-National Association), but favoured an aggressive industrial posture (more in keeping with the Lancashire union's). Not very successfully, he endeavoured to dampen down the conflict. This only served to exasperate all concerned. The *Northern Star*, a firm supporter of the National Association, claimed it had held back from making exposures of the Miners' Association out of deference to Roberts. Even so, the paper could not resist attacking his loyalty to the pitmen's union, which it characterized as 'the weakness of Mr Roberts'. Whether editorially inspired or simply a coincidence, the same issue of the *Northern Star* contained a forthright letter from an anonymous contributor, denouncing the Miners' Association. 'Chartist Collier' accused the union leaders of trying to lessen Chartist influence in the coalfields, and also, 'by the most disgraceful tricks and insinuations', of attempting to get rid of W. P. Roberts. For the Miners' Association, Martin Jude replied that the allegations were without substance.

Yet, they continued to persist, indicative of the interplay of complex pressures. Besides those arising from the dog-fight between the Miners' and National Associations, others arose whenever economic problems surfaced within the pitmen's union. Because of the amount of funds it absorbed, the legal department was always a prime target for curtailment, even closure. But further tensions came as a result of Roberts' scarcity of resources, the limited time and energy he had available. Should these all be swallowed by the miners' union irrespective of the urgent need for his services elsewhere? The *Northern Star*, suspicious that the Miners' Association might be behind the decline of Chartism in the coalfields, definitely favoured a wider approach:

> We have frequently thought, and we still think, that Mr Roberts' exclusive engagement with the colliers, although highly beneficial to that trade, is nevertheless a great national loss. In our opinion, Mr Roberts, as a local or sectional adviser, is thrown away. His legitimate place is in the metropolis – near the courts, in the vicinity of the Senate House, directing a national movement, instead of wasting his energies for mere sectional purposes. Booby solicitors can do better service under his training than those of a superior class without his instruction, not of the trades only, but of the whole working class, with Mr Roberts installed as their Attorney General and elected to the House of Commons.[16]

This magnificent vision of W. P. Roberts as a sort of central power-house of the trade union movement, supervising all the legal work from London as well as being its principal spokesman with a seat in Parliament, never came to fruition. Life was very much more messy. A protracted and inconclusive strike at Bolton in 1846 brought Roberts' position into question. A temporary setback, it almost certainly depleted the union's coffers. Roberts' salary went partly unpaid. He was compelled to seek legal work elsewhere. This did not prevent him from continuing to work for the pitmen's union, and he remained one of their leading orators. During the Bolton dispute he addressed numerous meetings. One local newspaper complained that 'Mr Roberts was as bitter as his more ignorant accomplices.' Certainly, his message always remained the same – stay out and stay solid – to which he added, with characteristic but unfounded optimism, victory was almost at hand.[17]

As a consequence of the Bolton setback, Roberts found himself involved in the most spectacular case, outside the coal industry, of the period. It arose out of a dispute in July 1846 at Messrs Jones and Potts, locomotive builders, of the Viaduct Works, Newton-le-Willows, Lancashire. The employers had engaged non-union labour and adult apprentices, intending to train them in two years instead of the customary period of seven years. In addition, they had introduced a wage cut for the labour force, reducing pay to below the normal district rate. The union, the 'Old Mechanics', did not directly support the strike; it contented itself merely with issuing appeals for voluntary contributions. These helped to keep the strike solid until November, when there was a general feeling that victory was in sight. On 26 November, however, Messrs Jones and Potts turned to the law. In the middle of the night seventeen men were dragged from their beds, handcuffed and, accompanied by officers with drawn cutlasses, taken to Warrington police station. A further ten arrests took place, including that of Henry Selsby, the union's general secretary. Boxes containing the private papers of the 'Old Mechanics' had their locks broken and contents removed.

W. P. Roberts entered the fray with gusto. To inform workers what was at stake, he addressed mass meetings in various parts of the country. Funds rolled in to pay for the defence. Heartened by the response, he confessed he enjoyed a 'good stand-up fight, to manage it as he liked, with a hearty and determined body of men for his clients'. He vowed 'he would give the law a terrible shaking.' Believing 'health, time and fortune favour the brave', he launched furious attacks on Messrs Jones & Potts from public platforms, ridiculing their claim that there had been a conspiracy to impoverish and bring them to beggary. The indictment, elaborating the claim, was a document unprecedented in legal history: it contained 4,914 counts, filled 990 folio pages and measured 57 yards long. When first he saw it, Roberts sarcastically remarked that he thought it was a petition calling for the release of John Frost and the other leaders of the Newport uprising. Later, after mature reflection, his creative imagination came up with some amusing alternative uses for the charge-sheets. Parliament had burnt down in 1834 and, by 1847, reconstruction had reached the stage where the House of Lords was to be redecorated. Amid cheers and laughter, he outlined his proposal to a public meeting:

> They were sometime ago advertising for a fresco painting to adorn the House of Lords, but if their lordships wanted something to adorn their walls which was extremely curious, though it might not be very ornamental, they had better send for our 57 yards of indictment. As far as my youthful reminiscences would allow me, I have made a pretty accurate calculation, and I find that 150 couples might safely dance to Polka upon it.[18]

The People's Attorney's first battle came before the Warrington magistrates. There he met two old adversaries, still smarting from the J. B. Edelston case. Thomas Lloyd, twenty-eight years a JP, and his colleague, William Stubbs, expressed their firm determination to keep at least four of the twenty-seven accused in custody until they came before the assize. Otherwise they threatened to resign from the magistracy. But this merely gave Roberts an added incentive, and on appeal the four were released on bail, amid calls from trade unionists for Messrs Stubbs and Lloyd to resign.

The case opened at the Liverpool assizes before Mr Baron Rolfe and a jury, consisting of eleven merchants and a banker. (Its composition was explained, tongue in cheek, by Roberts: 'The hope was that a jury, selected from the wealthier class of society, would be more removed from the operation of those low and petty influences, such as hunger and incessant craving for pelf.'[19]) The defence had engaged three Queen's Counsellors and three other barristers, an indication of the importance the working-class movement attached to the proceedings and its determination, if possible, to rebut all the charges. W. P. Roberts prepared the briefs. Sergeant Wilkins, opening for the prosecution, claimed that union funds totalled nearly £80,000, and were being used 'for the purpose of tyranny and despotism'. Even if the workers' requests had been reasonable, he stated, 'Dictation is not the language to be employed by workmen to their masters.' They had withdrawn their labour at a time when they knew their employers had a great many orders in hand. They had sought to persuade men in search of work not to fill the vacancies at Messrs Jones and Potts. By their conduct, they had thereby become active opponents of individual as well as national liberty: 'Every man has a right, a perfect right, to do what he will with his own labour, providing that in the exercise of that right he does not interfere with the rights and privileges of others. Every man has a right, if he thinks it proper, wisely or unwisely, to throw himself out of employment and reduce himself to want, but none to compel others to follow his example.'[20]

As one would expect, Roberts saw things slightly differently. He considered that the defendants, far from denying others freedom, were being stopped from exercising freedom – the freedom of speech – themselves. Behind the prosecution's vast legal panoply lay the detestation of a single act: 'The offence really tried in Warrington was walking up and down and talking,' he told trade unionists at a protest rally. It was referred to as 'picketing':

> This was a horrid word (laughter), and the learned counsel on the opposite side laid great emphasis, in deep sepulchral tones, as if it were only necessary to prove 'picket' and blood and murder were sure to follow.[21]

The intention, the People's Attorney told his audience, was to place the working class at a disadvantage compared to every other section of society: 'The magistrates, in their impudence, think that you are debarred the privilege which every other class claims – that while they may go to the Duke of Wellington and Sir Robert Peel, the working class, forsooth, are not to be allowed to speak to a brother in error – or going to commit an error.'

In court, the defence argued there had been no intimidation, merely the kind of advice a man might give to a friend. Moreover, it was done with a genuine concern for the community's best interests. The public welfare required locomotives to be built by skilled labour; from badly made steam-engines exceedingly dangerous and explosive consequences could ensue. As regards the charge of trying to impoverish Messrs Jones and Potts, it was argued that it had not been their intention; rather, their aim was to maintain the requisite level of skill. It was argued that just as the opening of a shop may lead to the bankruptcy of another shop in the same area, though this had not been the purpose behind the new venture, likewise the 'Old Mechanics' sought simply to safeguard their own interests, not to impoverish Messrs Jones and Potts.

Mr Baron Rolfe directed that some of the defendants be acquitted on charges which arose from industrial action intended to enforce a closed shop. His interpretation of the 1825 act's references to 'intimidation, molestation and obstruction' was, from the trade union standpoint, pleasingly narrow. For a strike to be illegal, he ruled, violence or threats of violence had to be made.[22] Gratifying though this judgement was, releasing nineteen of the twenty-seven men, it still left Henry Selsby and seven others in prison. So an appeal was immediately lodged. This was heard before Lord Justice Denham in the Court of Queen's Bench on 7 June 1847. As a result, all the sentences were quashed.[23]

The victory over Messrs Jones and Potts was complete. To celebrate, W. P. Roberts and Feargus O'Connor led a large procession through Warrington. News that the hated magistrate Thomas Lloyd had decided to retire added to the joy, but did not stop Roberts from making a final denunciation of him. He also attacked those responsible both for the time and manner in which Henry Selsby and other trade unionists had been arrested. He hoped that they would not again be dragged from their beds in the middle of the night and that a 'teetotal policeman would never break open a poor man's box again.'[24]

11 Politics, Parliamentary and Revolutionary

Although the summer of 1847 proved to be exceedingly busy for Roberts, during May he somehow succeeded in snatching a short holiday in Italy. During his trip abroad, his clerks – John Edwards in Manchester and George Chinnery in London – kept him fully briefed on developments. These included a quickly produced pamphlet on the Newton-le-Willows engineers' trial and the presentation of a miners' petition in Parliament, urging improved safety and ventilation in pits.[1]

When he returned to England the strike wave had not abated. Almost immediately, he became involved in a case arising out of a dispute at Hopwood's mill in Blackburn, where weavers claimed they were being paid below the prevailing district rate. Though Roberts won the court case, the workers lost the strike. Angry and disgruntled, they seized on a novel method of expressing their displeasure. A general election was pending and the millowner, Robert Hopwood jun., happened to be the returning officer for Blackburn. Therefore, the trade unionists decided to sponsor Roberts as their candidate. Not only could he be guaranteed to hurl oratorical thunderbolts at the local coalowners and millowners (including Mr Hopwood jun.), but it would also be a means of advancing the people's cause and ridiculing the grossly undemocratic electoral system.

At first it was proposed, as Blackburn was a two-member constituency, to put forward two people's candidates, with William Beesley as Roberts' running-mate. Believing its duty was to inform the public about these two dangerous and evil characters in its midst, the local newspaper explained:

If there be any ignorant of such facts as Mr Prowting (an

evident misprint for Spouting) Roberts and Mr William Beesley, it may be well to mention that the one is a contract lawyer for the Chartists, strikers, turnouts and unionists in this part of the country; and his associate is an operative weaver and chairman, fond of haranguing his 'fellow labourers' on 'the points' and took a prominent part in the recent strike in this town.[2]

The editor continued that he would have backed W. P. Roberts' candidature if 'representation was to have been in the beershop or on the Moor'; as it was, he needed to be shunned. Even more stringent criticism was reserved for the locally well-known – some would say, notorious – William Beesley. Since the collapse of the legal practice for the Durham and Northumberland miners, he had ceased being a solicitor's clerk and returned to his native Accrington, where he worked in a mill. Quickly victimized for his activities, Beesley turned to auctioneering and chair-making to make a living. That, despite adversity, he remained strongly imbued with Chartist principles was shown by the fact that he led an anti-enclosure campaign against Jonathan Peel, a large local landowner. To prevent what was common land being incorporated in Peel's stately home, Beesley and his colleague sallied forth at night and knocked down the recently erected stone-walls. Though such nocturnal activities had perforce to be kept secret from the authorities, he did nothing in other ways to conceal his support for Chartism. His political beliefs even shone through in the Christian names of his three children: Elizabeth Frost O'Connor Beesley, Julian West Robinson Beesley and Margaret Harney Kossuth Beesley. Moreover, Beesley had acquired the reputation of being the foremost trade unionist in North Lancashire. At all the mass meetings during the strike at Hopwood's mill, his voice could be heard.[3]

His remarks at one of these gatherings earned him a stern admonition from the *Blackburn Standard*. It felt constrained to comment:

We pass over the objectionable tone given to some parts of the speeches of last Sunday to notice a most wicked and dangerous attempt on the part of one of the speakers, named Beesley, to incite his hearers to a riotous attack upon the returning officer of the borough, Mr Robert Hopwood, junior. This man declared to thousands, assembled round him, that the returning officer was 'abominated, hated and detested' . . . if Mr Hopwood did 'dare to show his face' during the election 'there would be sure to be a riot and probably sacrifice of life'.[4]

Presumably, the *Blackburn Standard* was heartened to hear the news that Beesley would not actually be a candidate himself. Almost certainly, his withdrawal was prompted by tactical considerations. It seems that it was felt advisable to concentrate all efforts on securing the greatest possible number of votes for Roberts, who was the stronger candidate. Also, by doing this, it did not mean Beesley taking a back seat: the heavy load of legal work, with the crucial Newton-le-Willows engineers case top of the list, meant that Roberts was often unable to address meetings in the constituency. On these occasions Beesley had to deputize for him.

Conventional political opinion in Blackburn regarded the candidature of the Miners' Attorney-General as an unwelcome intrusion. His courtroom commitments elsewhere, as well as the hopelessness of his cause, may have led to hopes that he would not take the contest seriously. Consequently, when he issued his election address, Roberts was criticized not only for its content but also for the very act of publication.

The offending election address, espousing democratic and anti-aristocratic views, was published in full in the journal of the miners' union. It contained the seven points of his political platform:

1. He was a friend of the Ten Hour Bill, and would have rejoiced had it been an Eight Hour Bill. Nevertheless, he had no objection to grown men working as long as they thought fit.

2. He was a member of the Church of England, and favoured the separation of Church and State for the sake of the Church.

3. He was opposed to the existing law of primogeniture.

4. He was opposed to all taxes on food, commerce and manufactures, wishing them to be replaced, in the main, by additional taxes on property.

5. He was opposed to capital punishment, war, and the Game Laws. Moreover, he strongly objected to the continual increase in the powers of magistrates, abrogating the principle of trial by jury.

6. He was opposed to the rate-paying clauses of the Reform Act and anything giving greater rights to wealth and property.

7. The House of Commons would never be as it should be till every man had the right to vote.[5]

In conclusion, he dissociated himself from political parties – 'never was there less a party man than myself,' he admitted – and announced his intention not to incur more election expenses than the law permitted.

During the election campaign, Roberts held a number of public meetings and frequently reiterated his underlying reason for standing:

> It is time the working classes should be more adequately represented than they have been. This is the ground on which I appear before you. Popular principles are now and then brought before the House of Commons, but such principles are only regularly supported by one man – Mr Duncombe.[6]

His campaign aroused a welter of criticism; he was described as 'an illustrious nonentity'; he was said to be opposed 'to almost every existing element of the political scheme under which we flourish'. His opinions were called 'laughably absurd', although some shopkeepers may well have been concerned about the advice Roberts gave to non-voters: withdraw your custom from those traders who adopt an anti-Chartist line.[7]

On polling day, workers from Blackburn and the surrounding areas, most of them non-voters, swarmed to hear the candidates on the hustings. Customarily, out of deference and respect, millworkers had marched into town behind banners kindly provided by their employers. They might not have had votes; they definitely had a good pair of lungs. But on this occasion, there was a subtle difference: instead of supporting the candidate of their employer's choice, they supported the candidate of their own choice. W. P. Roberts, more popular and more eloquent than other candidates, was the hero of the hour. Amid enthusiastic cheers, he expounded Chartist principles at length. Inevitably, this involved attacking both the Whigs and the Tories. The Whigs, he declared, had indulged in a policy of legal repression: Dr Peter Murray McDouall, sitting with him on the platform, had been imprisoned merely for expressing his opinions; Feargus O'Connor had been gaoled for a newspaper article he did not write. Turning to the Tories, Roberts had a harder time dealing with their candidate. John Hornby, a textile manufacturer, had a relatively good record. He had not cut handloom weavers' wages in the 1842 depression. Since becoming an MP in 1841, he had voted for the Mines Act, the Ten Hour Bill and the release from prison of Robert Oastler. So Roberts, even on the hustings, generously did not shirk from complimenting his political opponent: 'He thanked Mr Hornby, in the name of the wives and mothers of England, in the name of the children of England' for supporting these progressive measures. Even so, Roberts could not forbear reminding him that he disagreed fundamentally with the Tories, who believed that 'there were two classes of men, a rich and a poor – the one to make the laws, the other to obey; one to levy the taxes, the other to pay them.'[8]

On the limited franchise, the result was a foregone conclusion. The People's Attorney came bottom of the poll. The figures were: Hornby 641, Pilkington 601, Hargreaves 392 and Roberts 68. Yet, despite the defeat, the election marked, albeit in a small way, a new departure. Like William Dixon, who stood at Wigan, he had enjoyed the full support of the miners' and millworkers' unions.[9] While the national structure whereby trade unions sponsored parliamentary candidates remained a thing of the distant future, nevertheless a step had been taken in that direction. To the National Association of United Trades, a demand came from its Sheffield branches that it should fund parliamentary candidates, but this became completely impractical as the union coffers were denuded by costly legal cases and the economic down-swing.

Twelve Chartist candidates fought the 1847 general election and the fate of W. P. Roberts was fairly typical. The one exception was Feargus O'Connor, the victor of Nottingham. He joined the small band of radical reformers in Parliament where, as Duncombe said, 'the most degrading and infamous proceedings take place.'[10] Undoubtedly, O'Connor's experiences within that house of ill-repute helped to enliven his weekly column in the *Northern Star* as well as his conversations. On 6 November 1847, he wrote: 'On Monday night I was at the Crown and Anchor, and sat up till three o'clock in the morning with our friend, Mr Roberts.'

By autumn 1847, economic depression had begun to damage trade unions, weakening their bargaining position. Falling profits and rising unemployment made wage cuts impossible to resist. Food riots occurred in Glasgow and elsewhere. Recently arrived Irish immigrants were reportedly dying of hunger in the streets of Liverpool.

On one occasion, when funds from the National Association failed to materialize, the People's Attorney dipped into his own pocket to alleviate the hardship of families involved in an industrial dispute. Problems, however, were beyond the powers of any individual or union to solve. The crisis seemed to have a destructive momentum all of its own. Soon newspapers were reporting, with ill-concealed glee, that trade unions were unable to pay Roberts his salary; perhaps he would have to abandon his work on their behalf.[11]

Largely as a defensive reaction, the focus of working-class activity switched from industry, where defeat followed defeat, to politics, where growing hardships gave added urgency to the need to win the Charter. The revival of Chartism, again holding mass meetings with enthusiastic supporters in attendance, gave Roberts a congenial milieu in which he could exercise his talents. Obviously, it was vital to secure the six points, but Roberts only regarded this as means to an end, namely, the fundamental transformation of society. As he told a Manchester rally: 'In war, in legislation, in government, in peace, in the arts, in wealth and all that wealth could bring; all that he ever had seen had been for the advantage of the rich.'[12]

As the crisis deepened, the state found itself assailed by threatening forces from three sides. Admittedly, it had seen off Chartism before. This time, however, the challenge came in a new context. In 1839, Ireland had remained quiescent, allowing General Napier to reinforce his mainland garrisons from there. No Irishman appears to have fought alongside Frost in the Newport uprising. Even in 1842, the Irish, both at home and in Britain, constituted no special problem.[13] But this had all changed by 1848: the seeds of Irish nationalism, the hatred of English domination, had emerged in Ireland itself as well as in the Irish communities of London and the industrial North of England. Here, for the first time, the Chartists found willing allies. To make matters still worse for the government, the growing menace of Chartist and Irish agitation was made more dangerous by events on the Continent. 1848 was 'the year of revolutions', which made it seem that no monarchy – not even the British one – was secure. Politics is often referred to as the art of the possible. By contrast, revolution is the art of the impossible. Suddenly, in a flash, mental horizons expand and a vista of limitless opportunities for hitherto undreamed of change opens up. Whereas politics has hitherto been the preoccupation of a minority, arguing about the desirability of making marginal adjustments, revolutions bring on to the stage of history the majority of the population, who feel a fundamental transformation of society is required.[14]

Obviously, to unite the various strands of resistance against the existing order, to have a triple challenge from Chartism, Irish nationalism and Continental insurrectionism, would maximize their mutual impact. A series of meetings was held, up and down the country, in an attempt to bond the struggle of the Chartists and the Irish Confederates. W. P. Roberts took part in this campaign. He addressed a meeting in Manchester Free Trade Hall. So memorable was his contribution that fifty years later a writer in the *Newcastle Weekly Chronicle* referred to it. Yet, the message was quite simple: 'whenever the peoples of both countries were united, the oppressors of both countries would fall.' This was followed the next day by a demonstration attended, according to one report, by a quarter of a million people, 'to promote the fraternisation of English Chartists and Irish repealers'.[15] Behind such open expressions of solidarity, other preparations were quietly proceeding. These led to elaborate plans being created for a simultaneous uprising in the two countries, with James Leach in command of operations in England. Likewise, contacts with the continent were established. In his day-to-day account of revolutionary developments in France, Lord Normanby recounts that news of the Chartists' big Kennington Common demonstration on 10 April – which many in Paris misread as the beginning of the British insurrection – caused widespread depression in revolutionary circles when it became clear that Lord Russell's government had survived the crisis.[16]

Confronting this mass of revolutionary menace, the authorities resolved to resist all Chartist demands. The least concession might have been construed as a sign of weakness. As one cabinet minister put it, they saw Britain as 'the Thermopylae of Europe', holding the pass, stopping the further spread of anarchy and disorder. Towards this end, the state strengthened its defences. New legislation sped through Parliament: the Aliens Removal Act, the Crown and Government Security Act and the Irish Crime and Outrages Act. Accompanying these measures went a stricter interpretation of existing laws. In order to achieve this objective, the army was placed on alert, thousands of special constables recruited and an extensive spy network devised. New technology in the form of the electric telegraph and railways was pressed into service. Before any uprising could occur, the forces of law and order intended to make a pre-emptive strike, bringing overwhelming might to bear on the trouble-spot, and thereby erasing the problem rather than letting it get out of control.[17]

Traditional narrative accounts suggest that in April 1848 Chartism collapsed in ignominy and ridicule; the Kennington Common demonstration was a fiasco; that Parliament decisively rejected the petition, and many of the 5½ million signatures turned out to be forgeries. But this is a highly distorted, selective version of events. For example, it omits to mention that Chartists argued that a lot of the forgeries – Pug-nose, Queen Victoria and the like – were written by government undercover agents, out to discredit the petition; nor that women's signatures were regarded as invalid since obviously, in the eyes of officialdom, they had no right to concern themselves with such weighty issues as the reform of Parliament. On a different level, the research of historians such as David Goodway and John Saville, has conclusively shown that Kennington Common did not mark the end of Chartism. After April 1848 the authorities faced their severest challenge. Simultaneously, the economic situation deteriorated and the loyalty of some special constables waned. By contrast, arming, drilling and conspiracies abounded. In many industrial areas of the north, disgruntled Irishmen joined up with physical force Chartists while in London 40,000 or 50,000 foreign political refugees, almost all of whom were of doubtful loyalty, added to the anxiety.[18]

W. P. Roberts appears to have taken no part in the insurrectionary plots. He only came into prominence once the revolutionary enthusiasm had waned and was followed by a reign of terror. The law was employed as a political weapon, a means of silencing dissenters as well as crippling Chartism. Two of the five-strong executive were arrested and fourteen of the twenty provincial representatives who attended the Chartist national assembly. The People's Attorney scurried around the country, defending prisoners himself in the magistrates' courts and arranging for barristers to defend others in higher courts.

Among the many cases was that of Dr Peter Murray McDouall.[19] The executive had asked him to do a speaking tour of the industrial north. His task was to co-ordinate resistance and gauge the popular mood. On 10 July 1848, he addressed a crowd of 500 in the Charleston meeting-room, Ashton-under-Lyme. Police, including deputy chief constable Robert Newton, were excluded from the premises. Later, however, after it had ended, McDouall and his supporters marched to the Oddfellows' Arms, where he was staying. From an upstairs window there, he again spoke, the police claimed seditiously. He told them that discontent was general, not confined to the unemployed; that several regiments had already revolted; and that people should organize themselves, at the same time acquiring weapons. He allegedly told them:

> There are only 10,000 disposable troops, and what are these against five million people? I wish they would call out the militia, but they dare not do that, for then we should have their guns and bayonets and cartridges, then we would let them see what we could do. Before the harvest, or very soon after, I'll promise you, you shall have the six points of The Charter and something more. Organise, organise, organise.[20]

Remarkably, at the magistrates' court, Roberts secured bail for McDouall. He argued the speech had not been violent or seditious. As for the references to organization, Mr McDouall was merely urging them to adopt the same structure as Methodist bible classes! But this line of argument was not so succesful at the Liverpool assizes. A succession of policemen entered the witness-box, giving virtually the same account of McDouall's speech. By some strange coincidence, as the *Northern Star* observed, 'their ears had all opened and closed at the same moment, and took in exactly the same.' They were, nevertheless, believed. And since every meeting was deemed unlawful that was liable to excite terror and alarm, not unexpectedly McDouall received a two-year sentence.

Prior to the trial, his prospects had not been enhanced by a disturbance at Ashton-under-Lyme on the night of 14–15 August. A group of Chartists and Irishmen, armed with pikes, swords and other weapons, encountered two policemen about 50 yards from their local club. PC Bright was shot through the head and killed. He had been mistaken for PC Pennington, who had testified at McDouall's committal proceedings. The second policeman managed to escape, hid in a cottage and eventually went to call up reinforcements. In the meantime, the group went in the direction of the army barracks, where it appears they hoped to gain support, but then decided to go to Hyde, pulling the plugs from factory boilers as they went. When serious opposition appeared, the Chartists and Irish quickly vanished. Apparently, there had been talk about holding the town against government forces.

In response, the authorities resorted to mass arrests. The following day twenty-two were arrested in Ashton-under-Lyme. During the night, Chartist and Irish clubs in Manchester were raided and leading members put behind bars. The same happened in Bradford and several other northern towns. It became clear that plans had been made, albeit rather crudely, for an armed rebellion. In London, some were arrested just as they were about to mount the barricades. Elsewhere makeshift arms factories and arms dumps were discovered. Those arrested were often members of quasi-military units, bearing titles like the Wat Tyler brigade and the Robert Emmett brigade.

Confronted with the formidable weight of evidence, Roberts for the defence faced a daunting task. Besides belittling the gravity of the prosecution's case, he seems to have largely relied upon two propositions: first, that the plots had been concocted by the police themselves; and, second, that the unsavoury character of many of the police informers – perhaps, the hold the police had over them – made them unreliable witnesses. The *Northern Star*, displaying more wishful thinking than realism, thought the Attorney-General would more than meet his match: 'The powerful genius, the legal accuracy and indomitable perseverance of William Prowting Roberts meets him, haunts him, paralyses him'.[21] In fact, the Attorney-General did not apologize for the spy system; he merely said that he regretted its necessity in order to protect state security. Turning to the jury at the big London trial, he told them they had to ask themselves the question whether an insurrection had been planned for that night: 'Of that fact he thought there could not be any doubt.' Members of the jury agreed. William Cuffay, Joseph Richie and the rest of the conspirators were sentenced to transportation.

Even so, the court proceedings definitely possessed unusual vitality. This was because a barrister named Dr E. V. Kenealy, an individual very much in the Roberts mould, conducted the defence. He began by likening the Attorney-General to the 'very worst of the infamous Attorney-Generals in the infamous days of the Stuarts and Tudors'. He went on to criticize prosecution witnesses and the police. Then, he clashed with the judge, Mr Justice Erle, who attempted to reprove him. But worse was to follow. The Attorney-General suggested that Kenealy himself had attended Chartist meetings and yet he had not informed the authorities about the criminal activities taking place, thereby making him an accessory. To this, Kenealy reacted with characteristic violence. As if to suggest that, up till then, he had been the epitome of moderation and restraint, he replied: 'I have said nothing as to the transactions of the Attorney-General at Horsham, nothing as to his private practices, corrupt as they are alleged to be.' This was a reference to the scandal surrounding the Horsham election of 1847, when there were allegations that the Attorney-General resorted to bribery and treating to secure the return of his son, John Jervis, jun. A committee of inquiry in March 1848 found there had been irregularities, but they were insufficiently serious to proceed with. Yet, this was hardly true: they included the charge that the Attorney-General had tried to pervert the course of justice. Obviously, for government ministers, the whole affair was acutely embarrassing. They could not afford to have Sir John declared corrupt. Not only would it embarrass the government, but the man who would succeed Jervis if he resigned – the Solicitor-General, David Dundas – was considered incompetent. Counsel, judges and the cabinet saw the problem and put their heads together. As one historian of the law laconically puts it: 'the legal profession closed ranks.' Consequently, at Lewes assizes, in March 1849, all thirty-two charges of bribery were dismissed.[22]

For Kenealy to allude to this matter may have been the height of indiscretion, yet for the general public it simply served to intensify the dramatic interest. They loved the verbal fireworks that so often accompanied the trials. Therefore, during the Chartist trials, attendance at court became very popular. Outside the Old Bailey, the doorkeepers touted for business, describing what was happening inside to whet people's appetites: 'Cockburn is knocking the servant maid to bits, and if you want to hear the best of it you'd better pay your half-crown or you'll miss the cross-examination.' The *Daily News* reported that the going rate was down to two shillings when Sergeant Wilkins came to address the jury.[23]

Such admission charges clearly limited entrance to the more wealthy. It may be this fact that helped to encourage Sir John Jervis to make some of his most biased remarks about one of the defendants. William Cuffay was depicted as the ringleader of the London conspiracy. A 61-year-old mulatto garment worker, he had a long, distinguished record both in the Chartist and trade union movements. Yet, Sir John Jervis seemed incapable of referring to him without mentioning the colour of Cuffay's skin. These expressions of class and racial prejudice prompted George Jacob Holyoake, an opponent of physical-force Chartism, to write 'An Open Letter to the Attorney-General': 'His deformed body but served as an inducement to your contempt; his lowly birth but an inducement to your contempt. Who can forget the pestilence of sneers that came hissing from your ranks on all sides at the mention of the poor tailor's name?'[24]

Another scandal of the Chartist trials, the sleazy world of *agents provocateurs* and political informers, remained the chief target of Roberts. Most of them were like Thomas Barnet, petty criminals, in and out of prison for short spells. Sometimes they were well paid for their services, a fact that may have tempted some to fabricate stories. Thomas Powell, known as 'lying Tom', became the most notorious. In the course of eight hours in the witness-box, he blandly admitted to a string of villainies: devising plans to assassinate the police, manufacturing caltrops to cripple cavalry and making die-caste for bullets. He also sold weapons to fellow Chartists and told the court: 'I encouraged and stimulated these men in order to inform against them.' He even sent a letter to Feargus O'Connor, threatening him that unless he joined the plot: 'you will be one of the first victims.'[25]

At Bradford, the prosecution's star witness was Robert Emmett. Under cross-examination, he conceded that he really was none other than 'Skipton Jack', a notorious criminal with convictions for embezzlement, false pretences and desertion. Even so, the court accepted his account of the Chartist conspiracy. The plan was to destroy Bradford Gas Works, putting out all the street lights and causing confusion. In the midst of the panic, three contingents of armed men would arrest the local magistrates and seize strategic buildings. When the defendants were found guilty, Robert Emmett, not unnaturally, discovered himself highly unpopular in his native West Yorkshire. Arrangements were made for him to move across to Lancashire, where the Manchester police provided money and protection. But this did not prevent him from contacting W. P. Roberts and making a full confession. He had kept a list of monies received from Chief Superintendant Beswick, as well as the £10 from Bradford magistrates. He admitted he had lied in court, and said he was ashamed of what he had done. To draw attention to the fact that the crown had secured convictions with the assistance of perjured evidence, Roberts arranged to hold a public meeting, where Robert Emmett would openly confess. Eleven MPs were invited to attend; naturally, none of them did.[26]

If this was an embarrassment for the notables of Bradford, worse was to follow from, of all people, William Briggs, their chief constable. Historical research reveals that even in 1840, when he was only deputy chief constable, Briggs had built up an elaborate network of spies and informers. Early in that year, this provided him with the necessary intelligence to forestall a Chartist uprising in Bradford. But in 1848, he was not so fortunate. On Monday, 29 May, apparently in a drunken state, he led a large contingent of his force into the Manchester Road area, a stronghold of the Chartists. There a pitched battle ensued. The police came off worse from the encounter and were compelled to retreat. They were only saved by the intervention of 200 soldiers with fixed bayonets and two troops of dragoons. Even then, William Briggs somehow succeeded in permitting the ringleader, Isaac Jefferson (alias Wat Tyler) to escape. The following year his career in the police force came to an inglorious end through a sex scandal. William Briggs was discovered in a compromising position in a young lady's bedroom and had to resign as chief constable.[27]

This is the background to the publication of his pamphlet. Acknowledging himself to be the author – William Briggs, ex-chief constable of Bradford – its remarkable title was 'The Spy System Exposed'. For good measure, he went to James Leach, a personal friend of Engels and one of those imprisoned for their part in the 1848 disturbances, to ask him to publish it from his premises in Turner Street, Manchester. Unfortunately, it seems that no copies of the actual pamphlet have survived, although a review did appear in the *Reynolds' Political Instructor* of 2 February 1850. It said the pamphlet contained 'useful information as to how spies are employed and evidence cooked up'. The British system of political surveillance, it claimed, had been modelled on that of Tsarist Russia. What probably made it unique for a work written by an ex-chief constable, it ended with a financial appeal for the political victims of police persecution.

Still more embarrassment for the authorities came three months later. In May, 1850, the Home Office received a letter from the Governor of New South Wales. It related to those involved in the Ashton-under-Lyme trial. Prosecution witnesses and their families, a total of thirty-four, had been shipped to Australia for their own safety. But, the letter said, their general behaviour was riotous, disorderly and deplorable. He protested about the Immigration Fund being used without the authorization of the New South Wales Commissioners. Darkly, he added: 'One of the party was suspected to have been the actual murderer of the policeman in those riots.'[28] In fact, there may well have been other fascinating encounters which involved police *agents provocateurs* and spies, sent to Australia for their own safety. Chartist and other working-class journals were well appraised of their movements. For instance, Thomas Powell, using the name Thomas Richards, arrived in Australia aboard the ship *Caroline*. The *Adelaide Observer*, on 9 February 1849, as well as the *People's Advocate & South Wales Vindicator*, reported he had been secretly provided with funds by the British government. It would be intriguing to know whether he met any of the individuals who had been sentenced to transportation as a result of his testimony and, if so, what happened.

One thing, however, is certain: the authorities were prepared to use anybody, irrespective of how disreputable they were, in order to defeat Chartism. There was even the suggestion, made in the autobiography of Thomas Frost, a London journalist with first-hand knowledge of 1848, that yet another member of the police undercover team may also have been a murderer:

> Does the reader remember the murder at Hackney of an old woman named Emsley, for the sake of a few pounds which she had in the house, and the base attempt of the murderer to divert suspicion from himself by placing part of the stolen property on the premises of an innocent man? That miscreant was the Home Office spy and informer Mullins, who had been dismissed from the police force for some misconduct, and went from crime to crime, until he ended his horrible existence upon the scaffold, to which he had so often striven to conduct others.[29]

Undoubtedly, in 1848 the authorities stooped to the employment of despicable individuals and despicable means. That fact was agreed across the political spectrum. But this does not mean, however, that W. P. Roberts and the *Northern Star* were correct in the assertion that government agents were the fomentors of the whole conspiracy.

Nor does it mean that such chicanery secured victory: the authorities were successful for much more profound reasons. Since 1842, Britain had enjoyed uninterrupted economic progress. Many of its population had benefited from this and the ruling class felt much more confident and secure, able to repulse any challenge.

12   Mid-century Malaise

Sometimes Roberts lacked political perception, the ability to discern profound changes that had taken place. The devastating defeat of 1848 was one such instance. It left Chartism fatally wounded. Its mass backing vanished while the few remaining supporters indulged in mutual recriminations, claiming physical force Chartism, Feargus O'Connor or somebody else was responsible for all the movement's misfortunes. They also quarrelled about the way ahead. But Roberts failed to address himself to these problems. Despite evidence to the contrary, he regarded 1848 as merely a temporary setback: the authorities had succeeded in temporarily bamboozling people into believing that Chartism was finished. The answer, in his opinion, was business as usual: the same policies, the same tactics.

In May 1850, contrary to the national trend, a flicker of life returned to Chartism in the Potteries. Roberts jumped at the opportunity to open the new People's Hall, a converted Primitive Methodist chapel, at Shelton. A triumphal procession took him and O'Connor from Stoke station, along streets of cheering people, to the new Chartist headquarters. Amid wild, albeit short-lived, enthusiasm, he contemplated moving his legal practice to the Potteries. To the assembled crowd he declared: 'The principles of Chartism were taking firmer hold on public opinion, which showed their cause was progressing.' He castigated all those favouring political innovations, be they socialists, red republicans or advocates of an alliance with the middle class.[1]

A couple of months later the same scene was re-enacted. Speaking at Blackstone Edge, the windswept Pennine ridge above Oldham, he told 30,000 Lancashire and Yorkshire Chartists to stay true to the cause. Almost drowned by applause, he ended his peroration: 'The Charter – the whole Charter – and no surrender'.[2]

Nevertheless, times had changed. Though it might still have been possible to get a large crowd for the occasional meeting, commitment of a more enduring kind, vital for the health of an organization – regular financial contributions, consistent attendance at business meetings, systematic paper-selling – had all vanished. Instead, crisis encompassed every facet of the movement, producing problems that had not previously existed. As J. B. Leno, one of the few new recruits, observed, 'Chartism was in a parlous state.' Many supporters of the movement, who thought their liberation from thraldom was near at hand, now had to make agonizing personal reappraisals. A Manchester barber, serving a mainly radical clientele, observed their disorientation: 'Poor old men! The time for the fulfilment of their prophecy has arrived and departed, but over themselves rather than over the State has the great change passed. Dispersed are the golden visions, the castles in the air, which formed their only heritage.'[3]

On others, the tragedy had a slightly different impact. Lack of money made it impossible for McDouall to appeal against his sentence. The hardship fund, set up to help prisoners' families, quickly dried up, leaving some without any food at all. When prisoners were released, they did not receive the widespread acclaim of their predecessors in 1839 and 1842; rather they emerged into a hostile, at best apathetic, world and discovered difficulties in finding employment. Many were forced to emigrate, thus depleting still further the already depleted ranks.

Roberts bore these political calamities with fortitude, but they proved too much for Feargus O'Connor. From the outset, O'Connor had been the main spokesman of Chartism, shouldering the greatest responsibility and, unlike Roberts, having no legal practice to distract his attention from the enveloping gloom. His personal disintegration mirrored that of the movement. In October 1851, he declared: 'Chartism is apathetic and dead.'[4] This inconsistency was symptomatic of his deteriorating mental condition. His behaviour exceeded the bounds of mere eccentricity: he addressed the queen as 'dear cousin', physically assaulted other MPs and disrupted parliamentary proceedings. Eventually, he was consigned to Dr Tuke's lunatic asylum, where he died on 30 August 1855. W. P. Roberts was one of the principal mourners at his funeral.[5]

Financial problems contributed to O'Connor's downfall. During the repression of 1848, he had publicly stated he would give financial assistance so that no prisoner would be without legal representation. The scale of the arrests, however, made it impossible for Roberts to cope with all the cases himself; other lawyers had to be engaged. Naturally, these gentlemen expected to be paid for their services, and looked to O'Connor to honour his commitment. In the aftermath of the 1848 débâcle, as the whole movement fell apart, O'Connor found himself harassed by threatening letters from lawyers. There is more than a hint that these sometimes demanded deliberately inflated amounts, a malicious attempt to apply Lord Melbourne's dictum: 'Ruin him with expenses.'

The situation left O'Connor very distraught. 'I tell you I can't stand it,' he said, 'and I won't stand it.' To worsen matters, solicitor James MacNamara, who O'Connor called 'a young shark', successfully sued for damages. He followed this up with another legal action to secure payment of fees and costs incurred defending Ernest Jones and other Chartists. Another solicitor named Nixon repeated the same process. O'Connor, who claimed to have spent between £50,000 and £70,000 of his personal money in the people's cause, now found himself in severe financial difficulties.

His political friends tried to rally round. South Lancashire Chartists formed a three-man committee, of which Roberts was one, to raise money. But at the first public meeting, they found the audience none too supportive, and reluctant to part with their money. Many former activists blamed O'Connor for Chartism's present debilitated state. Indeed, some heckled Roberts' speech and, led by Thomas Clark from London, created a disturbance.[6] Attempts to raise funds were causing still more dissension in the divided movement. But the most serious obstacle to success remained O'Connor himself. Reputedly drinking fifteen glasses of brandy daily, his grasp of reality as well as his tongue tended to slacken, leading to more discreditable incidents and legal actions. He might well have had another problem: from his symptoms, modern medical opinion suggests that he was probably suffering from terminal syphilis.[7]

Whatever the cause, O'Connor seems to have become psychologically much more frail than Roberts. A setback that one could take in his stride, the other could not. A good illustration of this point was the collapse of the Land Plan, with which they were both closely involved.

The collapse of the National Land Company – established first as the Co-operative Land Company in 1845 – came as a result of many factors. Some suggest that the size of the plots of land, varying from two to four acres, made the smallholdings economically unviable. Then there were the tenants, most of whom possessed scant knowledge of agriculture and little capital equipment. Another difficulty arose, in an age before modern secretarial techniques had developed, of keeping down the cost of the collection and administration of many thousands of members' tiny contributions. Add to this the generally hostile environment in which it operated as well as the effects of the economic depression that began in 1847, and it hardly becomes surprising that the Land Company stopped trading – that is to say, taking in members' contributions and purchasing more land – in August 1851. It had by then purchased a total of 1,100 acres of land for £42,544, of which £10,500 remained the debt outstanding.[8]

As this darkening economic cloud descended, O'Connor took it very personally. On top of all the other calamities, he now had to witness the demise of the Land Plan, his most cherished project. He bemoaned his misfortune: 'If it was not for the infernal Land Company, in which I have expended £7,500 of my own money, I would have devoted more of my time to Chartism.'[9] He fulminated against the tenants, and rejoiced when some were evicted. In his eyes, they were 'ruffians, who have been located by the money of the poor, are ousted from the land they have held for four years and paid not a fraction of the rent.'[10] To him, their conduct constituted a personal betrayal, a stab in the back, that helped to unhinge his mind.

By contrast, Roberts, although as treasurer he was at the eye of the whirlwind, came through the ordeal with equanimity. Alice M. Hatfield, the author of a history of the Chartist Land Plan, has suggested that he unscrupulously derived personal gain from the bankruptcy. Another historian was still more critical. Dr J. T. Ward, believing he did little or nothing to earn his rewards, refers to him as 'the idle Roberts'. But the opposite seems to have been true. In the final stages, he worked energetically to stave off disaster. He personally advanced loans to the Land Company, money that was never repaid. His descendants contend the family lost a lot through the venture. In 1853, the *People's Paper* reported wrongly that outstanding debts totalled £10,000 and went on: 'We know for certain that the debts of the Company have not been paid: Mr Roberts's bill for law expenses is still unsettled; the money that that gentleman advanced towards the expenses of passing the Bill has not been repaid; nor has any other creditor.'[11]

Time passed and the debts remained unpaid. So in April 1857, the Master of Chancery wound up the company, placing the estates on the market. The following year a man named Hibbert offered £19,200 for all the properties, much less than the original purchase price of £42,544. This allowed the liquidators to pay £17,000 to debtors.[12] As a consequence, the costs of management and administration, as well as W. P. Roberts' legal expenses, still remained outstanding. Little or nothing was left for creditors or shareholders. (Presumably the remaining £2,200 went in the official costs of the Chancery legal action, estate agents, and so on.)

Roberts seems to have received the ground rent for some of the cottages in lieu of repayment. He wanted to retain an interest in the settlements and, if possible, help to preserve their Chartist character. He also purchased the schoolhouse at Heronsgate, which he found a congenial place in his final years – living among old friends and recounting the battles of yesteryear.

This, however, had not been his original intention. When the Land Company ceased operating in August 1851, some of its supporters regarded it merely as a temporary setback. Among those urging that money be raised 'for repurchasing some of the estates' was Martin Jude, the miners' leader. In the summer of 1852 Ernest Jones and Roberts also sought to revive the scheme. A *People's Paper* editorial said: 'The Company has fallen but not irremediably.'[13] Though this proved to be unduly optimistic, everything was not entirely lost: the spirit survived though the structure had been wrecked. At Heronsgate, for example, radical-minded tenants sought to perpetuate the Chartist principles. They formed the nucleus of the North London Anti-Enclosure, Social and Sanitary Mutual Improvement Society. Then, in 1855, a Mutual Improvement Society was established. This played a pioneering role in campaigning for branch libraries in rural areas. Its own library, an off-shoot of Hampstead Public Library, was open every evening. Tenants also established retail outlets in London, encouraging potential customers and well-wishers to visit Heronsgate.[14]

Chartists from all parts of Britain, and foreigners too, journeyed there. On one occasion, a Polish–Hungarian band took part in a special commemorative party, attended by a large number of people, for 'the victims of 1848'.[15] At holiday times there were frequently, to quote the tenants' own words, 'The excursions of friends to O'Connor's paradise'. A public announcement in 1857 assured visitors 'all pilgrims to that Holy Land (holy to freedom and all that is dear to it) will be welcome. Though the farms have a retired villa-like appearance, they are like the Hospice at Mont. St. Bernard, open to all.' It added that refreshments would be provided.[16]

Whereas Feargus O'Connor only saw the negative side of the Land Company's collapse, W. P. Roberts could see that some positive features remained. Through those hard, unrewarding times, Herons-gate must have been a comfort to him, a little oasis of friendly and like-minded people in an otherwise largely inhospitable world. His wife Mary continued living at Heronsgate after his death. But by the 1880s, the Chartist character of the place was dwindling. The last of her children, a son born in 1856, had long since left home. The schoolhouse was too big, too costly to maintain. In straitened financial circumstances, she moved to a small flat in London.

Even so, the mid-century was definitely a discouraging period. It left Roberts with very few political and industrial cases to fight. Therefore he had to rely upon routine work (petty crime, conveyancing, etc.) that is the bread-and-butter of most conventional solicitors. But this kind of work was hard to come by. People from the upper and middle classes were hardly likely to turn to a disreputable Chartist for legal advice. Boycotted and ostracized, both Roberts and Ernest Jones suffered financial difficulties. But Jones, being a barrister, appears to have felt the problem more acutely. In his diaries, Lord Derby reported that Jones begged from him. He also received money from Disraeli. And George Howell stated that, at least on one occasion, he was forced by financial necessity to represent an employer against a trade union in a court case at Bolton. Yet, even these desperate measures did not end his penury: the poverty of his appearance was so striking that, forty years later, a correspondent wrote to a newspaper to describe how, campaigning for Chartism, Ernest Jones had journeyed around County Durham on a donkey, slept in miners' cottages, his poverty being obvious to all because of his well-worn clothes.[17]

In the post-1848 period, many workers had come to regard

Chartism as an old, worn-out garment, a symbol of failure with which they no longer wished to be associated. When the Society of Arts convened a conference to discuss social problems, Ernest Jones had the humiliation of experiencing this change of attitude. Chairing the proceedings, Lord Grosvenor ruled out of order an attempt by Ernest Jones to move a Chartist resolution. Jones appealed to delegates for support, hoping they would back him in his dispute with Lord Grosvenor. But W. Newton, of the engineers' union, declared that 'the representatives of the working class had come there to place themselves in the hands of the Society of Arts and had full confidence in them.' Later, when Jones made a second attempt to move his resolution, quoting paragraph 4 of the conference rules which said resolutions could be moved, again he was refused permission. 'The chairman and his friends seemed greatly annoyed.' Lord Grosvenor pronounced the content of the motion to be 'offensive'. To this, Jones retorted: 'Truth is often offensive.' Enraged, the chairman brought the argument to an end with 'I will hear no more.' Despite the presence of many who had been sturdy advocates of the People's Charter, including Thomas Cooper, George Holyoake and Samuel Kydd, none came to the aid of Ernest Jones. Lord Grosvenor might pay labourers on his estate only eight or nine shillings a week; yet, they would rather grovel before His Lordship, hoping that their good behaviour might gain them a few crumbs of comfort, than continue with the kind of confrontation politics Chartism implied.[18]

Even so, the political ice age did not last forever. The first signs of a thaw, albeit a very modest one, became discernible around 1852–3. By then, Britain was emerging from the depression and trade unions were springing into life. This meant that workers began once more looking for the services of legal advisers. In a limited way, too, there was also a revival of Chartism. Ernest Jones decided to start and edit a new journal, the *People's Paper*. Naturally, Roberts did whatever he could to assist him with the venture. Soon the two men became political companions and friends, a partnership which survived for the rest of their lives.

The politics of Roberts and Jones were similar but not identical. Both acknowledged that Chartism, to make progress, required a socio-economic programme. The slogan was 'The Charter and something more'. For years, Roberts had, by implication, accepted this position. All his trade union work had been based on the assumption that workers needed greater industrial as well as political freedom. But for Ernest Jones, this freedom meant socialism. He had come under the influence of Marx and Engels. They recognized him to be 'a fellow who knew his business', was 'on the right lines', but 'would not have got on the right road without our teaching'. The revival of Chartism, Engels predicted, would have to appeal to 'the instinctive hatred of the workers for the industrial bourgeoisie'.[19]

Nobody could accuse Roberts of not having a healthy hatred for the industrial bourgeoisie. He loathed the Gradgrinds and Bounderbys. His daily hand-to-hand fighting with them gave him a practical knowledge of their little dirty tricks, probably greater than that of Marx or Engels. This did not, however, make him a socialist. From the beginning of his political career, his line remained the same. At Bath in 1838, he had debated with Alexander Campbell, an Owenite socialist. He argued that all efforts should be devoted to the attainment of pressing immediate demands; time and energy should not be dissipated on discussions about a new society, which might well be unobtainable.[20]

Roberts personally knew Marx and Engels but, unlike Ernest Jones, he does not appear to have been influenced by them. Probably the acquaintance arose through his interest in continental movements against oppression. In the aftermath of 1848, when the defeat of European revolutions was much more demoralizing and divisive than among the British Chartists, a violent quarrel erupted inside the German Workers' Education Society, a London-based organization that encompassed a wide range of political and social functions. In 1850, the moderates objected to the activities of the Communist League within its ranks. They tried to seize control of the society's assets. Its treasurer, a Jewish lace dealer named Heinrich Bauer, of 64, Dean Street, Soho, happened to have the Marx family living with him as temporary lodgers. Legal action was taken against Bauer and another official, Karl Pfender. Employing Roberts as their solicitor, they succeeded in defeating the move. Then a statement was issued by Bauer and Pfender (though actually drafted by Marx and Engels) reporting that the money had been deposited with a London citizen – the editor of the Marx–Engels Collected Works thinks this might have been Roberts – and would ultimately be used for its original purpose.[21]

Apparently, Marx had considerable confidence in Roberts' legal abilities. He used him again as his British solicitor during the protracted Herr Vogt affair ten years later. This was precipitated by the publication of a book by Herr Vogt. It accused Marx of being a forger and blackmailer, living off contributions from working people while only having respect for thoroughbred aristocrats, such as his brother-in-law, the Prussian Minister of the Interior. These allegations, extensively circulated, had a considerable impact. Newspapers both in Britain and on the continent repeated the charges. So Marx decided to sue the *National Zeitung* in Berlin and the *Daily Telegraph* in London. Ernest Jones was responsible for first bringing the matter to Marx's notice in a letter saying 'you should answer the falsehood and malignancy of the writer.' On 13 February 1860, Marx wrote to Engels telling him he would be travelling to Manchester as he had arranged an appointment with Roberts on Wednesday.[22]

Generally, historians believe Marx over-reacted, wasting eighteen months of his life rebutting Herr Vogt's charges.[23] Both in Britain and Germany the libel actions were failures. A book which Marx wrote on the issue, going into elaborate detail, is now regarded by most scholars as a misuse of his intellectual abilities. Legal consultations must have frequently brought Marx and Roberts together. It is inconceivable that two such politically-minded individuals never discussed politics. Yet, their approaches were so dissimilar. One sought to overthrow the existing system, the other simply to eradicate its injustices. Marx had already begun his theoretical labours that were ultimately to lead to the writing of *Capital*, a book of lasting importance, whereas Roberts operated on a much more practical, mundane level.

Far from the lofty flights of abstraction, he found himself involved in the class struggle at a raw, basic level, which sometimes provided insights that would otherwise have been lost. For example, much has been written on the issue of child labour, both by writers of the time and by historians later. What is often overlooked is that child labour inevitably means child involvement in industrial disputes, with children confronting each other as strikers and blacklegs on the picket line. Although a Select Committee in 1860 admitted that 'disputes are frequent among females and young people', adding that they are frequently 'ignorant of the laws and means of redress', the significance of its remarks has never been properly assessed.[24]

Such a conflict led, on 7 June 1851, to a case being heard before M. C. Trafford, Salford stipendiary magistrate. The court case arose out of incidents that had happened outside Sir E. Armitage's mill a few months previously. Strikers shouted and hooted at employees returning to work. It was alleged that stones had been thrown. Early in the proceedings Roberts tried unsuccessfully to get the case against each individual heard separately, believing this procedure would enhance the chances of acquittal, particularly for two child defendants. Thwarted in this move, he then sought to prove the millowner was, at least in part, responsible for the dispute by paying such low wages. The public gallery, crammed with strikers, exploded with incredulity when this was denied. Whereupon the stipendiary magistrate threatened to clear the court if the disturbances continued and the prosecutor described the interruption as 'very indecent in a court of law'. Immediately Roberts riposted. 'Against that indecency is the fact that a boy of 11 and a girl of 13 are summoned to be imprisoned for three months.'[25]

A second case, almost identical to the first, involved three boys. They were alleged to have intimidated girl power-loom weavers at Crossley's Salford mill. They had, it was alleged, shouted 'knobstick' at the strikebreakers and thrown clods of earth. Roberts sought to disprove these claims, but found it impossible to penetrate the prejudices of the stipendary magistrates. Asked if he placed any reliance on defence witnesses, the magistrate replied, 'No, I do not,' adding 'There will be a conviction in this case.' To which Roberts replied: 'Your mind is very closed.' Naturally, this remark did not endear him to M. C. Trafford, who, incidentally, belonged to the wealthy family of cotton merchants that gave its name to Trafford Park. From his privileged position, the magistrate saw the case arising not from an industrial dispute, the result of a struggle between masters and men, but from an internecine conflict between workers. He told the court: 'There was no tyranny more unbearable than the tyranny of one worker over another, and it was a painful thing for him to send children to prison, but he could not help it.'

When he heard the sentence, the youngest child burst out crying. His mother also started to shout, imploring Trafford to reconsider the verdict. In turn, this only served to make her child shriek louder. Excited and distraught, the boy – probably an epileptic – fell on the floor, rolling about unconscious. The sergeant-an-arms tried to restrain him; but his conduct simply frightened and angered the mother, who struggled to release her son from the sergeant-at-arms' grip. Above the mêlée, the voice of Roberts could be heard: 'Don't hold him so . . . Oh, you cursed rascals . . . Isn't it a shameful thing? The child shall not be sent to prison.' But the stipendiary magistrate, quite unmoved, still had his way. He was determined the boy would serve his sentence. Before leaving the court, Roberts shouted at the stipendiary magistrate: 'As truly as there is a God in heaven, there will be punishment for sending that child to prison.'[26]

From the standpoint of the entire trade union movement, one of Roberts' cases that happened roughly at the same time as the child-pickets was of much greater importance. It related to Messrs Perry, tinplate manufacturers of Wolverhampton. In the spring of 1850, the National Association of United Trades, liaising with a semi-secret local union, took up workers' grievances there. Their main demand was to receive the going pay rate for similar workers in the Black Country. In this they received the support, rather unusually, of other tinplate manufacturers in the area. Perhaps they did not want to see Messrs Perry gain an unfair competitive advantage through lower labour costs. Even George Robinson, the Mayor of Wolverhampton, and four magistrates, who tried to mediate, sided with the men.[27] But Messrs Perry refused to budge, arguing that the introduction of costly new machinery made the work not strictly comparable.

The ensuing strike was conducted in an ultra-cautious manner. In the wake of the Chartist disturbances of 1848, the National Association had received unwelcome attention from the authorities. One of its leaders complained that the union had been falsely accused of being a physical force movement, with bloodshed and robbery as its objectives. In September 1848, at a union recruitment at Bilston, only a few miles from Wolverhampton, a posse of policemen had entered the hall immediately the doors were opened and maintained an intimidating presence throughout the proceedings.[28] With such unpleasant memories at the back of their minds, union leaders resolved from the outset of the dispute to make every effort to keep within the law, giving neither the employers nor the police a pretext for intervention. No picketing whatsoever took place against the blacklegs (about a fifth of the labour force) or against the foreign workers brought over from France. Strikers contented themselves with simply keeping the place under surveillance. They tried to discover where those working for Messrs Perry lived; then they would visit the strike-breakers, inviting them for a drink and a discussion in a local public house. In this way, many of those working were persuaded to stop, and production was seriously disrupted. Faced with the inability to meet pressing orders for home and export markets, Messrs Perry turned to the law.

The firm's prosecutions of the trade unionists came before Mr Justice Erle, at the Staffordshire summer assizes, in July 1851.[29] Three officials of the local union and three officials of the National Association were charged with conspiracy. The jury, consisting of twelve Staffordshire businessmen and traders, returned a verdict of guilty on all counts. Even more disturbing were some of the judge's remarks. Whereas the Newton-le-Willows trial of Selsby in 1847 had left workers some loopholes, Mr Justice Erle now went out of his way to close them. His judgement clearly laid down a much more restricted framework within which trade unions could function. These limits were so circumscribed as to make their continued existence, as legal entities, virtually impossible.

Mr Justice Erle conceded that workers had a legitimate right to work, or not to work, at a given rate of pay. They even had the right to combine. However, what they did not have a right to do – indeed, it would be highly dangerous to allow them to do – was to try and induce others to break their contracts of employment: 'There might be no threats or intimidation used by the defendants, but he thought it clear that they conspired to induce men to leave Mr Perry in order to compel him to alter his mode of doing business. If the jury were of the same opinion, they could, of course, find the defendants guilty.' The case was sent to the winter session of the Queen's Bench for sentencing, where each defendant received three months imprisonment. In the course of these proceedings, Lord Campbell, the Lord Chief Justice, queried the *raison d'être* of trade unions, whether 'such associations are necessary for the protection of working people'; while his colleague, Mr Justice Pattinson, expressed concern about the size of the National Association's funds. He alleged that it had a bank balance of £20,000, and expressed the fear that this money might be used for sinister purposes. So he told the defendants: 'You must not interfere between employers and their men.'[30]

Greatly shaken by the imprisonment of its leaders, the National Association reacted by adopting an even more conciliatory approach. It sought to transform itself into an industrial peacemaker rather than being a trade union. Even while the trial continued, the National Association made tentative steps towards disassociating itself from industrial conflict in all its forms. This included a plan to try and save its own three officials on trial by repudiating the actions of the three officials from the local union. This provoked instant anger from the People's Attorney: W. P. Roberts' response, as the *People's Paper* put it, was 'more energetic than polite'. Even so, once the court proceedings were over, the National Association executive explained to its membership that their leaders had been imprisoned because of the acts of others, of which they disapproved. The general secretary, William Peel, stated that he saw the union's new role as that of 'bringing antagonistic parties to submit their conflicting claims to arbitration'. The defeat of the engineers in the 1852 lock-out merely served to reinforce his belief in industrial pacifism – 'the desire to see the strike system entirely superseded'.[31]

Many workers, though not enamoured by strikes, nevertheless thought it essential to keep the strike weapon for protection, something to use as a last resort. Consequently, they did not go along with the National Association's policy of unilateral industrial disarmament. Many left the organization. Unconcerned, the National Association thought it could still continue as a political pressure group: it launched a campaign to improve trade unions' legal position. A petition to Parliament gained 77,377 signatures, but the legislators took not a scrap of notice. There followed years of effort, backed by no industrial muscle. All that was ever achieved was a futile exchange of mutual pleasantries. For example, in 1861, representatives of the association 'waited upon the new Lord Chancellor to congratulate and thank him for his constant readiness to assist them in industrial legislation. The chancellor, in reply, spoke of frequent communications with the association, which had impressed him by its intelligence and moderation.'[32] Apparently, ordinary workers were much less impressed than the Lord Chancellor, for membership continued to dwindle. In 1860, one of its officials stated that membership was only 5,000 and 'we do not care much about it.'[33] Whether or not the National Association had acquired some other, non-working class, source of funds, it is impossible to say. What is clear, however, is that it was able to continue its twilight existence, making occasional statements and giving evidence before royal commissions, until 1867.

The fate of the National Association, its growing enfeeblement and lingering death, should remain an object lesson to workers on the role of industrial law under capitalism. Its function is not merely to fine or imprison trade unions and trade unionists. More important still, it imposes acceptance of the attitudes and values of the existing system. The law can have a powerful symbolic significance, altering behaviour and perception of the world. The relatively trivial punishment meted out to officials of the National Association had a disproportionate effect on its subsequent activities. By complete compliance with the law, the National Association became no threat to employers or government – and no use to workers either.[34]

Other workers did not see the need to make such an abject surrender. Rather, by 1852, realizing there was an upturn in the British economy, they used their bargaining strength to the full. On 10 July 1852, *Reynolds Newspaper* reported: 'From all parts of the country we receive the most cheering accounts of the labour movement. Employers in most instances ultimately found it expedient to submit to the just and legitimate demands of their workpeople.' Where strikes did occur, four-fifths were successful. While Peel, of the National Association, was declaring strikes for higher wages were 'impolitic and injudicious', skilled shipyard workers on Tyneside were able to increase their pay by 25 per cent in a year. Naturally, none of this could have happened had workers kept strictly within the law.

What had been decided by the courts and what then happened in practice were two entirely separate things. After the Wolverhampton trial, Sir Richard Bethell, the Solicitor-General, explained the import of Mr Justice Erle's ruling to the House of Commons. It meant, he stated, 'that the law as it stands at present, and after the decision of the Court of Queen's Bench, makes it illegal for workmen to combine to persuade. Such conduct is tantamount to intimidation and molestation.' The Erle ruling meant that to try and compel a master to raise wages was, under the 1825 Act section 3(c), criminal under the common law. In a later judgement, it was held that for those wanting to work during an industrial dispute even 'to encounter black looks' or have to experience any acts 'calculated to have a deterring effect' would mean a criminal offence had been committed.[35]

Obviously, W. P. Roberts regarded these judgements as unfair and unjust. His objections were echoed by trade unionists generally. *Reynolds Newspaper* observed that they lacked balance. They branded trade unionist action to increase wages a conspiracy; no similar ruling was made when employers tried to lower them. The editorial went on to cite the example of railway directors who had loaned another railway company, which was involved in an industrial dispute, some of its staff to replace workers on strike. These railway directors had not been charged, as trade union officials had, with meddling in a dispute of no concern to them.[36] Also, almost instinctively, there was a feeling among workers generally that it was an example of class injustice, of the rich condemning the poor. Yet, such was the chasm that divided the two Englands that they had no conception of – and therefore never actually gave the figures for – the vast disparities of wealth that existed. Wolverhampton tinplaters, earning roughly a pound a week, had been prosecuted by leading Queen's Counsel on between £5,000 and £8,000 a year. Sir John Jervis, then the Attorney-General, was making over £20,000, plus £300 for retainers, while Sir Richard Bethell, the Solicitor-General, who informed Parliament of the significance of Mr Justice Erle's judgement, was earning only slightly less.[37]

This judgement, however, had little or no immediate effect. Workers continued to pursue their pay claims aggressively. In the prevailing boom conditions, with high profitability, employers usually continued to make concessions. They did not want strikes or protracted legal actions that might disrupt and embitter productive relations. Their attitude changed when, temporarily, the economy reached a downturn. It was then that the confident mood of the weavers and spinners of Preston, aware of the recent success of their counterparts in Stockport, met resistance. The Preston millowners, better organized than elsewhere, were determined not to concede to the workers' demand of 'ten per cent and no surrender'. By October 1853, there was what amounted to a general strike of mill operatives in the city. The dispute gained nationwide publicity. Charles Dickens visited Preston, wrote an article about it in *Household Words*, and may have used some of his experiences there in the novel *Hard Times*.[38] From almost every industrial centre in Britain, money was sent to swell the strike funds.

The dispute dragged on for thirty-two weeks. In February 1854, the millowners began bringing in new labour from outlying agricultural districts, augmented by shipments of impoverished, semi-destitute Irishmen. This angered the strikers, yet the vast majority still obeyed the leaders' advice and stayed calm. Then came further provocation with the prosecution of eleven members of the strike committee on conspiracy charges and the imposition of heavy policing on the city.[39]

There seems to have been a definite, well worked-out plan to foil the defendants' attempt to secure the legal services of the People's Attorney. Probably a police informer had infiltrated the strike committee. Hence it was known that one of its spokesmen was going to W. P. Roberts' offices in Manchester, and he was arrested on Preston railway station. At the same time, a rumour was spread that Roberts would be unable to attend because of illness. The first Roberts knew of the eleven arrests was when a reporter approached him and asked whether he would be representing the men:

> I was compelled to reply I had not been sent for – know nothing about it – and that I thought it likely that the case would go to a local attorney. Later in the day, I heard that Mr Cobbett, of Manchester, had been sent for and was in Preston, defending some of the men. It is hardly necessary for me to say that this last information was a very great disappointment, a heavy blow. I could not overstate it nor can I describe it. Ten thousand recollections of old contests rushed at once to my memory. Still, there was no help for it. That the defendants had a perfect right to be defended by any one they thought fit.[40]

Eventually, a letter came from Preston, putting an entirely different complexion on things. It stated that they were all surprised and disappointed by his non-appearance; everybody thought he had been sent for. Immediately, Roberts set off for Preston, where he was cordially welcomed. All the arrested men wanted him to act as their solicitor. On 28 March 1854, at the Liverpool assizes, he managed to secure the release of all the prisoners. Mr Justice Cresswell deferred the case until the autumn assizes.

In the meantime, the strikers and their families were being subjected to police harassment. This, it was hoped, would make their lives such a misery that they would resolve to return to work. Though Roberts gained the admission in court from a police officer that he had never known the city so peaceful, this did not prevent the local constabulary from asserting an oppressive presence in Preston. The reaction of the people of Preston to this finds expression in a poem, stuck at the front of a collection of documents on the dispute, deposited in the Lancashire Public Records Office:

Police Street Regulations

Move on, move off, move away,
Stop not for frolic nor fray;
Stand still not, lie down not, sit not,
Dirt not, puke not, sit not,
Ballad not, psalm not, sit not,
Break window-panes not nor glim not
Over pedestrians ride not,
Throw not orange peel nor slide not,
Fruit baskets carry not,
Late out at nights tarry not;
Commit no nuisance, indulge not a lark,
Drive not mad bullocks, wear not pattens in the park,
Pull not off bell-pulls, however inviting;
Pull not men's noses, which leadeth to fighting;
Cry 'Sweep' not, folks wake from sleep not,
Be not tipsy, nor stagger not,
Servant maidens list not off,
Pears, apples, nor gingerbread sell not,
Nuts, walnuts, nor chestnuts shell not,
Fire not cracker nor squib.
Beg not, steal not, nor fib,
Hoop trundle not, in street tumble not,
At policeman grumble not,
Quietly to the station-house go,
Whether you like it or no.
At woman look not, nor squint not;
To woman talk not, nor hint not.

Once the lock-out ended, so did the authorities' excessive zeal over minor infringements of the law. Indeed, even the case against the eleven strike-leaders was dropped. To have pursued it would have been counter-productive from the employers' standpoint, rekindling memories of strife best forgotten. Anyway, insofar as the millowners wanted to punish the ringleaders, they could easily do so without invoking the law by the quietly effective method of victimization.

In the autumn of 1853, an industrial dispute was also taking place in the neighbouring town of Wigan. But there was a stark contrast between the violence that occurred there and the tranquillity of

TAKING A LEAF OUT OF THE FRENCH BOOK.

THE LICENSER OF PLAYS INTERFERING WITH THE PANTOMIMES.

Police were regarded as corrupt killjoys. One drawing (1851) shows police arresting two street clowns for obstruction and the other (1841), captioned 'A strong attachment', shows a plain clothes officer and a gonoph (i.e. a minor thief or pickpocket) in mutually advantageous business.

A STRONG ATTACHMENT

(*Punch*)

Preston. At Wigan, angry miners, largely unorganized and leaderless, went on the rampage once they heard the coalowners had rejected their wage claim. Public houses, the town hall, grammar school and numerous shops were damaged. The masters, chased through the main thoroughfare, took refuge in the Dog and Partridge Hotel. Similarly, the police, greeted by a volley of missiles, turned and ran, barricading themselves in the comparatively safe police barracks. Meanwhile, men roamed the streets, destroying or stealing whatever they chose. An attempt to blow up Moss Hall colliery, using a home-made bomb, blew off the roof and damaged nearby buildings. For five hours, Wigan was left to the tender mercies of John Leadbetter, known as 'John the poker', and his friends. Only the arrival in the town of the Lancashire Hussars, galloping down from strike-torn Preston, restored tranquillity.[41] The absence of an effective police force meant that most rioters got off scot free: only five were prosecuted, and then merely for petty thievery.[42]

The strikers in Wigan as well as Preston were ultimately defeated. Far from allowing themselves to become demoralized and question-ing whether all their sacrifices had been worthwhile, Jones and Roberts urged workers not to jettison the principle of industrial action. What was needed, they said, was greater industrial action and more solidarity. Had the Wigan workers linked their struggle for higher wages with their brothers and sisters in Preston – better still with workers throughout Lancashire – the outcome could well have been rather different. The *People's Paper* affirmed: 'A unity of action through all trades would strike terror in the employers.'[43]

Roberts endeavoured to put these defeats into perspective. Addressing a widely-reported public meeting at Accrington, he spoke from first-hand experience, having defended in court those workers charged in both Preston and Wigan. He advised his listeners not to be discouraged and to recognize that 'a great social war was now going on', a conflict which he likened to the Crimean war, then taking place:

> Their war against capital must be fought as the war in which we were now engaged was to be fought against Russia. They could not expect that, as they whistled, the enemy would lay down his arms and confess himself conquered. They must be content to gain, step by step, always looking to the certainty of ultimate victory.

Despite the prevailing mood of pessimism, Roberts still remained confident of final victory:

> He knew it must be by a succession of struggles. He did not hold out, as some might think, that in the next struggle they would be victorious. He thought they were doomed to be beaten again and again, but that each time they would rise with renewed intelligence and additional power to resist their oppressors.

In this war, Roberts thought that class organization and the withdrawal of labour were their most powerful weapons. They had already borne some fruits:

> If it had not been for their continual strikes, wages would at this time have not been half what they now were. In the agricultural districts they had had no strikes, and consequently the agricultural labourer was glad to get whatever he could. With regard to the factory operatives – and he said this emphatically – he believed their whole, their sole power consisted in striking.

To secure maximum advantage from industrial action, Roberts considered that a general strike was necessary:

> The whole combined power of the masters of this country had not been able to put down Preston until after 32 weeks of struggling. (Hear, hear) What were they to learn from that? Why their movement must be extended . . . As soon as they had the power to strike altogether, there is no power in the land, nor in any other, can prevent you obtaining all that you are entitled to. (Hear, hear and cheers)[44]

Roberts' speech gives a fascinating insight into his intellectual development. Vanished is the easy-going optimism of 1844, when he thought that the miners alone could bring about their social emancipation at one single stroke. It had been replaced by the politics of the long haul, a realization that each battle might be vital but constituted only a small part in the protracted conflict, a struggle that must actively involve all workers. What distinguished Roberts from others in mid-Victorian Britain was the strength and duration of his commitment to the workers in the class struggle. Unlike so many others, he had not joined in the headlong rush into respectability and moderation.

13 The Collapse of Chartism

In the 1850s, Chartism fell into terminal decline, wracked by faction and fragmentation. Its branches either ceased to exist or contained only a handful of members. Meanwhile, there was a proliferation of small groups, led by disenchanted ex-Chartists, that sought to compete for the diminishing clientele. Among these were Bronterre O'Brien's National Reform League, Holyoake's Social Reform League which was trying to unite socialists and Chartists, the National People's Party of Fussell and Reynolds, while Tom Clark was employed by Sir Joshua Walmsley's middle-class Parliamentary Reform Association.

Its record of failure had left Chartism in an impasse – neither petitioning nor physical force provided realistic ways forward. Three petitions had been presented to Parliament. The number of signatures had risen from 1,280,000 in 1839 to 5,700,000 in 1848, yet while thirty-nine MPs voted for it on the former occasion, on the latter the House of Commons dismissed it with a laugh. Many were so disillusioned that they said they would never again put their names to a petition. If, as one Chartist put it, moral force was like 'striving to drive in a nail with a feather', the state's firm and resolute response to the troubles of 1848 clearly indicated that physical force could not win.

During the 1850s attempts were made to associate what remained of the movement with some acutely felt current grievances of the working class. For example, to link it with the campaign to democratize the army, a product of the outcry over the scandalous inefficiency displayed by the geriatric generals during the Crimean war; to give extra punch to campaigns about the scarcity and high cost of food; to become involved with the growing trade union movement, a move that it was thought could be to their mutual advantage.

W. P. Roberts welcomed the new emphasis. In the 1830s, he had seen the mass discontent engendered by the Reform Bill, Poor Law Amendment Act and economic crisis channelled into creating and sustaining Chartism, an unprecedented movement of protest. Perhaps the same thing could happen again. In any case, Roberts had always regarded the workers' struggle as indivisible, devoting himself equally to trade union and Chartist matters.

He therefore saw the convening of a Labour Parliament at Manchester in March 1854 as step forward. Originally proposed as a means of helping workers involved in the Preston lock-out, it sought to provide workers throughout the country with a forum, where they could discuss their mutual problems and formulate a common policy. Ernest Jones predicted: 'A unity of action through all trades would strike terror in the employers.'[1]

From the Labour Parliament's deliberations, the Mass Movement was born. Alas, from the outset, it was riddled with inner contradictions, being neither mass nor a movement. But this did not prevent its organizers, backed by Roberts, from formulating grandiose plans for expansion. In the initial optimism, they envisaged that money would pour in from all parts of Britain, providing sufficient finance for those involved in industrial disputes and for the Mass Movement to purchase its own agricultural and industrial enterprises. Reality, however, proved to be rather less kind. The Preston struggle had ended in defeat, its leaders, like Mortimer Grimshaw, victimized and wandering around begging. This had a chastening effect on others, increasing their reluctance to become associated. The leaders of the National Association refused to belong to the Mass Movement, which they stigmatized as 'a political adventure'. Even Roberts' old friends the pitmen drew back: they had just made an unsuccessful attempt to form a national organization of their own, which they considered to be a much more pressing task than to join the Mass Movement.[2]

All this was part of a powerful tendency towards separatism then prevailing among workers – for occupational groups to look to their own salvation while shunning involvement with others. Moreover, many thought the political overtones of the Mass Movement, its Chartist links and lack of respectability, might jeopardize their chance of securing their industrial objectives. It soon became obvious, however, that Chartism, diminutive and disaster-prone, did not possess the power to weld disparate groups of workers into some sort of unity, giving them cohesion and coherence. For a short time, Roberts was treasurer of the Mass Movement, which was not a particularly onerous job. Three months after its formation, it was reported that the income of the Mass Movement for a fortnight had fallen to only two shillings – in others words, less than the cost of postage and writing paper![3]

Nevertheless, all was not despondency and gloom. Despite the débâcle of the Mass Movement, one of the creations of the Labour Parliament survived: the United Brothers grew into a highly successful friendly society. W. P. Roberts also became successful in his defence of friendly societies. His involvement in the Labour Parliament and Mass Movement had been minimal because of his work elsewhere. Besides the rash of court cases arising from the Preston and Wigan strikes, he played a prominent part in the campaign to resist moves in Parliament to destroy friendly societies. Attitudes to them in the upper echelons of society remained ambivalent. While they were examples of self-help, where ordinary working people practised thrift, saving for death or infirmity, at the same time they were perceived as vehicles for mischief.

Many friendly societies were trade unions, even when they had no such avowed purpose. For example, in 1847 the Blackburn weavers' strike was largely financed by money from the Grand Order of Modern Druids.[4] Not only did those in authority wish to end this misuse of funds, they also wanted to eliminate, as far as possible, the opportunities which friendly societies provided for corruption and dishonesty. These dangers were enhanced because many had officials without even an elementary knowledge of accountancy and other relevant subjects. On one occasion, the Registrar of Friendly Societies, T. D. Pratt, received a statement of accounts from a burial club in Hyde, Cheshire, where the secretary persisted in referring to the town as 'Hide', could not add up, and conceded that most of the money had been literally swallowed up in the form of 'licker'.[5] Much more serious, many in polite society suspected that working people killed their children in order to secure benefits from their friendly societies. In a well-publicized case, Mr Hudson, the Cheshire coroner, declared that he thought parents should never receive more money than it cost to bury a child. Otherwise it gave an incentive to infanticide.[6] Others thought the practice extended well beyond the killing of the new-born: they attributed the high mortality figures in some working-class districts not to poor housing, sanitation, ventilation, and so on – rather it arose from the survivors' desire for monetary gain. As a consequence, to deal with these abuses, the Friendly Society Bill proposed to introduce restrictions. First, it would make it impossible for trade unions to secure Friendly Society protection. Second, before benefits were paid out, people would have to prove that the deceased had not been unlawfully killed.

Trade unions and friendly societies combined to attack clauses 3 and 4, which contained the offensive provisions, and it was agreed to petition Parliament. W. P. Roberts was approached and asked to arrange for their views to be put to favourably disposed MPs as well as government ministers. Officials of the Oddfellows seem to have led the campaign. They argued that the proposed clauses would mean the end of many societies and were 'a direct insult upon every working man, inasmuch as it stigmatised every parent as a murderer and compels proof to the contrary.'[7] The extent and intensity of the opposition forced a rethink, delaying the parliamentary passing of the legislation. When, eventually, the Friendly Society Act, 1855, reached the statute book, Roberts and his colleagues had secured almost total victory, with the objectionable clauses expunged. Trade unions received the protection of the act so long as they had been established for the furtherance of legal purposes; and friendly societies also obtained virtually everything they sought. The Registrar of Friendly Societies had to receive their constitution and annual statement of accounts, both to assure himself that they were being properly run and for legal purposes, after which they could pursue their business without let or hindrance. Mid-Victorian Britain was experiencing a boom, with prosperity gradually percolating down through society. Thanks to the 1855 Act, friendly societies in England and Wales flourished, possessing 2,000,000 members and £10 million assets by 1860. As the wealth of workers grew, so did their stake in existing society, making them a conservative force.[8]

Something similar was happening with trade unions. Although the victory over the 1855 act, as originally drafted, owed a lot to Roberts' pertinacity, they were not as a result drawn closer to Chartism in gratitude. Far from it: the removal of the source of irritation helped to smooth the path to their greater integration within existing society, also giving them a vested interest in the *status quo*.

Another highly contentious legislative issue, which aroused Roberts' wrath, happened almost concurrently with that of the friendly societies. In 1854, Parliament passed an act which closed all English establishments for the drinking of alcohol between 2.30 p.m. and 6 p.m. and after 10 at night. The following year, Lord Robert Grosvenor introduced a bill that would further restrict the hours of Sunday trading. The only exception to the prohibition would be bona fide travellers. But 'What is a Traveller?', to quote the title of the pamphlet W. P. Roberts wrote on the subject. His fear was that the upper and middle classes would be able to escape the penal clauses; the restrictions, in practice, would only apply to the working class. A lot of people endorsed the sentiments expressed by James Finlen: 'Six days a week we are treated like slaves and now Parliament wants to rob us of the bit of freedom we still have on the seventh.'[9] On 24 June 1855, a mass protest took place at Hyde Park. The police tried to disperse the crowd as they were on crown land, but disturbances lasted for three hours. However, the following Sunday – 1 July – the situation became even more violent. An irate crowd of 200,000 assembled in Hyde Park to express their disapproval. In the opinion of *The Times*, all would have been peaceful but for 'the outrageous conduct of the police'.[10] In retaliation to an onslaught by the Metropolitan constabulary, thousands of people surged out of Hyde Park and into fashionable parts of London, harassing and molesting any of the rich who happened to be passing by. There was widespread rioting. Frustrated by their inability to clear the area, the police resorted to mass arrests, during which some of the rich were inadvertently swept into the Black Marias. Wishing to avoid a repetition of these disgraceful scenes the next Sunday, a group of MPs, led by Colonel J. Lindsay, considered that the authorities should resort to a simple expedient – the trial of six-pounder cannons in Hyde Park. The irate populace were not deterred by such threats and on Sunday, 8 July, another demonstration took place. Again, the crowd swarmed out of Hyde Park and into Belgravia, smashing 749 window panes.

One of the participants in the mayhem on both Sundays had been a German emigré named Dr Karl Marx who, according to Wilhelm Liebknecht, came close to being arrested. Marx thought he was witnessing – or, rather, playing a small part in – the beginning of a great movement. Writing in *Neue Oder-Zeitung*, he forecast wrongly: 'We saw it from beginning to end and do not think it an exaggeration to say the English revolution began in Hyde Park yesterday.'[11]

W. P. Roberts was as much opposed to Lord Robert Grosvenor's bill as was Karl Marx, but they saw matters differently. Whereas the founder of communism saw it as 'a conspiracy of the Church with monopoly capitalism', to the People's Attorney it was 'the agony Bill', a vindictive piece of legislation, designed to encroach upon the enjoyment and liberties of the poorer classes. His pamphlet is probably the most powerful reasoned statement of the case against the legislation. He points out that most working people were paid on Saturday evenings, and therefore did their shopping on Sundays. So far as public houses were concerned, in an age of bad housing and overcrowding, Roberts argues that for the average man and woman the public house performed a special function:

> To the poor man, his little ones and their hard-worked mother, the public-house – it may be a pity, but it is so – is for the Sunday afternoon a seat, a room, neighbourly talk, shelter from the rain and cold. The mistake is in supposing that the beerhouse is nothing more than a place for drinking. Drinking is certainly its means of support, but equally certain is it that drinking is not the only taste to which it ministers: to the poor such a house is what a hotel, a reading-room, a carriage, the club, the country seat is to the rich.[12]

A coalition of diverse interests had promoted the Bill. Naturally, the church figured prominently, expressing puritan and sabbatarian views. Public houses competed with the churches for customers. Then, some employers, wanting to curb absenteeism and drunkenness among their labour force, also supported the legislation. Finally, there were the big brewers: they did not open their establishments on Sunday afternoons – rather it was the small beershops – and they begrudged their small rivals getting the extra custom. The Bill's critics regarded all this as a mean, killjoy attitude, expressed by the high and the mighty. While Chartists were active in the agitation and Chartist leaflets were distributed at Hyde Park, there was no evidence it won them widespread lasting support. Of course, many British people were not enamoured by 'their' Parliament; this did not mean they were sufficiently incensed by the range of parliamentary activities to go to the enormous trouble of reviving Chartism.

A flicker of hope that this might happen came when the authorities granted an amnesty to John Frost, leader of the Newport uprising. On his return to England in 1856, he set out upon a speaking tour. By then, he was an old man, white-haired, but remarkably active. His long absence from political debate, coupled to his lack of knowledge of current developments in Britain, made him a not particularly impressive speaker. One person, hearing him for the first time, was disappointed because Frost 'seemed to lack the dignity and mental force that might be expected from a man who has led a great movement.'[13] Many other listeners were disturbed by his speeches. Frequent references were made to the prevalence among those transported to Australia of sodomy and other homosexual practices, taboo subjects to Victorian audiences. Yet, Frost persisted in mentioning them. 'The authorities in Van Dieman's Land,' he said, 'were indifferent to the commission of this great offence.' He even suggested that this might have been a calculated policy: to have morally degraded prisoners, lacking all self-esteem, made them less likely to revolt. Even so, anybody who did step out of line could expect the severest punishment: 'The knout was made of the hardest whipcord, of an unusual size. The cord was put into salt water till it was saturated; it was then put into the sun to dry; by this process it became like wire, the 81 knots cutting the flesh as if a saw had been used.'[14]

As a recognition of his services to the movement, Chartists decided to set up a testimonial fund for John Frost. They appointed his old friend W. P. Roberts as the treasurer, and Frost stayed with him at Seedley House, Pendleton, while doing the Lancashire part of his speaking tour. He must have spent many happy hours talking to Roberts, reminiscing about old times.

From Frost's speeches, two interesting points emerge. The first is that he made no attempt to resurrect the arguments put forward by the defence counsel at his trial – namely, that the Newport uprising was merely a demonstration that went hideously wrong. By implication, the absence of protestations of innocence meant he accepted the prosecution's basic case. However, Frost did consider that the government might have been guilty of dirty tricks and provocative behaviour. Unbeknown to the three leaders of the Newport uprising, after the trial when they were awaiting their execution, the authorities had been closely monitoring their private conversations. As a result, they had known that the prisoners were discussing a plan to cheat the hangman of his task by committing suicide. In retrospect, Frost thought that the date of execution could well have been deliberately postponed to add to the psychological pressure and lead the three to do themselves what many of the cabinet ministers thought should have been done for them. When they were aboard the vessel which transported them to Australia, Frost had been approached by a man who he believed to be an *agent provocateur* with a plan to take control of the ship and free the 212 prisoners on board. Frost had been suspicious of the plan, which he thought had little prospect of success, but would have given those in charge a pretext for killing them as mutineers. He therefore replied: 'We have made one mistake – do not let us make another.'[15]

In the course of his speeches, Frost made an interesting comparison between the state of Chartism in the thirties and the fifties. Delegates to the 1839 convention were, he argued, a very different breed to those being elected to the forthcoming conference in London. Though not wanting to belittle the talent or intelligence of those attending the earlier gathering, he thought Chartism had been able to benefit from the lessons of experience: 'I believe the men about to be elected will have more knowledge in their little fingers than most delegates of '39 had in their whole bodies. Democracy, then, was a blind influence – now it is a calm, thoughtful, reasoning movement.'[16]

Profound changes, much more significant than those mentioned by Frost, had been taking place over those twenty years. To understand future developments, the transformation of Chartism must first be grasped. It can be illustrated both in terms of person and place. A good example of changing attitudes can be found in Thomas Cooper. In the Potteries riots of 1842, as we have already seen, he had made a fiery speech, indicting the existing system and holding it responsible for mass murder. But eleven years later, a rather different Thomas Cooper addressed a public meeting at Congleton, only a dozen or so miles from the Potteries. He spoke 'in eulogistic terms of old England and its laws. He said it was the land of the free . . . a nation of pleasant smiles and independence.' Not that Cooper was a renegade – he still stood by his Chartist principles. However, he was at pains to point out: 'Our Charter does not propose the abolition of the Monarchy; nor any alteration in the constitution of the House of Peers. Our Charter does not propose the abolition of private property.' He warned his audience that the times when 'we were compelled to show our teeth have gone . . . Since then, our doctrines have been widely spread among the middle classes, and openly expressed by thousands of them.'[17]

A similar move towards moderation can be discerned on Tyneside. On New Year's Day, 1838, the Reverend John Rayner Stephens addressed a massive Chartist rally on Newcastle Town Moor. He, like everybody else there, was incensed by the inhumanity of the new Poor Law, the way it broke up families, segregating husbands from wives in infamous workhouses. After declaring himself to be 'a revolutionist by fire, a revolutionist by blood, to the knife, to the death', he had urged people to arm themselves. Any attempt to implement this bill, passed by Parliament, should encounter all-out resistance: 'Newcastle should be one blaze of fire, with only one way to put it out, and that with the blood of all those who support this abominable measure.' According to T. A. Devyr, Stephens' call to arms had been widely heeded: ironworkers on Tyneside busily manufactured cannons, hand grenades and pikes for the coming struggle.[18]

What a contrast with proceedings precisely twenty years later! The form was the same, the content very different. The few who attended the meeting in 1858 still called themselves Chartists. They still believed in the six points, as Thomas Gregson, who moved the resolution, made abundantly clear. Yet his reasoning had subtly changed: his main argument for the Charter was that, since working people were the most law-abiding section of the community, they should have a say in making the laws. Another speaker claimed that manhood suffrage was necessary for good and cheap government. He said that it cost five times as much to govern Britain as it did America. Working people, accustomed to having to count their pennies, would not be so profligate with the public purse as were the country's rich rulers.

The transformation of attitude and behaviour over those twenty years was highly important. To have conceded the vote in 1838 would have had very different consequences to conceding it in 1858. At the earlier date, the working class, angry and intransigent, would have used their newly-acquired power to upset the political system. The impoverished many would have elected representatives to dispossess the affluent few. In 1858, however, as was subsequently proved when the franchise was extended a few years later, workers could be relied upon to operate within the parameters of the existing system, loyally supporting candidates of the two traditional parties. The extension of the franchise by the 1867 Reform Act only involved minor changes – indeed, Chartist talk about the need to cut wasteful public expenditure might even gladden the hearts of right-wing politicians today.

Intertwined with these changes in working-class political outlook went rapid economic progress. The mid-Victorian boom resulted in higher real incomes for almost every section of the community. The fact that so many had visions of a better tomorrow had tended to blunt the sharp edge of extremism. Meanwhile, the expansion of business opportunities, managerial posts, the professions and labour aristocracy helped to provide the prospect for upward mobility, the type of self-advancement for the individual that, as ex-Chartist Samuel Smiles predicted, would accompany the advancement of Britain as a whole.

Many of those who had graduated through the school of Chartism were peculiarly well-suited to seize some of society's glittering prizes. While Britain's continued progress depended upon a rapid increase in knowledge and skills, the educational system remained inadequate, unable to provide the quantity or quality of labour required. So the gap was often filled by individuals who had acquired knowledge along less orthodox channels. Underlying all its political activity, Chartism had a reverence for the value of education. It believed that ignorance caused manifold social evils. Enlightenment, on the other hand, was the road to emancipation: they liked to quote Francis Bacon's dictum 'knowledge is power'. Holding lecture courses, maintaining reading rooms, publishing journals were the visible signs of their commitment to education, but unwittingly many other activities helped individuals to develop their talents. From learning how to produce leaflets, write accurate reports of meetings or letters to newspapers, many acquired skills that later could be transferred to a variety of occupations. Likewise the organization of meetings and selling of pamphlets gave people experience that could subsequently be applied in business. In the circumstances, therefore, it was hardly surprising that, from a Chartist background, a disproportionate number moved on, gaining wealth and influencing people.[19]

As a consequence, the 1858 Chartist convention – the last held – was a vivid contrast with what the movement had been twenty years earlier. For one thing, it was presided over by Alderman T. Livesey, a good Lancashire radical, who was chief constable of Rochdale, and thought nothing amiss in chairing a Chartist meeting in the town, urging everyone to remain true to the six points, while he held that high office.[20] For another, on the fourth day, a middle-class deputation, which included two MPs, came from the Parliamentary Reform Association and asked for an audience. It wanted to investigate whether sufficient common ground existed for a joint campaign. On the sixth day, a resolution was passed agreeing to hold a conference with middle-class reformers. A committee of thirty – W. P. Roberts was one – had the task of smoothing the path to progress. After the Chartist convention had concluded, *The Weekly Times* observed: 'So far from Ernest Jones and friends seeking to assassinate their opponents, they seek to come to reasonable terms. The Reformers and Chartists shook hands; and the last, grown politically wise in their generation, have determined to act in a practical manner.'[21]

In the more relaxed atmosphere of the 1850s, the pre-conditions for the compromise had gradually ripened. Mutual contact had overcome mutual suspicions. Wanting to increase their own parliamentary influence, the middle-class reformers envisaged an enfranchised working class having a supportive, yet subordinate, role. In return, Chartism hoped to acquire renewed credibility. Over the years, it had lost literally millions of supporters, not because they had reneged on the six points and accepted the post-1832 Reform Bill political situation, but because they thought that Chartism was stranded in a cul-de-sac. From bitter experience, it seemed that neither petitions nor physical force could accomplish the desired aims. Developments in 1858, however, provided fresh hope. As so often happens, early optimism proved to be excessive – an attempt to widen the franchise, made by sympathetic MPs in 1859, failed. Nevertheless the road could be dimly discerned to the 1867 Reform Bill.

As W. P. Roberts and Ernest Jones discovered to their chagrin, this could only be accomplished at a price. Initially, they had hoped Chartism would continue as before. But this would have meant unnecessary duplication, having two organizations basically fighting ostensibly for the same thing – when surely it would make sense to concentrate all efforts on the newly-formed and more influential Political Reform League. Furthermore, to many in the league, particularly its middle-class leaders, the silent passing away of Chartism was an added bonus. Its string of failures and catastrophes, its outbursts of violence, did not harmonize with the positive image of moderation and respectability they wanted to project. They were determined that henceforth the extension of the franchise would be fought for with the middle class in control while the working class acted merely as a junior partner.

Soon Roberts was made painfully aware of the limitations imposed by the new alignment. The result of a parliamentary election at Manchester, where veteran radical bookseller Abel Heywood stood as candidate, showed that there were to be no quick, easily-won gains. With Roberts as his election agent, he just avoided coming last in a four-horse race. The lesson of Manchester, a two-seat constituency, remained obvious: middle-class radicals welcomed working-class support when it meant an accretion to their own electoral strength; they refused to reciprocate, however, by voting for Heywood. Rather than back this well-known champion of workers' rights, they cast their second vote for a Palmerstonian candidate named Turner or an outright conservative called Denman.

Admittedly, the election in early 1859 did not take place at the most auspicious time for Heywood. His election agent had just gained considerable publicity in a legal drama, defending Wigan colliers involved in a violent industrial dispute. Miners had stopped work, claiming a rise of twopence in the shilling. To persuade others to join them, they marched over the Leeds–Liverpool canal, where their way to Ince Hall Coal and Cannel colliery was blocked by a posse of policemen. An all-night battle ensued, in the course of which the police were forced to retreat inside the colliery premises. Only the arrival of 100 troops quelled the riot.[22] As another crowd of strikers approached a sawmill at Standish, just outside Wigan, its owner, Col. Lindsay, MP, gave the order that a volley of shots be fired. Two men were wounded.

Wigan gave the appearance of a besieged town; local magistrates issued a proclamation, forbidding all assemblies and giving the chief constables special powers; shops and stalls stayed boarded up or opened for a very limited period; around the collieries, strikers continued to congregate, waiting to accost anyone who might consider returning to work. A massive crowd stood outside Wigan Moot Hall to await the arrival of W. P. Roberts, who came to defend fourteen miners employed by Pearson and Knowles, summoned for leaving work without notice. He secured an adjournment till a hopefully less emotionally-charged time, but this meant return visits, not only to defend these pitmen but also others charged with more serious offences. For several weeks, the press prominently reported both the battles on the picket-line and in the courtroom.

Notwithstanding unfriendly newspaper comments, Roberts, always the eternal optimist, did not think his association with the strike would in any way prejudice Heywood's electoral prospects. In buoyant mood, the People's Attorney addressed a series of election meetings. He told his audiences they had an opportunity to bring to fruition working-class hopes and aspirations. They should regard John Bright's bill for the extension of the franchise as simply the first instalment.

Abel Heywood himself seemed less confident. Repeatedly, he encountered more affluent Mancunians who had contributed to the funds of Bazley, supposedly his running partner, but refused to support him. In his speeches he sought to allay misgivings. He told his audiences that he was not standing as a Chartist; he strove to make a much wider appeal. But, despite his protestations, in the opinion of many middle-class electors he still remained tainted with unacceptable extremism. Even before polling day, the *Manchester Guardian* editorially commented: 'If we belonged to the Chartist Party, we would be strongly inclined to think Mr Heywood has been shabbily treated by the Lancashire reformers. He has been welcomed like a poor relation and sent away empty handed.' The result was: Bazley 7,545, Turner 7,300, Heywood 5,445, Denman 5,201.[23]

That Roberts had become a political misfit, unable to adjust himself to the new mood of moderation, was clearly shown later in 1859 when he addressed a big meeting in the Manchester Free Trade Hall. He did not disguise the fact, as he told his listeners, that he bemoaned the passing of Chartism:

> He implored them to maintain their integrity to the principles of Universal Suffrage. He thought it had sustained much damage when it departed from its glorious name, The Charter. The Charter was a name known not throughout Manchester, but throughout England and the world. It had been sanctified by the sufferings of the martyrs and the assistance of great and good men, who had given all their energies to its principles. He had yielded to the stream, and gone for a more moderate measure for the purpose of being genteel in his old age, seeing that The Charter was deemed too vulgar; but he implored them

to look to Universal Suffrage as the only thing which would really benefit them.

Roberts then revealed how uneasy he found the new alliance with the middle class. He turned his attention to the current craze of the more affluent section of society – the creation of rifle clubs. Not only did he realize that the weapons, avowedly for sporting purposes, could have political uses, but he envisaged the possibility of armed conflict between the working and middle classes, supposedly allies:

> He did not think the Rifle Movement would divert the attention of thinking people from reform. He thought the only way to meet the middle class movement towards the possession of arms was not to be grumbling at them, but by obtaining arms for themselves (cheers) – and he for one, as his jolliest bit of furniture, meant to have one of the best Enfield rifles he could purchase. Then, he thought that Peterloo would not occur, or, if it did occur, it would have a much more cheerful character (cheers).[24]

His friend Ernest Jones also thought the rifle movement might lead to a second Peterloo. In a short-lived journal he published, named *The Cabinet Newspaper*, he alluded to the 'general arming of the respectable cut-throatry of England' and endorsed Roberts' call with an editorial headed, 'Arm, Arm, Arm or you are lost':

> Drilling is troublesome, buying a rifle or pike expensive – nevertheless, for your material and moral health, for your wives and childrens' sakes, you could do nothing more salutory or commendable. To drill is far more healthy than to stretch your legs under the table of the pot-house parlour; to lay out money is a far better investment than expending it on gin, beer or tobacco.[25]

Both Ernest Jones and W. P. Roberts misread the political situation. Far from entering a period of intense class struggle leading to armed conflict, as greater wealth percolated down through society, it became a time of growing class collaboration, a bridge-building not barricade-building. Moreover, their proposal was impractical. The authorities, much more in control than a few years previously, would not have tolerated its implementation. In mid-Victorian England, the possession of rifles by the middle class was an entirely different proposition to their possession by the working class, just as the British state today would treat with much more concern the owning of large quantities of shot guns by coal-miners than it currently does by farmers.

What W. P. Roberts' speech does reveal is how enduring and firmly held were his fundamental beliefs. At Trowbridge in 1838 he had held up a gun and spoken to his audience in affectionate terms similar to those used at Manchester twenty years later. At Trowbridge he had described it as 'an elegant specimen of physical force workmanship'; now it had become an Enfield rifle, 'his jolliest bit of furniture'. Yet, the passage of time had brought a change. Now he frequently spoke of 'his old age' – although he was only fifty-three – giving it as the grounds for yielding to the stream, adopting a more moderate stance. It is possible that he did not enjoy good health, that the gruelling regime of the past was no longer possible; but there could be another explanation. From its beginning through to its end, Roberts had remained one of Chartism's foremost spokesmen, making sacrifices and identifying with the cause. No other national leader had a personal record of longer duration or greater intensity. But with Chartism's demise, he became politically homeless. In mid-Victorian respectable society, the litmus test of political respectability was to keep W. P. Roberts at arm's length.

14 Back to the Coalfields

By the late 1850s, the feeling was emerging that it would again be feasible to form a national union of miners. In most parts of the country local or area organizations existed; the problem was to unite them. Other groups of workers had shown this could be done. Despite being severely mauled by the 1852 lock-out soon after its formation, the Amalgamated Society of Engineers quickly recovered its strength, and by 1858 had amassed funds of £80,000. Why, if the engineers could succeed, should pitmen not recapture lost glories, building a second Miners' Association?

Two men, more than any others, symbolized the links with the past. One was Martin Jude, the other W. P. Roberts. Almost from the outset in 1842, Jude had been a leader of the Miners' Association, and even after its demise he had tirelessly tried to revive it. He organized conferences and petitions to Parliament, calling for better safety and ventilation. His efforts for the cause over many years, his personal sacrifice of time and money, endeared Martin Jude to pitmen everywhere, keeping his name fresh in their minds.

Similarly, W. P. Roberts had continued to do whatever he could to assist in the dark age, the time when union organization was either weak or non-existent. In particular, the North East had a special affection for him. He loved to return to the scene of his former triumphs. Whenever the opportunity arose, he jumped at a chance to address public meetings or represent pitmen in court. And, in even the most unfavourable circumstances, he still sometimes scored minor victories. For instance, he secured greater security of tenancy for pitmen living in tied cottages. This arose out of a dispute in 1850 at Marley Hill colliery, near Gateshead, where the owners had evicted families without giving notice. Though he won the issue of principle – the right of tenants to be given notice to quit – Roberts failed to gain compensation for those thrown out.[1]

As long as employers went through the proper procedure, they still retained the power to evict. Lord Londonderry did just that during a dispute with 'his' pitmen at Seaham in 1855. One of the families was turned out of their home as one of their young children lay dying. This act of inhumanity aroused great anger, which erupted in a full-scale riot. Again, the Miners' Attorney rushed up from Manchester to defend those charged. A few months earlier, he had been called up by the men of Woodhouse colliery, Crook, where a strike had led to a midnight raid of the men's leaders. Four were arrested, one was cut by a policeman's cutlass while being taken into custody. The authorities denied them the right to legal representation. Immediately Roberts heard about this outrage, he dropped what he was doing and travelled by train, arriving at Crook in the early morning. Besides securing freedom for the four men, he also counselled the pitmen to petition Lord Palmerston, questioning the legality of the procedure of arrest and the denial of the right to legal representation. In County Durham pit communities, the news of the success of the Miners' Attorney spread quickly. The men of South Hetton colliery approached him and he won for them the right to come to the surface once they had finished their allotted tasks.[2]

Once courts had given a ruling on such a question, other coalowners in the district, wanting to avoid similar litigation, would often fall into line. In this fashion, one legal victory could affect an entire coalfield. But occasionally a recalcitrant owner cropped up, prepared to contest lost ground again. In 1858, a Durham coalowner wanted two pitmen and six boys sent to prison because, after finishing a day's work, they insisted on being drawn up from the pit bottom. What was in dispute – what the men thought had already been legally settled – was whether a man could go home after finishing the stipulated amount of work or whether he would be expected to wait at the pit bottom until the shift officially ended. In court, Roberts successfully argued that the pitmen's conduct had been perfectly reasonable: 'rather than stay in a ricketty cage, which had "got stuck", they jumped out of it and went home.' In a letter addressed to the miners of Durham, Northumberland and Yorkshire, a jubilant Miners' Attorney reported: 'Friends, I have just returned to Manchester from a glorious and successful contest with your Durham oppressors at Houghton-le-Spring and, after an arduous fight, I compelled them to bite the dust!'³

Conveniently, the Houghton-le-Spring victory came while moves were afoot to reform the union. To many workers, it gave a tiny glimpse of what could be won once the Miners' Asociation and its legal department had been properly re-established. Towards this end, a mammoth meeting was arranged at Black Fell, one of the highest hills in County Durham, on 18 September, 1858. At this gathering, old and new were well represented on the platform. Alexander MacDonald, the young Scottish miners' leader who was later to figure prominently in trade union affairs for a quarter of a century, journeyed down to address his first demonstration outside Scotland. Naturally, Martin Jude was also there and, as the organizer, he invited Roberts. Not only did the Miners' Attorney readily agree, he appealed to pitmen to remember the good old days. In an open letter, he told them that Martin Jude 'writes – and I believe him – that my presence there will give you courage and this, and in other ways, will aid the cause of the union. Heartily and sincerely, I respond to the invitation – God permitting . . . Come in your thousands as you did 14 years ago.'⁴

A warm reception greeted Roberts when he rose to address the demonstration. He began by reminding them of the historic significance of their meeting place: 'They had met before on that hill; they had triumphed before by the spirit of union – they had made their oppressors bite the dust more than once – and it was in their power to do so again.' Colliers lived and worked under basically the same conditions, shared common interests, and this gave them the identity of interest needed to build a successful trade union. He urged them to support financially the Yorkshire miners, then on strike against a 15 per cent wage reduction. For if the coalowners succeeded in Yorkshire, then Durham and Northumberland would be next on the list. He reminded his audience that a contented slave was a degraded slave, adding that, with a universal spirit of resistance, 'they would scatter oppression to the winds, never to rise again.'⁵

Similar meetings were taking place at roughly the same time in other coalfields. These led to the convening of a national conference at Leeds on 9 November 1858. Delegates attending officially formed – or re-formed – the Miners' Association of the United Kingdom. Its aim was not to regulate wages and hours, having a centralized structure and nationally agreed policy on these matters; rather, less ambitiously, it sought to create a loose organization, consisting of independent local unions that would struggle to secure legislative improvements. The tenth resolution passed agreed to approach W. P. Roberts offering him £800, inclusive of office and other expenses, if he would become the association's legal officer. He agreed, and helped to draw up a petition to Parliament, hopefully to bring pitmen into activity as well as to secure legislative improvements.[6]

The national petition, eventually presented to Parliament in February 1860, pointed out that, whereas the average expectation of life in Britain was 33.4 years, for a collier it was only 27 years. It also stated that the collier was likely to have 67 per cent more time off work through injury or ill health than the average worker. The petition suggested this was primarily caused through inadequate safety and ventilation. Legislators saw the logic behind this argument: to cut down the carnage in the coalfields, to have a fitter labour force, less prone to illness or early demise, was in the interest of the coalowners and community as well as the colliers. The 1860 Mines Act was their response. It represented a significant advance. Besides making provision for more adequate standards of safety and ventilation, it improved mines inspection, thereby providing an informed judgement on how further advances could be made. It also further restricted child labour. But, most important of all, from the standpoint of the development of miners' unions, the act contained a clause permitting pitmen to elect a checkweighman. The underlying reason for this provision was to lessen mutual suspicion and conflict over whether or not a hewer was being paid for all the coal he was entitled to be paid for – by placing the men's representative alongside the master's to supervise the actual weighing operation. Various historians have pointed out that, in providing for checkweighmen, the act unwittingly allowed the miners to elect their full-time (union) representative at each colliery.[7] While this was true, it was equally true to suggest that the coalowners had a deep personal interest in these elections, as well as having subtle ways of influencing the outcome, since it was vital that the checkweighmen who had daily contact with management were moderates, not militants.

The whole evolution of mining trade unionism, the force that in the early 1860s gave such power to Alexander MacDonald, was closely linked to the creation of the post of checkweighman. It fostered unionism, albeit of a conciliatory, moderate kind. Until its

advent, progress with organization remained much slower. This may
be seen by considering again what happened in the North East. The
first meeting on Black Fell, addressed by Roberts, MacDonald and
others, was in September 1858. Only 11,000 Durham pitmen
attended; virtually none came from Northumberland. While it was
agreed to hold regular meetings at local level, very few areas actually
implemented this decision. The defeat of the Yorkshire colliers
reinforced the prevailing feeling of apathy and demoralization. On 11
March 1859, a second meeting was held on Black Fell in an attempt
to rouse the colliers. Ostensibly called to honour W. P. Roberts –
many speakers, including Alexander MacDonald, praised him for the
work he had done for pitmen over the years – it also had a second
function: to strengthen the precarious organization created on the
previous occasion.[8] Roberts referred to the woefully inadequate
nature of existing mining legislation. He showed how other groups of
workers enjoyed much better legal safeguards. Finally, he mentioned
that the union was trying to improve the position, by its campaign for
better safety and ventilation as well as its petition to Parliament, and
concluded by emphasizing that it was in their own interest to join the
union, giving added strength to the struggle for improvement.

However sound Roberts' line of argument, it had to be considered
against the background of the existing relationship of forces. At that
time, most pitmen possessed an immense fear of the coalowners, of
their ability to hold them in servitude. This was not appreciably
lessened by Roberts' rhetoric. He had told the second Black Fell
meeting that 'it seemed he was, even in old age, to be a terror to evil-
doers and a means of holding working men together.' He went on to
warn coalowners 'that the existence of this power gave him the
determination to use it, and he would never feel satisfied until he had
succeeded with the aid of those he addressed today.'[9] But every day
pitmen came across the realities of power. All too well they knew
that, whatever threats Roberts might make to the coalowners, much
more powerful were the threats coalowners made to any collier found
involving himself in union activity. In the distant future when the
union had everyone organized, then it might be a terror to evil-doing
coalowners. In the meantime, it was the evil-doing coalowners who
possessed the rod for use on the pitmen's backs. Indicative of this
fear is what happened at Bishop Auckland, only a few miles from
Black Fell, three months after the demonstration there. A union
meeting could not take place because there was no chairman. Four

individuals were approached, but none accepted. 'They knew if they dared say one word on their own behalf, they would in all probability get a ticket to leave their employment, and might travel from colliery to colliery, county to county, and get no work. Such is the power of the Coal Kings of the North of England.'[10]

The same seems to have been true elsewhere. A national conference, held at Ashton-under-Lyme, 2–7 May 1859, heard reports of the meagre progress being made. The proceedings were given added urgency because the existing Mines Act came to an end in 1860. If they wanted to influence the new legislation, it had to be done quickly. Conference issued an appeal for funds, revised the petition to encompass the gamut of pitmen's demands, and agreed to campaign for them with reinforced vigour. It was in the course of these discussions that Alexander MacDonald sprang into national prominence. His flair for influencing people and quietly persuading politicians of the need for improved legislation paid off in the much improved 1860 Mines Act. Section 29 of the act, permitting the appointment of checkweighmen, had great consequence for the direction in which trade unionism in the coal industry henceforth developed. Slowly, a checkweighman started to appear at each colliery, an individual who was not paid by – and therefore not beholden to – the coalowner. Admittedly, as their paramount concern was supervising the weighing of the coal and they were therefore paid by the hewers on the coalface, the aristocrats of labour, they often did not fully express the frustrations of the less well paid. Even so, the advent of checkweighmen made less likely the kind of mass intimidation which had occurred at Bishop Auckland.[11]

With both sides of the coal industry familiarizing themselves with the new legislation, there was little work for W. P. Roberts to do. Although he had the title of head of the legal department, he does not appear to have received the salary to accompany it, since the union's finances were too meagre. He continued, as before, to take commissions from other working-class organizations. In the building industry, a ferocious battle was taking place over 'the document', a declaration which employers expected all workers to sign, renouncing union membership. Roberts represented the men on a number of occasions. For example, he defended a man named Perham, accused of intimidating a blackleg. The prosecution admitted there had been no violence or insulting language; he had merely warned the strikebreaker: 'If you go to work, you will be called black.' Yet, he was still found guilty, and Roberts lost the appeal. Another menacing extension of the definition of 'intimidation' came after the dispute had ended. A London builder, Auley, found only two of his 100-strong labour force were prepared to become blacklegs. On the resumption of work, the trade unionists demanded that the two strike-breakers be sacked. In doing so, the court held the men had acted illegally.[12]

An equally alarming case occurred at Staindrop in North Yorkshire. An employer there inveigled his workers into a public house, supposedly to pay back wages. On entry, however, the men discovered a squad of policemen waiting. They were arrested at once, then marched through the town in handcuffs, consigned to a damp cell, without food or beds; and arraigned before a single magistrate under the Master and Servant Act, at a special hearing, at seven o'clock the following morning. Their pleas for postponement and the right for legal representation were turned down. All of them were fined. When they refused to pay, the magistrate authorized the employer to deduct it from the wages they were owed. Later W. P. Roberts sought unsuccessfuly to obtain redress. First, he sued the employer for the docked wages. Then he tried to get a criminal prosecution of the magistrate. When this failed, he tried in vain to get the conviction quashed. Aggrieved and frustrated, the People's Attorney described the whole affair as 'a series of the grossest outrages that ever occurred in a civilised country.'[13]

Once the troubles in the building industry had died down, and the miners remained quiescent, Roberts thought it would be a good time to take a well-earned holiday. Since his wife always yearned for foreign travel, he decided to accomplish a cherished ambition of his – to make a pilgrimage to the Holy Land. Always a devout Christian, it was clear from the alacrity with which he gave talks to church audiences on his return how much he treasured his memories of visiting biblical places.[14] En route they journeyed at a leisurely pace, taking time off to view the splendours of Italy. It seems probable, though no documentary evidence exists, that on some occasion he had helped the Italian nationalist leader, Mazzini, with a legal matter while he was exiled in Britain. The Public Records Office contains files revealing that the authorities were concerned about 'the revolutionary designs of M. Mazzini' and close surveillance was maintained on him because it was believed he was in Britain with the intention of purchasing arms and ammunition to resume the revolution back home.[15] Whether it related to this or not, one thing is clear – the two men were close personal friends. Mazzini gave Roberts a handwritten note to use as he deemed fit. This appealed to his fellow countrymen to give his esteemed friend any assistance he required as he travelled through Italy. The outward journey seems to have been enjoyable; only on the return did troubles arise. Roberts was taken severely ill in Constantinople and, although it is not known what he was suffering from, it is certain that for a while there were fears for his life.[16]

During his absence, the national development of the miners' union took a different direction. Though the earlier inaugural meeting at Leeds in November 1858 was never disowned, tacitly a relaunch was decided upon, also to be held in Leeds, in November 1863. By then, thanks to his contacts, MacDonald had emerged as the key person. Significantly, he sought to model the conference upon the same lines as the proceedings of the National Association for the Promotion of Social Science, a completely non-working-class organization. As if to enhance the aura of respectability, he decided to exclude W. P. Roberts from it entirely.

To understand why this happened, it must be appreciated that two schools of thought were beginning to emerge. First, there were those who looked back nostalgically to the Miners' Association of the 1840s, stressed the need for continuity and saw its demise as arising from inadequate industrial muscle. In essence, these people wanted a replay of the 1840s, hopefully with a happier outcome. The second believed it vital to learn the lessons of the 1840s, not to have the union obliterated in an all-out war with the coalowners. Class collaboration harmonized with the generally prevailing view. Amid the growing prosperity and social peace, political extremism had virtually vanished. A new breed of employers, ready to reach an amicable understanding with their workers, created a challenge trade unions could not shirk.

If W. P. Roberts was the outstanding representative of the first school, then Alexander MacDonald was of the second. The young Scot's emergence as a figure of national importance caused a flutter of excitement. Never before had a working miner written articles containing phrases like 'post-prandial effusions', corrected a distinguished mining commissioner's errors of logic, or known Latin and Greek. His life epitomized the Victorian values of moderation, sobriety and, above all, hard work. From a humble colliery community, by his own efforts he gained a place at Glasgow University, where he qualified as a schoolmaster. But soon he returned to his roots, helping to build the colliers' union. Although in the initial phase some employers tried to destroy the organization, subsequently he strove to establish an understanding with them. This process, the gradual erosion of mutual suspicion, was aided by his ability to see the other person's viewpoint: 'the bulk of the capitalists are right at heart and at least have the welfare of the workers in view.' Alexander MacDonald, the self-made man, became a shareholder in several collieries and a close personal friend of Lord Elcho, Scotland's biggest coalowner.[17] The character of the coal industry in mid-Victorian Britain helped to foster MacDonald's amicable approach to class relations. Sinking shafts, developing new coal-faces, installing haulage and proper ventilation, all tied up large amounts of capital. Not surprisingly, therefore, the coalowners were among the first to avail themselves of the provisions of the Limited Liability Acts (1885–7) to raise the requisite money. Moreover, they remained anxious, unless the price was too high, to maintain uninterrupted production, thereby maximizing their returns. A pitmen's representative like MacDonald helped to reassure them: loyal service would be rewarded with moderate wage increases granted.

Obviously, Roberts was an anathema to MacDonald. The wild rhetoric, the advocacy of strikes, the gladiatorial court battles, where rejoicing followed coalowners 'biting the dust' – to a Scottish moderate, all these were signs of a primitive bygone age. The Miners' Attorney-General, moreover, constituted both a personal and organizational threat. Whenever he felt strongly on an issue, Roberts had no compunction about meddling in internal union affairs, advocating actions that might have disastrous consequences. Even worse, if thwarted by union leaders, he was liable to turn to the rank and file, inciting them to disaffection. In eliminating Roberts from union business, or at least taming him, MacDonald faced a dilemma – his powers were limited. Local coalfield unions had virtual autonomy; they could engage whatever lawyer they chose. All MacDonald could do was to try and persuade.

The indications are that MacDonald began to move against Roberts during the Methley riot in September 1863, and grew more pressing from then onwards. At Whitwood and Methley collieries in

South Yorkshire, the masters decided to try and break a strike by introducing blacklegs from Derbyshire. Their arrival aroused widespread anger among the 1,400 men and 500 boys on strike, who feared they would lose permanently both their employment and their homes.[18] Anger turned into violence. In court, subsequently, the prosecution claimed that, once the new pitmen had been seen in Methley, a mob marched up and down the village, throwing stones. Doors were broken, window frames knocked out, even cottages demolished. For the defendants, Roberts denounced the masters: they had 'the greed which only looks on the bones and sinews of the working class as a means of their advancement'.[19] He went on to accuse the coalowners of conduct liable to cause a breach of the peace. Provocatively, they had reduced pay, brought in strike-breakers from Ilkeston under false pretences, and described an incident where six children threw stones as if it were a major riot. They wanted this minor disturbance designated as a riot since this would entitle them to have their 'rotten cottages' rebuilt at public expense. Despite Roberts' defence, the magistrates still committed the prisoners to the next York assizes.

Before this happened, W. P. Roberts found himself involved in one of the biggest cases of his career. At the small South Wales village of Blaina, employees of Messrs Levick and Simpson felt deeply aggrieved. They claimed they were being robbed, paid only for a ton of coal when they hewed between 30 and 35 cwts. A deputation visited the manager and asked for the right to appoint a checkweighman, as they were entitled to do under the 1860 Mines Act. The manager replied he could not give them an answer. As a protest against being denied their legal rights, they decided to have a one-day strike. This led to arrests and sackings. In the middle of the night, pitmen were dragged from their beds, handcuffed and taken, through the snow, the nine miles to Tredegar. Under the Master and Servant Act, they were then charged with breach of contract.

The South Wales local union approached the Miners' Attorney to conduct the defence. The case opened at the Oddfellows' Hall, Tredegar, on 28 January 1864, with the Reverend Edmund Leigh as presiding magistrate. A packed public gallery signalled the intense local interest. In reply to the breach of contract charge, Roberts argued, first, that there was no contract; second, if there were a contract, then by law wages should have been paid in coin of the realm; and, third, that in the circumstances the pitmen's conduct was completely justified. Placing great emphasis on the owners' violation of the Truck Act and Mines Regulation Act (1860), he asserted: 'I say, as a matter of law, that where the law gives protection to a contract, and one party refuses to grant that protection, the contract is broken.' The presiding magistrate refused to accept the submission, ruling that the case simply related to the Master and Servant Act; whether any other laws had been broken was irrelevant to the matter in hand. However, Roberts remained undaunted. Time and again, much to the annoyance of the magistrate, he disregarded this ruling and returned to the issue of truck.

From the outset, Roberts realized he was in a hostile court. The presiding magistrate was a friend and neighbour of the coalowners; both Levicks, father and son, were also magistrates. In some respects proceedings at Tredegar resembled those at Thornley, two decades before. Angry scenes were common and on several occasions the magistrate accused Roberts of insulting the bench. Once he adjourned the case for, he said, self-protection. But the Miners' Attorney, undeterred, still continued to denounce the coalowners, describe the men's sufferings and elicit the maximum public sympathy. 'The present struggle,' he told the court, 'was for the existence and continuation of that mighty domestic institution, the truck system. They called slavery in America "the domestic institution", and he heard the truck system had a similar title in South Wales.'

As at Thornley, Roberts waged a war of attrition, bringing large numbers of witnesses to testify. One of these, an orphan girl named Janet (or Jeanett) James, caused a sensation. She described how she had worked for two years, pushing coal-tubs around the pit-brow, without being paid a penny:

> My wages have been 5s. 6d. and 6s. a week. During the whole time, I did not receive any money. I never received a farthing in money, but all in goods at the shop. The whole of my wages were swallowed up in shop bills for bread and tea, on which I lived.[20]

The truck shop held her responsible for her dead father's debts. Since she never received any money, she had no prospect of every repaying them. In perpetuity, the truck system kept her in bondage, tied to the same masters.

The proceedings were starting to gain nationwide publicity, damaging to the reputation of the local business community. The presiding magistrate, therefore, resolved to adjourn the case till 27 January 1864, presumably, hoping that the interval would act as a cooling-off period, perhaps providing the basis for an out-of-court settlement. But he had not reckoned with Roberts.

The Miners' Attorney used the adjournment to whip up further public feelings of anger and outrage. He wrote an open letter to the Lord Chancellor. It warned His Lordship of the 'probability of a serious and irreparable injustice being committed at the petty sessions at Tredegar unless your authority can be used to prevent it'. The accused faced the prospect of three months imprisonment, with no right of appeal. Yet, the magistrate had prevented a fair trial from taking place, putting many obstacles in the way of the defence: 'The magistrate stopped very many of my questions; he told witnesses they were not bound to answer them; he desired the witnesses not to answer them.' Frederick Levick, jun., had refused to answer any of the questions about the company stores, slaughterhouse and bakery. In conclusion, the open letter explained that the wealthy were guilty of hiding much of their own law-breaking behind their own legal positions: 'Many of the large iron and coalmasters in South Wales are magistrates; and that a large proportion of these magistrates keep truck shops is a matter of common notoriety.'

These activities bore fruit. On 29 January 1864, a thousand people crowded into the Tredegar Temperance Hall at the end of the trial, to hear the verdict. The magistrate found the accused guilty. He sentenced them to imprisonment for one day. As they had already been incarcerated for longer than that, it meant their immediate release. In triumph, they returned to Blaina. W. P. Roberts was the hero of the hour. Amid the jubilation, he stood up and told them that now was the time to press home their advantage – to go on the offensive. He advised them to sue Levick and Simpson for wrongful dismissal and for Janet James's two years unpaid wages: not to do so would be 'the grossest folly you could possibly commit. The combination of circumstances in the present truck case is most favourable to your attack.'

Widespread indignation about the treatment of the orphan girl of Blaina, from many quarters of society, gave the campaign added momentum. Even the government felt compelled to respond to the pressure. The Lord Chancellor replied to Roberts, asking him to list the South Wales coalowners who were both magistrates and broke the Truck Act. While nothing was done with the information it did act as a stimulus, prodding the government into setting up a Select Committee on the Master and Servant Act a couple of years later. It did, moreover, highlight the generally unsatisfactory state of affairs. To prosecute offending employers for truck violations was, as the South Staffordshire Anti-Truck Association pointed out, often too expensive and too dangerous for most workingmen to contemplate. The average case cost £80 in legal expenses. On top of this, there would be the cost of paying witnesses as well as sustaining the complainant, who also certainly would have been victimized by his employer.[21]

The national outcry caused by the Blaina revelations, therefore, created a rare and unusually favourable situation for turning to law to give an offending employer a good thrashing. People generally in South Wales endorsed this course of action with alacrity. They backed Roberts' proposal that a fund be opened. Concerts were held to raise money, as well as street and public house collections. The Miners' Attorney made his personal contribution. While there would be barrister's costs, court fees, expenses of journeys and witnesses, he said he would waive his own expenses: 'As to myself, I require nothing. My reward will be the pleasure of serving you.'[22] Going still further, he published at his own expense 10,000 copies of a transcript of the Blaina trial to assist the agitation. In a preface, he explained they were playing for high stakes. He estimated Levick and Simpson's truck shop had 2,500 'customers', giving the company a 9 per cent profit on wages – the equivalent of £10,000 a year.

Meanwhile, Alexander MacDonald and other members of the national council of the Miners' Association watched developments in South Wales with mounting anguish. From its formation, the national council had repudiated strikes. At its first meeting, on 9 December 1863, it had issued a statement denouncing all forms of industrial action. Yet, only a few weeks later, miners at Levick and Simpson were not only on strike but unofficial strike. To make matters worse, instead of apologizing for their bad behaviour, they had continued to display a lack of caution and were widening the conflict.

On behalf of the national council, secretary Richard Mitchell wrote to D. R. Thomas, secretary of the South Wales union, after the court case had begun, advising the union to terminate proceedings: 'The case ought never to have been defended; it was one of those cases that cannot be defended successfully because there is no defence. Two wrongs do not make a right; and if A violates the Truck Act, B is not justified in trampling the Master & Servants Act under his feet.'[23] When it became clear that the national council advice was not being heeded, Mitchell again wrote to D. R. Thomas: 'You are not, in my opinion, being well advised in those matters at present.' Another national councillor, Thomas Stephenson, tried to reinforce this judgement by sending Thomas a second letter which ended: 'Mr Roberts will do you no good.'[24]

At first, Roberts did not appreciate the significance of the moves being taken against him; he thought there had simply been a misunderstanding. Both the national council and he shared the same objective, the elimination of truck. In a letter to the South Wales miners, written on 24 February 1864, he wrote: 'Now I do not wish to be thrown into a collision or antagonism with the National Council (though I think they cast an implied censure they might, in justice and honesty, have given me an opportunity of explaining what might be doubtful or difficult).'[25] However, it soon became obvious that there was no lack of understanding – the members of the national council understood only too well Roberts' essentially belligerent approach – but a fundamental disagreement over tactics. They envisaged the law functioning primarily as a means of resolving industrial conflict; he saw it as a weapon that might, at times, foster industrial conflict when that was in the interest of rank-and-file miners.

Feeling so strongly on the issue, the national council decided to encourage local unions to dispense with Roberts' services. Its first success came in Yorkshire, where another lawyer was engaged for the latter stages of the Whitwood–Methley riot case. Naturally, Roberts felt deeply hurt, especially as he had personally stood bail for some of the accused. In an open letter to the Yorkshire miners, he described his sacking as 'a foul wrong', adding 'I tried hard for the honour of defending you.'[26] All this happened amid a spate of persistent rumours: Roberts had retired, Roberts was ill, Roberts had been charging exorbitant fees. After a short while, Roberts discovered that all this misinformation had been concocted by Richard Mitchell, secretary of the national council, abetted by its president, Alexander MacDonald.

In an attempt to counter these lies, Roberts wrote a number of open letters. Initially, he thought that Mitchell – 'my bitter enemy' – was the source of the trouble; only later did he realize that it had been masterminded by MacDonald. On the point at issue, he remained content to allow ordinary miners to decide. Speaking of Mitchell, he wrote: 'I can only say, as before, I have no intention of contending against him. If he faithfully represents you, keep him; if not, turn him out.'[27] In letters to colliers in Durham, Northumberland and Yorkshire, he recounted his past work on their behalf, his triumphs and his eagerness to continue. But the poignancy of his own personal position, if left bereft of union work, came through: he said he had become 'known as the poor man's friend . . . to my severe pecuniary loss'. As a consequence, he had 'been recognised as the rich man's enemy'. It meant that, whereas other lawyers do not care which side they represent, 'I have no such choice.'[28]

All this was taking place against the backcloth of Blaina. As was his custom, Roberts synchronized his action in court with agitation outside. He issued an appeal to all British workers, calling upon them to launch a campaign against the truck system. To this, he added a warning for the national council: 'Let these gentlemen then be quick or I will jog them again. Public opinion is urging them on. Let them answer the lash, or somebody will take the business out of their hands.' A thinly-veiled appeal to rank-and-file revolt against the moderate leadership, it drew the reaction from Alexander Mac-Donald that Roberts was disregarding union conference decisions, a fact that was undoubtedly true. When pressure stirred them into action, the national council carefully saw that the campaign against the Master and Servant Act used the services of John Strachan, a Scottish lawyer, not W. P. Roberts.[29]

Undoubtedly, MacDonald and his comrades were incensed by what had happened at the initial hearing at Blaina magistrates' court. They would dearly have liked to prevent more ugly courtroom scenes and therefore brought pressure to bear on the South Wales union to dispense with Roberts' services. Ultimately, this was agreed, but it did not solve the immediate problem. Obviously, having never received a wage, Janet James had never been in a position to join a trade union and pay its subscription. In their entirety, her legal costs were being covered by public donations, largely from people who had confidence in the personal abilities of the Miners' Attorney. The South Wales union therefore had no control over what happened. Even had it wished to, the union would have been powerless to dampen popular enthusiasm, or stop people with collecting boxes going around and saying things like: 'We have a noble commander in Mr Roberts and he is not afraid to use the Armstrong gun if we will only find the powder. Come, then, brothers, if you will be true now, the truck system will flourish no more.'[30] People with such an attitude would not be fobbed off with minor concessions, with the kind of compromises sought by MacDonald and the national council. Rather, they wanted a complete and utter victory over Levick and Simpson.

Remarkably, that was what they got. At the Monmouth assizes, on 28 March 1864, Roberts secured two years back pay for Janet James. Levick and Simpson also had to pay the £200 to £300 legal costs. On certain points the verdict was ambiguous and Roberts threatened to take the case to the Queen's Bench. To avoid further unpleasant proceedings and publicity, the employers settled out of court, making what was tantamount to a complete surrender. Workers had the right, they conceded, to buy goods wheresoever they chose; there would be no victimization; and three-quarters of wages would be paid weekly. When the news reached South Wales, celebrations began and continued well into the night. Tar barrels and bonfires were lit outside the homes of prominent activists. People joyously cried: 'We have killed the monster truck.'

W. P. Roberts did not try to conceal his happiness about the outcome. He declared, 'Truck was the Sebastopol against which I had from the first decided to direct by artillery.' He went on to warn the magistrate, the Reverend Edmund Leigh – he persisted in calling him highly 'irrelevant Edmund' – that he would return to South Wales with his cannon at the first sign of renewed trouble. And as for Janet James, the heroine of Blaina, he had nothing but praise for the way she had withstood her court ordeal: 'She was the stick with which I gave her former master a sound thrashing'. Roberts knew that employers in South Wales would never forgive her for her courage; they would hunt her wherever she went. Consequently, he advised her to use her small fortune to emigrate and start a new life in Australia. Lastly, turning to the colliers of South Wales, he hoped the significance of the victory had not been lost on them. From now onwards, the future lay in their hands. 'It has been my privilege,' Roberts concluded, 'to teach you how to fight.'

That was precisely what MacDonald and the other members of the national council did not want. They did not want cannons and the battles of Sebastopol; rather they envisaged using the law as a means of securing class reconciliation. A month later, on 30 April 1864, they demonstrated the type of legal procedure which they desired, with give and take by both sides. Having prevailed upon the secretary of the South Wales union to engage a solicitor named Barrett rather than Roberts, the case of the six Blaina pitmen, the original cause of the dispute, came to court. An amicable settlement was reached. Levick and Simpson agreed to reinstate the six men and pay all the legal costs (but no compensation), while the men agreed to withdraw all other charges.

When the national miners' union held its half-yearly conference, at Leeds from 9–13 May 1864, it became obvious how deeply the South Wales case had divided the membership. Many criticized the national council, believing it should have backed Roberts. Replying to the charges, Alexander MacDonald claimed the national council had merely implemented conference decisions; for this opposition to unofficial industrial action, it had been subjected to an unparalleled barrage of lies and vilification. The climax of his highly emotional speech came when MacDonald, on behalf of himself and the rest of the leadership, offered to resign *en bloc*. Whereupon delegates immediately re-elected them all. That issue settled, the conference turned to the question of the union's legal adviser. Amid loud cheering, a resolution to appoint W. P. Roberts was defeated by thirty-nine votes to two.[31]

Afterwards, the pro-Roberts faction claimed the conference had been rigged. Non-miners had been admitted as delegates while bona fide miners had been excluded. Richard Fynes, a prominent North-East pitman, even claimed that those largely responsible for the union's formation had been debarred.[32] As news of the conference spread, so did the anger. Some of the opposition stopped paying subscriptions; others resolved to be better organized for the next half-yearly conference.

Buried beneath the ferocious debate lay the issue of strategy. Conditions had changed since the 1840s, when coalowners like Lord Londonderry had single-mindedly sought to destroy trade unions and punish the activists. In the more relaxed tolerance of the 1860s, co-existence became feasible. Wanting to use the opportunities thereby opened, MacDonald believed it was vital to preserve industrial peace, gaining improvements by parliamentary means. But to accomplish this, an image of moderation and respectability was essential. Friends in high places, too, had to be sedulously cultivated. From MacDonald's standpoint, it did not matter whether a person had ever been besmirched with coal-dust; the vital thing was that he could state a case in a cogent, lucid manner. Consequently, MacDonald was assisted on the national council by Stephenson (a chemist) and Miller (a doctor).

John Holmes, treasurer of the Miners' National Association, was the most powerful of MacDonald's assistants. The explanation, at least in part, for his key role lies in his wealth. He was in the fortunate position of having no need to work. Whatever time he chose could be spent supporting the national council. In 1865, Holmes took a visitor on a tour of inspection, showing him 'an experiment of my own to furnish improved dwellings for miners' and boasting of 'the 500 volumes in the library provided by me'.[33] The rest of his time and energy was largely devoted to collecting books, paintings and pre-historic objects. Towards the end of his life, he sold these to Leeds Corporation at less than their market value, conditional on their being put on public display.

Assisted by such respectable and wealthy individuals as Holmes and the other members of the national council, MacDonald was able to establish a London committee. It, also, was comprised of wealthy and influential non-miners, including the Marquis of Townsend, Lord Raynham and General Zaba. The London committee's task was to smooth out any difficulties that might arise in the legislative process when the national council's proposals had been submitted to Parliament.

Both to the coalowners and the cabinet, MacDonald and his supporters had a certain beguiling charm. They not only avowed their deep detestation of all strikes, they even put their words into deeds, acting as almost a private security firm, trying to deal with disorders whenever they broke out. In the report of the National Association for Social Science (1860), John Holmes was largely credited with bringing the West Yorkshire coal dispute to an end. What coalowner could fail to be impressed by such a gentleman? He openly stated that the best union leaders were those who were 'the last to strike and the first to concede'. Still more vital, he was the main organizer of the 1863 Leeds conference, which did just what the masters had wanted the miners to do for years – it excluded W. P. Roberts.[34]

Naturally, traditionalists were outraged by the new brand of trade unionism. They believed a miners' union should be run by miners, not by middle-class people, friendly to the coalowners. The standard of revolt against the MacDonald leadership was raised in the coalfields. A circular advised pitmen: 'Select from among yourselves for the offices that are to be filled.' It accused 'the cursed triumvirate – MacDonald, Holmes and Miller – of 'squandering your money and laughing at your credulity – today amusing you with a grand petition, tomorrow a Royal Commission, the next with an account of interviews with My Lord This and Mr Esquire the Other.' And their sacking of W. P. Roberts was easily explained: 'They wanted a lawyer appointed by themselves – whom they may terrify and cajole, whom they can dismiss as they please, rather than he should gain the hearts of the colliers – of the real men, the workers in the pit.'[35]

Matters came to a head at the half-yearly meeting, which began at Manchester on 8 November 1864. From the outset, there was trouble. *The Beehive* reported:

> The meeting, having opened by singing and prayer, a very long discussion ensued, mingled with a great deal of personality, as to the right of Mr MacDonald to preside over the meeting. Several delegates appeared determined to summarily eject the President and Council, without even before receiving their report or hearing what they had to say in defence about the charges.[36]

Stephenson opposed the resolution to remove MacDonald from the chair. He argued that business could only commence once delegates' credentials had been checked. A Durham delegate smartly made the riposte that that was precisely why MacDonald should not be in the chair – his credentials were not in order!

In fact, MacDonald was on extremely shaky ground. He came as a representative of the Scottish miners, yet only one lodge in the whole of Scotland – the Hope Lodge of Linlithgow – had up till then contributed to union funds. In fact, the first monthly payment of the Scottish miners was paid five months later, in March 1865. It amounted to £12 5s 6d, being a penny for 2946 members. Alexander MacDonald's biographer, Dr Gordon M. Wilson, has criticized me earlier for making this point, but it appears quite incontrovertible to me that for seventeen months MacDonald held the post of president while the body he was supposed to represent was not affiliated. Indeed, he later conceded as much. Writing in *The Beehive*, of 18 March 1865, MacDonald stated: 'The fact is at once admitted, but for this reason – the Scottish miners at one time half believed in a hungry lawyer, who feasted upon the very vitals of the poor miners for many years. They have had almost nothing to do with the Miners' National; they feared a repetition of the same story.'[37]

Despite his dubious personal position, MacDonald continued to chair the Manchester conference. Similar disputes arose over Holmes and other national council members. The most fiercely contested credentials were those of Dr Miller. South Staffordshire delegates, insulted by Miller's criticisms of their recent strike, made it abundantly clear that he did not represent them. Whereupon North Staffordshire delegates threatened to walk out if he were added to their number. Eventually, MacDonald achieved a compromise: Dr Miller would be allowed to stay, although in what capacity, delegate or visitor, remained obscure.

Apparently, MacDonald used delaying tactics, leaving the crucial question of the election of officers until the fourth day. By then, the situation had become more favourable for him. Some of the opposition had walked out in disgust. They were particularly incensed by the decision to disassociate the union from W. P. Roberts' legal work in South Wales and by MacDonald's remarks: 'Let us hear no more of Janet James, the Blaina truck case,' he told conference. 'The very name Blaina stinks in the mind of every collier in England.' As the opposition was weakened by defections, MacDonald continued to augment his support. It seems he wrote to the Cleveland miners, unrepresented at the conference, asking them to authorize him to appoint a delegate on their behalf. When it became clear he had employed this subterfuge to gain voting rights for Dr Miller, there was uproar. *The Beehive* reported that 'almost half the delegates rose to their feet arguing that Dr Miller, not being a practical miner, had no right to represent the Cleveland district . . . One or two of the same party also endeavoured to close the conference by singing a hymn.' Order, however, was temporarily restored.

John Normansell, a close colleague of MacDonald, was appointed chairman during the election of officers. Election of the president came first. The two proposed were MacDonald and Kimberley, of

South Staffordshire. The result was nineteen votes each, whereupon Normansell gave his casting vote for MacDonald:

> This was the signal for a great uproar, accompanied by bellicose demonstrations, such as shaking fists by some of the more excited, and it was suggested that the police should be called in, but not carried out. A number of delegates at once left the room, and it was not until after a considerable period had elapsed that order was restored. It subsequently transpired that a number of delegates had instructions from their districts to secede from the conference if Mr MacDonald was re-elected.[38]

All the anti-MacDonald faction then went to the Swan Inn, Shudehill, Manchester, where they formed a breakaway union. Two days later, when the constitution and policy had been agreed, they were invited to W. P. Roberts' residence, Seedley House, for a celebratory meal.

After the split, quarrelling continued unabated. MacDonald prevented the £90 collected by the London Trades Council from reaching the families of striking pitmen in South Staffordshire. Challenged about his action, MacDonald replied that he feared it would all have been pocketed by 'a greedy Manchester lawyer'. Instead of giving the '3,600 men, women and children sixpenny worth of bread and soup', the money would have found its way to Roberts, that 'legal cormorant'. These attacks were part of a barrage of accusations. The MacDonald camp claimed that he had deliberately promoted industrial strife in order to secure lucrative legal work. From the Blaina case alone, it was alleged, he had made £200.[39]

In South Staffordshire and elsewhere, the newly-formed union – called the Practical Miners – was completely smashed. It could not withstand the combined might of the coalowners and the national association. Through his links with the junta, a group of rising union leaders, MacDonald was able to influence much of the labour movement against the new organization. Many ordinary trade unionists, heeding the advice of their leaders, were reluctant to show solidarity with workers branded as militants. The campaign against the Practical Miners, in the press as well as on the platform, also served to isolate the Miners' Attorney. Now he had virtually no legal work in the coalfields.

W. P. Roberts' position was the quintessence of personal tragedy. Over the years he had learnt to shrug off, even treat with contempt, the lies and slanders that came from the coalowners. But now they came from an entirely unexpected quarter – the trade unions, which he had dedicated his life to defending. Frail and in failing health, he could no longer trade blow for blow as he had done in the internal union disputes of the 1840s. Instead, Lear-like, he had to endure base ingratitude, a position made more poignant because he was motivated not by a desire for pecuniary gain but for popular acclaim:

> He was a man who loved to be thought well of by his fellow men, but how much in hard cash did he put into his pocket over the transactions? Will any of his detractors say he was anything like adequately paid for his labours by his miserable fees which he charged? In his latter days when he was getting old and feeble, but still anxious to serve miners, instead of giving him an opportunity of doing so, they ungraciously turned their backs upon him and added to the injury they had done with an unmerited insult. Well might Mr Roberts, adopting the lines of Amiens, exclaim:
> > 'Blow, blow, thou wintry wind,
> > Thou art not so unkind
> > As man's ingratitude'.[40]

Nothing could conceal that Roberts had suffered a grievous blow, a completely unexpected blow, delivered from persons for whom he had a great affection. Yet, the Miners' Attorney was made of sterner stuff. During his entire lifetime, his conduct had been determined by what he regarded as being morally right. So he shrugged off this setback and continued operating.

15 The Manchester Martyrs

One of the most famous cases with which W. P. Roberts became involved was the Manchester Martyrs in 1867. This arose out of the murder of Police Sergeant Charles Brett, who was one of a group of members of the Manchester constabulary transporting Irish nationalist prisoners to Belle Vue gaol. When the police van, proceeding along Hyde Road, reached the railway viaduct, a group of Irishmen suddenly attacked it. They hit it with stones, a hammer and a hatchet, but all in vain; they could not get into the van. Then a man fired a revolver to break the Black Maria's lock and they succeeded in liberating the two Fenian prisoners, Kelly and Deasy, detained inside. In the process they had shot Sergeant Brett, who had his eye close to the keyhole. Whereupon the police, angry and panicky, started arresting all Irishmen whom they considered might be remotely connected with the murder. A wave of anti-Irish fervour swept through the country.

It was in this atmosphere that a group of Irish people – afraid both for the large number who had been arrested and the even greater number who might be – approached W. P. Roberts, pleading with him to take on the case. Quite rightly, they considered a miscarriage of justice might easily take place. They believed it imperative to secure the services of a man with a strong personality, undaunted by the wall of anti-Irish prejudice, to conduct the defence.

The nine-day committal proceedings opened before the Manchester stipendiary magistrate on the 27 September 1867. Arraigned in the dock were twenty-eight Irishmen; the number finally rose to around fifty. Each of them was in danger of being brought before a special commission, where they could be sentenced to death if complicity in the crime were proven. W. P. Roberts and Ernest Jones, along with three other lawyers, appeared for the defence.

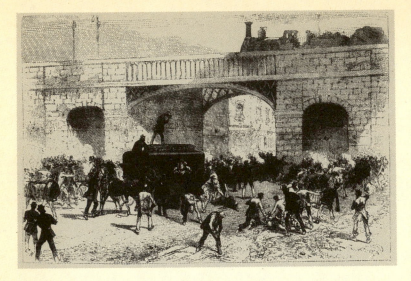

Attack on the prison van at Manchester, and rescue of the Fenian leaders (*Illustrated London News* 1867)

From the outset, the defence lawyers encountered immense difficulties. Everything possible was done by the authorities to overawe, intimidate, obstruct. Immediately the procedings began, so did the protests. Ernest Jones jumped up to object to the presence of soldiers on the bench. John Cottingham criticized the confined space in which the prisoners were kept, likening them to sheep in a pen. All the defence lawyers united to condemn the practice of keeping the prisoners in irons. Besides the inconvenience and indignity, some of them remained in constant pain because the manacles were so tight-fitting. Roberts told the court 'the conduct of the police is wickedly cruel.'

Mr Fowler, the stipendiary magistrate, tried to allay criticism. He said the soldiers sat beside him on the bench by invitation, in the capacity of personal friends and spectators. As for the well-being of the prisoners, he promised to have a doctor in attendance for any of them suffering discomforture. He even went so far as to concede that the prisoners' handcuffs might be removed when he deemed it prudent. Nevertheless, he made it clear that overall responsibility for the security of the court remained with the police.

These concessions did not satisfy the defence. They persisted in their demands and, when these failed, Ernest Jones stood up to announce:

Then as a member of the English bar I decline to sit in any court where the police override the Magistrate. I will not lend myself to any such violation of the ordinary course of justice. There is your brief, Mr Roberts, I am sorry to return it but I cannot disgrace the bar by proceeding with the defence.

Handing over his brief and gathering up his papers and umbrella, Jones marched dramatically out of the court to the accompaniment of loud hisses from the public gallery.

Then four of the prisoners, till that point represented by Ernest Jones, demanded to have the lawyer of their choice. Unless this right was conceded, they would take no further part in the proceedings. One of them, by the name of Gould, went on to complain about continually being kept in handcuffs, even at the identification parade – a procedure that must have simplified the problem of identification – adding: 'If this is English justice, then I am done with it.'

The stipendiary magistrate hinted that he might be prepared to compromise. He hoped Ernest Jones, believed to be somewhere in the building, could be prevailed upon to change his mind. When this proved to be wishful thinking, Mr Fowler decided to have further consultations with the police over security. Once the outcome of these discussions was announced – namely, that the manacles would remain – the public gallery, filled with the better-off members of Lancashire society, started cheering. This annoyed W. P. Roberts intensely. With the manacled Tolpuddle martyrs at the back of his mind, he shouted: 'Remember we are in Manchester, not Dorset.'

As well as the objections raised by the defence, the prosecution was having problems of its own. These related to the quality and quantity of the evidence. Only a handful of policemen had escorted the Black Maria, quite insufficient to identify the large number of Irishmen said to be involved in the Fenian escape. Moreover, once Sergeant Brett had been shot, as one witness picturesquely put it, 'the police ran every way from the van, except through a wall.' Most of the civilian eye-witnesses had equally restricted vision. At the time of the attack, the street was almost deserted. As for the other prisoners in the van, confined in a cramped space, catching only glimpses through the small slits in the sides of the Black Maria, it would have been a miracle if they had gained a coherent idea of what was happening.

Remarkable as it may seem, however, the prosecution evidence possessed great coherence and uniformity. All members of the Manchester constabulary gave virtually the same testimonies. Similarly, the prosecution's civilian witnesses repeated the same story, almost word for word. Of course, all this could have been just a happy coincidence, a lucky break for the prosecution – but for some suspicious individuals, both in and out of court, it appeared to stretch credulity too far. The *Reynolds' Newspaper*, rather unkindly, referred to 'the infamous system of police tutorship', and went on to offer sarcastic praise for the way in which civilian statements 'harmonized, in a most beautiful manner, with the assertions of the police.'[1]

Seeking to heighten doubts, W. P. Roberts sought to question the character and reliability of prosecution witnesses, particularly those in the van. One of them was a drunkard, who entered the witness-box still under the influence of drink. He admitted that for the past three or four days 'I have had a drop too much.' Asked if he had ever had delirium tremens, he replied that he had read about persons who were much worse than him. A second witness seemed to be motivated by hatred of Allen, one of the prisoners. He admitted that he hoped to go and see him being hung. A third was alleged to have shouted at a man he picked out at an identification parade that he would see him dead. Although he denied this in court, it still did not prevent him finding the subject of capital punishment humorous. Roberts commented: 'And that makes you grin? You're a bad 'un.' The stipendiary magistrate considered this judgement too harsh: 'Now, Mr Roberts. I think he has given his evidence very fairly, and I think you have no reason for that.' To which the People's Attorney retorted: 'I don't think he has. I know he told a lie about hanging; and I shall express my opinion.' W. P. Roberts thought he was typical of prosecution witnesses: 'He hoped to see him hang and it is evident all his thoughts were of blood. The prosecution was made up in its intensity of such men. A convicted thief or two; an immoral woman or two.'

The defence devised a trick to upset the police. Believing that they had taught witnesses to identify specific prisoners by where they stood in the dock, Roberts obtained the magistrate's permission to move them around periodically – shuffling the pack, as it were – and a greater error rate ensued. Then Roberts brought a succession of people into court to corroborate alibis. At the time the police-van was attacked, one man was working for the Lancashire and Yorkshire Railway. Others were employed in Oldham Road market, as a tailor, as a schoolteacher in Ardwick, and so on. In this way, he succeeded in having the case against them dismissed. But as quickly as he secured the release of some, police raids resulted in others being charged. The dock remained full.

W. P. Roberts worked under prodigious pressure. His day started at six o'clock in the morning, when he left his hotel and walked to the City Gaol. There he would hold hurried, inadequate consultations. He tried to secure some idea of the witnesses who were likely to be called that day. Then he would be off to do battle in court. Sometimes even these brief preliminaries did not take place: on 2 October he threatened to throw in his brief when asked to defend three men he had never seen before, particularly as the stipendiary magistrate told him he could not advise the defendants in open court.[2]

The ongoing nature of police inquiries also tended to damage the judicial process itself. Raids on the Irish community created a reign of terror, making people fearful to come forward to testify on behalf of individuals publicly branded as notorious Fenians. Newly-arrested prisoners, appearing in the dock for the first time towards the end of the prosecution's case, found the prosecution reluctant to recapitulate for the umpteenth time all the relevant details. Still more important, since police were still making arrests, information was withheld from the proceedings which it was believed, might be of assistance to those still on the run. This unsatisfactory situation, probably unique in legal history, led Roberts to complain on behalf of the defendant named Allen that he would only hear the full evidence against him when he appeared before the special commission. 'I have never known a prosecution attempted on the principle that only part of the evidence will be taken before the magistrates and part at the trial.' He pleaded with the magistrates that they 'should not soil their names by sanctioning a practice which would let in every account of injustice which could possibly be permitted under the name and sanction of law'.

But the whole proceedings were taking place in an atmosphere of race hatred, where thoughts of judicial impartiality were liable to be the first casualty. When a witness was asked to say what he thought was meant by Fenianism, the reply came 'persons who upset the country and who murder anyone who resists them'. The press generally endorsed this 'objective analysis'. Even the supposedly fair-minded *Manchester Guardian* described Fenianism as 'aimless, idle and perfectly hopeless', adding 'the law must be invoked with unsparing vigour.'[3]

Respectable society endorsed the newspaper's opinion. Access to the public gallery was by ticket. The affluent and powerful sat there out of a sense of duty, waiting to see retributive justice done. Throughout they maintained a noisy presence, heckling defendants and their lawyers. W. P. Roberts frequently asked for them to be ejected, but his requests were not heeded. So, when the hissing came from the public gallery, he usually contented himself by exclaiming, 'And there goes the swell mob' or 'The swell mob are at it again.'

By making these remarks, Roberts was questioning the probity of the occupants of the public gallery. In Victorian society the term 'swell mob' was used to denote a high-class, well-dressed kind of pickpocket. In his *London Labour and the London Poor*, Henry Mayhew stated that the swell mobster 'moves generally in the best company, frequenting – for the purpose of his business – all the places of public entertainment and often being a regular attendant at church and the more elegant chapels, especially during charity sermons.'[4] Quite naturally, the visitors in the public gallery were enraged by such insinuations and interrupted all the more.

Both inside court and outside, Roberts felt himself to be confronting the prevailing feeling of blood-lust, quite immune to rational argument. 'How dreadful it is to have to address such a spirit that reigns against these men!' he told the court: 'It paralyses the tongue.'

Nobody was prepared to listen to Roberts' argument that the political motivation of the prisoners' actions differentiated them from ordinary criminals: 'There are some features that remove it a long way from the ordinary description of murder.' Nor was anyone in a mood to consider seriously his practical objection to hanging as an answer to the Irish question. He mentioned Robert Emmett: 'The Government hanged him and did themselves no good by it.' Unquestionably, what remained in most people's minds was a desire for vengeance. Under the circumstances, it was a considerable triumph for Roberts and Cottingham that they whittled down to twenty-six the number of prisoners actually committed to trial before the special commission.

At the time, Britain was experiencing what was probably its most violent outburst of anti-Irish hysteria. Mobs descended upon the Irish quarters of large cities, particularly in Lancashire, smashing homes and terrorizing the inhabitants. To give an example from the Scholes district of Wigan: a mob entered a small court, with a dozen houses, smashing and looting eleven; the twelfth had 'English' scribbled on the door and was left alone. Another mob turned up outside W. P. Roberts' hotel, determined to get him. They only dispersed when a blood-soaked sheet, which they took to be his blood, had been displayed from an upstair window. In fact, Roberts had succeeded in making his exit by a back entrance.[5]

The press fanned the feelings of hatred. Newspapers carried stories about attempts to shoot or kidnap Queen Victoria. It was claimed that Fenians planned to seize Dover Castle, to occupy Stockport and to burn down London. It was alleged that an attack on the Harrow Volunteers' armoury had been made by them. The death of a bandsman of the 40th Middlesex Rifles regiment was automatically – and wrongly – attributed to them. One Irishman, unconnected with the Fenians, asked to be kept in police custody to avoid the frequent arrests and interrogations.

The excited mood of the populace led W. P. Roberts to have further fears that a miscarriage of justice would happen unless the trial was postponed or, at the very least, moved to London. Along with the other defence lawyers (John Cottingham and Ernest Jones, who had resumed his involvement with the case), he petitioned the Home Secretary, Gathorne Hardy, to plead for a postponement. Their letter referred to death threats made to individuals associated with the defence, demonstrations made inside the courtroom, rumours spreading anger and panic, the hostility of the press, the alarm occasioned by the extensive military preparations for the trial, as well as the poor health of the prisoners.

But the Home Secretary rejected the plea. Apparently, he felt the country's best interests would be served by dealing with the matter expeditiously. Possibly he thought an early trial was a precondition for a return to tranquillity; it would be impractical to await tranquillity and then hold the trial. What weight he attached to the possibility of a miscarriage of justice happening cannot be said.

Undoubtedly, his decision to press on had general endorsement from newspapers and public alike. *The Times* devoted an editorial to attack 'the insolence of Mr Roberts'. It argued that 'the prejudice which Mr Roberts deprecates is not, we suspect, local as much as national, being no other than a prejudice against organised conspiracies for the defiance of the law and the murder of its authorized agents.'[6]

As planned, the special commission began proceedings on 28 October 1867. Annie Besant, the well-known feminist, was a friend of the Roberts' family. A young woman of twenty at the time, she describes in her autobiography what it was like to accompany Mrs Roberts and her daughters to court:

> We drove up to the court; the streets were barricaded; soldiers were under arms; every approach was crowded with surging throngs. At last, our carriage was stopped in the midst of excited Irishmen, and fists were shaken in the windows, curses levelled at the 'damned English who were going to see our boys murdered.' For a moment things were uncomfortable, for we were five women of the helpless type. Then I bethought myself that we were unknown, and like the saucy girl I was, I leant forward and touched the nearest fist, 'Friends, these are Mr Roberts' wife and daughters'. 'Roberts, Lawyer Roberts! God bless Roberts. Let the carriage through.' And all the scowling became smile-wreathen, and cheers sounded out for curses, and the road was clear for us to the steps.[7]

W. P. Roberts believed the authorities were deliberately manipulating the proceedings to secure the result they wanted. Annie Besant described his reaction to the news that Mr Justice Blackburn was to preside: '"They are going to send that hanging judge," groaned Mr Roberts when he heard it, and we felt there was small chance of escape for the prisoners.'[8] But matters did not end there: he thought the authorities had resorted to blatant jury-vetting. Seven of the grand jury were Members of Parliament, all for Manchester constituencies. One was heard to remark before the case began that he 'didn't care what the evidence was, he would hang every damned Irishman.'

Being a solicitor, Roberts had no right of audience in the high court. To make an unauthorized speech rendered one liable to professional disqualification and imprisonment. Yet, so flagrant was the jury-vetting, and so strongly did Roberts feel about it, that personal consequences did not enter his mind. He contended that, as a solicitor, he had the legal right to substitute himself for his client, raising points of law on his behalf.

But Mr Justice Blackburn thought otherwise. When Roberts stood up and made objections to the names of the jury being read out by the clerk to the court, the judge told him he could not interfere. Nevertheless, Roberts persisted: 'These men's lives are at stake, my lord.' Angry, Mr Justice Blackburn retorted: 'Mr Roberts, if you speak once more, I will order that you be taken into custody.' 'That's perfectly uncalled for, my lord,' the People's Attorney replied. Whereupon the clerk to the court resumed reading the names. Unable to contain himself, Roberts shouted out: 'I object on the part of Allen.' Instantly, the judge ordered: 'Take that man into custody.' Only later, as a result of the pleadings of Digby Seymour, QC, did Roberts secure his freedom again. For the rest of the trial, he sat in silence.[9]

Annie Besant was right in her prediction – 'the verdict was a foregone conclusion.' Of the twenty-six prisoners tried, five were convicted for murder, seven for riot and assault. Many of the remainder were found guilty of lesser offences. The Home Secretary granted pardons to two of the five men sentenced to be hanged. The circumstances surrounding the release of one of these two men is probably unique. Twenty-two journalists, who had been covering the trial, petitioned the Home Secretary, expressing their opinion that he was innocent. Thomas Maguire happened to be a private in the Royal Marines, hapless enough to be scooped up in one of the numerous police raids while home on leave. Evidence emerged that made it obvious he had nothing to do with Sergeant Brett's murder. But this created an awkward problem for the Home Secretary: so many witnesses had testified to seeing Maguire participating in the attack on the Black Maria, his release was certain to cast doubt on the quality of the evidence against other condemned men. Even so, this was eventually done. Maguire returned to continue his career in the Royal Marines.[10]

The three men to be hanged – Allen, Larkin and O'Brien – accepted their fate with dignity. After the judge had pronounced sentence, each addressed the court. The first, Allen, declared his regret at the death of Sergeant Brett, denied his own involvement in it, but said he expected no mercy: 'I will die proudly and triumphantly in defence of republican principles and the liberty of an oppressed and enslaved people.' He concluded by giving 'Mr Seymour and Mr Jones my sincere and heartfelt thanks for their eloquent and able advocacy regarding my part in the affray. I wish also to return to Mr Roberts the very same.' Likewise Larkin declared: 'I call my God as a witness that I used neither pistols, revolvers nor any instrument that day that would take the life of a child, let alone a man.' He, too, concluded by expressing gratitude to his counsel: 'They have done their utmost in the protection of my life; likewise my worthy solicitor, Mr Roberts.' Then, lastly, came O'Brien, speaking in roughly the same vein: 'I shall commence by saying that every witness who has sworn against me has sworn falsely.' But he did not try to deny his Irish nationalism: 'Ireland, with its beautiful scenery, its delightful climate, its rich and productive lands, is capable of supporting more than treble its population in ease and comfort. Yet, no man, except a paid official of the British Government, can say there is a shadow of liberty, that there is a spark of glad life amongst its plundered and persecuted inhabitants.' He ended as well by thanking his counsel and Mr Roberts.[11]

As they awaited execution, the condition of the prisoners gave grounds for concern. The long hours in manacles began to tell. Similarly, the poor food, solitary confinement, lack of exercise and lack of sleep all took their toll. The *Manchester Guardian* reported that they were only getting a remarkably niggardly two hours sleep a night. According to Roberts, the stress and strain had not merely damaged Allen's health, it had altered his appearance. He made attempts to secure improvements in their prison conditions without success.[12]

All efforts were now concentrated on trying to get a reprieve. The defence counsel, denied leave to appeal, enlisted the assistance of some eminent figures. They submitted a long and complex memorandum to the Home Secretary, who was also subjected to parliamentary pressure from MPs opposed to the executions. Then there was an extra-parliamentary campaign, with the Irish naturally to the fore. A large demonstration of London Irish marched to the Home Office, demanding to see the Home Secretray. When this was refused, a disturbance broke out in Whitehall. One of the leaders, ex-Chartist James Finlen, predicted that this was but a small foretaste of what was to come: the presence of 10,000 troops in Manchester would not prevent them from stopping the executions. Up and down the country there were mass protest meetings.

But, despite all the pressure, the Home Secretary remained unmoved. On 23 November 1867, the three condemned men walked to the gallows erected outside Salford prison. The immediate vicinity was thronged with soldiers, an overwhelming display of military might that made any rescue attempt quite impossible. Further away, thousands of members of the public stood to witness the executions. The authorities hoped that, by demonstrating their firmness and resolve, they would deter potential Fenian recruits. Yet, even at this dark moment, Irish nationalists still had something to cheer. The two Fenian prisoners, Kelly and Deasy, whose liberation from the Black Maria had sparked off the whole affair, had escaped to America and were never recaptured. The same was true of Peter Rice, the man who, it seems, actually fired the fatal shot.[13]

Almost from the beginning of his involvement, W. P. Roberts appears to have known that none of the prisoners were Sergeant Brett's murderer and that the man who had pulled the trigger was safely out of the country.[14] This may have made the People's Attorney even more determined and spirited in his defence of the victims in the dock. Early in the trial he had told the stipendiary magistrate: 'I will resist oppression wherever I meet it, and this is oppression.'

In the aftermath of the hangings, highly emotional meetings took place in many towns and cities. A demonstration of 20,000 occurred at Clerkenwell Green. A few days later, on 13 December 1867, an attempt was made to free Fenian prisoners by blowing up Clerkenwell prison. Naturally, in the northern centres of Irish immigration, too, unrest was intense.

W. P. Roberts and Ernest Jones were, as one would expect, much in demand to address protest meetings. Interestingly, Karl Marx was supposed to have been on the platform at one of them, but at the last moment another speaker took his place. In a letter to Engels, he wrote that he was relieved at this, 'as I don't like to mix with a crowd like Roberts, Stephens and the rest.'[15] The reasons for his objection remain unclear, although his letter may provide a clue. He told Engels that, as a result of the passions inflamed by the Manchester executions, he 'would have been forced to hurl revolutionary thunderbolts instead of soberly analysing the state of affairs and the movement as I intended'. Undoubtedly, W. P. Roberts was always a man of passion and excitement; deep political analysis was never his strong point.

Had he been a sober political analyst, he probably would have realized that Engels had explained most satisfactorily the long-term significance of the Manchester Martyrs. He likened it to the execution of John Brown following the raid upon Harper's ferry, which had greatly boosted the struggle against slavery in America: 'All the Fenians lacked were Martyrs ... Through the execution of these men, the liberation of Kelly and Deasy has been made an act of heroism which will be sung over the cradle of every Irish child. The Irish women will take care of that.' It constituted, Engels believed, 'the definite deed of separation between England and Ireland'.[16]

That the authorities had not achieved their desired objective by executing the Manchester Martyrs had soon become obvious with the explosion at Clerkenwell prison. It had been an unsuccessful attempt to liberate Fenian prisoners by blowing a hole in the wall during their exercise period. But the authorities had foreknowledge of the plot and took precautionary steps. Even so, the hole in the wall was of impressive dimensions and the huge explosion also damaged 400 houses, mainly slums, in the vicinity. Three passers-by were killed and thirty-seven others needed medical treatment, of whom three died in hospital. In the ensuing panic, 50,000 special constables were enrolled and the establishment of the Metropolitan Police permanently increased.[17]

If the outcome had not been so tragic, police conduct could easily be fitted into a slapstick comedy by Laurel and Hardy. In their determination to maintain super-secrecy, it would seem that each of the authorities operated independently, not informing the others of what they were doing. The Irish constabulary knew a conspiracy was afoot; likewise, the Metropolitan Police knew of the plan to blow up the wall of Clerkenwell jail. And the prison governor and his staff were also appraised of the situation. Hence, it came as no surprise when, on 12 December 1867 – 'at the exact time indicated by intelligence sources' – two men rolled a barrel of gunpowder against the prison wall.[18] The fuse, however, was damp, and the two men rolled the barrel away again. A policeman, watching them, took no action. According to the official statement, he saw no reason to apprehend anyone; although a more plausible explanation is that the authorities hoped to catch a greater number in their net on the second occasion. This opportunity arose the following day. Six people were seen trundling a barrel, resting on a trolley, along the road towards the prison. From his home, one man who saw this happening called to his wife. He thought the group had placed a rag over the top to conceal the fact that the barrel contained beer! But then things happened very quickly – too quickly for Warder Cope, who was standing outside the prison with a gun. Later, at an inquest, the coroner asked him: 'What were you watching the wall for?' 'In case of an explosion,' he replied.[19] When the big bang came, not only Warder Cope but also a swarm of plain clothes policemen in the vicinity had an excellent view of events. One of them, Edward Moriarty, standing a short distance from the bomb as it was thrown, subsequently testified at the trial. He told the court, in a disarmingly innocent manner, that when he saw the burning fuse, he 'had stepped back eight to ten yards to see what would happen next'.

As the dust began to settle, three arrests were immediately made. PC George Ranger seized Jeremiah Allen, who had been loitering outside the prison all day. He was beaten up and then taken to Bow Street police station. Embarrassingly, he too turned out to be a policeman! At the committal proceedings, several witnesses testified that they had actually seen Constable Jeremiah Allen planting the bomb. The inquests on Humphrey Evans, Martha Thompson and Sarah Hodgkinson also reached the verdict of wilful murder against six individuals, including PC Jeremiah Allen.[20] Yet, no action was taken against him. At the trial, opening on 20 April 1868, the prosecution was greatly aided by Patrick Mullany. He turned police informer after being presented with an impressive 20-foot-long document. The authorities claimed they had sixty-two individuals prepared to give evidence against him. Among many other offences, they would prove his complicity in the murder of Sergeant Brett as well as the Clerkenwell explosion. This meant he would certainly face the death sentence. In the circumstances, Mullany decided to become a prosecution witness in return for a new identity and safe passage to Australia.

At the trial, Patrick Mullany admitted that he had turned informer for the sake of his family and because he thought that if he did not another Irishman would do so anyway. He told the court he now regarded himself as the property of the English crown, which always paid for its services. But his testimony was distinctly shaky. Under cross-examination, he conceded that he could read very little and he could not read a key letter he quoted in his evidence. Other dubious things occurred at the trial. Defence lawyers pointed to the contradictory and conflicting evidence that had been given. Several witnesses who at earlier hearings had said they saw Jeremiah Allen plant the bomb now changed their testimonies, claiming they saw it done by the accused. As two historians subsequently observed: 'The odour of perjury at the trial was uncomfortably strong.'[21]

W. P. Roberts was the solicitor of one of the accused, a middle-aged Irish woman named Ann Justice, who happened to be near the prison at the time of the explosion. The wife of a poor Soho tailor, she had no money whatsoever to engage a barrister. The prosecution, on the other hand, would have the experienced and skilled law officers of the crown, with all the back-up they required. Even the right of a solicitor to substitute for his client, at one time allowed in English courts, was now being denied, as Roberts' treatment at the Manchester Martyrs' trial had shown. Roberts wrote to the Home Secretary on behalf of his client, pointing out the injustice of her position. His plea did not succeed in influencing the Home Secretary. Nevertheless, the publicity given to it helped to increase the collections being made, largely by Irish newspapers. As a result, she and the other defendants did obtain sufficient money to engage barristers, albeit young, inexperienced ones prepared to take the briefs for a small fee.

Ann Justice secured an acquittal. The judge agreed that all she had done was to loiter in the vicinity of the prison and talk to police agent Jeremiah Allen; there was nothing to connect her with the explosion. Similarly, four others were acquitted. But the sixth, Michael Barrett, was not so fortunate. He was found guilty and on 26 May 1868 a crowd of 2,000, some cheering, others hissing and booing, watched him mount the scaffold for what was to be the last public execution in Britain.

The trials of the Fenians had revealed, in W. P. Roberts' opinion, some defects in the English legal system. The first had been highlighted by Ann Justice's plight, her lack of money preventing her from obtaining adequate legal representation. Commenting on Roberts' letter to the Home Secretary, *The Law Journal* agreed that the situation was unsatisfactory. It contrasted the situation here with that in France, Germany and the United States, 'where counsel to all cases of any moment are assigned to prisoners and suitable remuneration is provided.'[22]

The second criticism, often made at protest meetings, was the emergence of the common law principle of constructive murder. Obviously the Fenians who attacked the Black Maria had no intention of killing Sergeant Brett; they had no way of knowing he would be peeping through the keyhole as they came to break the lock; and therefore, Roberts contended, his death was simply an accident. Usually, for an individual to be found guilty as charged, the prosecution has to prove he had a guilty mind – *mens rea* is the legal term. But there is no need to prove malice aforethought, i.e., intention to murder, to secure a successful conviction for constructive murder. All that is required is to show that (i) an illegal act was committed and (ii) in the course of it somebody lost their life. Ironically, though not mentioned at the time, W. P. Roberts' relative, Lord Justice Tindal, played an important part in the development of the principle of constructive murder. In the case of Fenton (1830), a person had committed the unlawful act of trespass and thrown stones down a mine shaft. He was unaware that a man was at the pit-bottom, looking up, and the stone killed him. Tindal directed the jury, if they found the victim had died as a result of Fenton's actions, to bring a guilty of murder verdict.[23]

The third criticism Roberts made concerned the authorities' extensive use of police spies, *agents provocateurs*, the devising and encouragement of illegal acts. As the Clerkenwell case revealed, the explosion was caused by a plain-clothes policeman, yet it was impossible for the accused to claim entrapment, a legitimate defence in United States law. Moreover, in passing judgement, Judge Cockburn had ruled that any illegal act committed for political purposes but known to be dangerous would be treated as premeditated murder if loss of life ensued.[24] Though he accepted that the Fenians had not intended to kill Sarah Hodgkinson, they had undertaken a reckless act with the full knowledge that loss of life might result. To W. P. Roberts, such a judgement was far too sweeping and liable to lead to misuse of powers by the authorities.

Soon afterwards, the treatment of Michael Davitt appears to have underlined Roberts' misgivings. In 1870, while this famous Irish patriot and labour leader was detained in Clerkenwell prison, his communications with his solicitor were regularly intercepted and read. The authorities did this under the pretext that they had to foil a second plot to blow the place up. As a consequence, the Crown not only acquired prior knowledge of Davitt's defence case, but they were able to whip up a hysterical press campaign against him. Not content with prejudicing the possibility of a fair trial before an impartial jury, the prosecution relied upon perjured evidence to secure a conviction. Their vital witness was an Irishman named John Corydon. He testified that he had seen Davitt at Chester, one of those involved in a conspiracy to attack the castle there. In fact, Davitt had never been to Chester in his life. But there was a second lie, as the historian F. Sheeny-Skeffington explained:

> As a matter of fact, Corydon had never seen Davitt before. So it was deemed necessary to facilitate the identification. He was therefore allowed to stand in the corridor of the prison with a warder while Davitt was being transferred from one cell to another. After this it was not a very difficult task for the informer to identify the one-armed man in the cell which he had seen him enter.[25]

As Roberts realized, a pattern for political trials involving people from Ireland was beginning to emerge. The crucial objective to be achieved, an aim over-riding any thoughts about justice, was to secure a conviction at all costs – to catch a man, not the man. This was what had happened to the Manchester Martyrs, to Michael Barrett over Clerkenwell, and then to Michael Davitt. Involved in the first two cases, Roberts displayed no inhibitions about denouncing the way the authorities were perverting the course of justice. Yet, his utterance of the truth also had a cost. It made him intensely unpopular with the jingoistic section of the public.

Though well able to withstand hatred and obloquy, the ageing Roberts seems to have found it increasing irksome. This may have been one of the reasons why he decided to move from Seedley House, Pendleton, Manchester. For many years, he had lived happily there amid congenial company. His next-door neighbour, a fellow lawyer and friend, was Richard Marsden Pankhurst, whose wife and daughters later championed the cause of women's suffrage.[26] But Roberts was getting old and needed tranquillity. He decided to curtail his legal activities, loosening his ties with Lancashire. He moved to the School House at Heronsgate. There he could spend most of his time living quietly among his old Chartist friends.

16 The Final Tragedy and the Ultimate Triumph

As W. P. Roberts' life drew towards its close, the main feature of modern labour relations began to emerge. Unions became stable, more durable, more structured. A meeting at Manchester in 1868 formed the Trade Union Congress. This helped the union leaders, the high and mighty of the movement, to speak to government with greater coherence and impact. Similarly, employers also became more highly organized. In response, the state felt compelled to take cognizance of these developments. Between 1867 and 1869 a royal commission made the most detailed investigation of trade unions ever carried out in this country. It provided valuable information for the spate of legislation then enacted, which laid down the concepts and procedures that remain with us to the present day. While many union officials regarded this as unmitigated progress, it received only two cheers from Roberts. From the workers' standpoint, he regarded the changes as falling well short of what was desirable and necessary.

A significant initiative was taken on 20 April 1864. On that date, the Glasgow Trades Council convened a conference to discuss the Master and Servant Acts.[1] As a consequence, a memorandum was drawn up and published. It showed how these acts were unjust and inequitable. Throughout the country, working people heeded the call for a campaign. A second conference was held, this time in London. All the leading figures of the movement attended, and it was agreed to request an audience with the Home Secretary and President of the Board of Trade. The ultimate outcome in 1867, after further campaigning and a select committee inquiring into the question, was 'An Act to amend Statute Law between Master & Servant (30 & 31 Vict c 141)'.

Quite deliberately, W. P. Roberts was excluded, as far as possible, from proceedings. On Clydeside, his arch-enemy, Alexander Mac-Donald, was highly influential. He owned the *Glasgow Sentinel* and largely controlled the Glasgow Trades Council. From the outset of the campaign, therefore, it was easy for MacDonald to arrange for another lawyer, John Strachan, to act as legal adviser. Even so, his powers did not extend to preventing Roberts from testifying before the select committee. This, at least in part, had been set up as a result of Roberts' exposure of the scandals of Blaina.

In his evidence to the select committee, Roberts' approach stands in marked contrast to that of the union leaders who appeared with him. Men like MacDonald were content to see minor modifications, leaving the basic structure unchanged. When pushed into a corner, they conceded that owners required a weapon with which to maintain discipline. Roberts, on the other hand, wanted to see the Master and Servant Acts entirely swept away – a position which was naturally quite unacceptable to the employers. Yet, while not prepared to countenance such drastic changes, many of the more far-sighted masters saw that modifications to existing legislation were required. Therefore, they were looking for a compromise. The fact that the union side was led by moderates like MacDonald was helpful. Still more help came from the Bill's sponsor – Lord Elcho (then Lord Wemyss) who, as already stated, was Scotland's biggest coalowner and a personal friend of MacDonald. He piloted the necessary compromise successfully through Parliament.[2]

As they then operated, the Master and Servant Acts were becoming counter-productive, angering workers rather than coercing them. Their lack of even-handedness was increasingly obvious: to break a contract remained a civil matter for the master; for the worker it was criminal. The worker was liable to up to three months' imprisonment with hard labour. Not only that: to take action against a master was fraught with difficulties. Besides the expense, in the unlikely circumstances of victory, the worker usually received only a proportion of his claim. For the employer taking action, the position was very different. He had merely to go to a magistrate, assert that the servant had broken his contract and an arrest immediately followed. What it meant in practice was described by a Lancashire pitman. He said miners could wake early in the morning, walk a long distance to work to be there for 6 a.m., only to discover the coalowner had decided not to open the colliery that day. While they had no redress against the owner, who could plausibly give lack of demand or countless other reasons as his excuse, if one morning the miner did not turn up at 6 a.m., then they would probably be punished. Amid cheers, he told a Wigan rally the acts were 'a relic of a barbarous age' and continued: 'If John the miner was liable to be dragged from his bed by the neck for breaking his contract, John the master must be liable, too, or the laws of England were unequal.'[3]

From his personal experience, W. P. Roberts gave the select committee other instances of injustice:

In 1865, at the Phoenix ironworks in Rotherham, a worker who had been dismissed was told to teach his replacement the tricks of the trade before he left, but he refused. Whereupon the employer prosecuted him. The man was arrested in the night, put in a police-cell and taken at 8 o'clock the following morning to the magistrate's home. There, with only a clerk to the magistrates, the representative of the employers and two or three policemen present, the man was tried and sentenced to a month's hard labour. When Roberts heard about the case, he tried to secure the man's immediate release from Wakefield gaol. He contacted J. A. Roebuck, MP, who wrote to the secretary of state. In reply, the minister expressed his regret, saying nothing could be done about the sentence.[4]

In 1861, building workers in County Durham were arrested without being told the charges against them. They were taken from their beds, handcuffed, marched three miles to Barnard Castle, where they were imprisoned and kept without food. Once friends heard the news, they frantically attempted to secure the services of a solicitor. Unsuccessfully, three were approached. So desperate were they that one of the friends went to an attorney's residence and, having 'being refused admittance by door, got in by his window, and tried to induce him, sitting in his bedroom, to come and defend the men'. Again unsuccessful, they went to the magistrate and pleaded with him to adjourn the case until the hungry prisoners had been fed and obtained a solicitor to defend them. But the magistrate refused and the building workers were gaoled.[5]

In North Staffordshire, a pottery worker named Baker was imprisoned for breach of contract. After he had served the sentence, the master expected him to return to do the same work as before, which Baker declined to do. Since his contract had not expired, he was charged with the same offence and imprisoned again. W. P. Roberts took Baker's case to the Court of Queen's Bench. There it was held that a man 'might be committed over and over and over again; that there was, in fact, no end to the power of commitment.' However, the persistence of the People's Attorney finally paid off: Roberts took the case to the Court of Exchequer, where, by a bare majority, he secured Baker's release.[6]

Roberts gave the select committee three reasons why he advocated the repeal of the acts. First, he argued that 'their laws were all derived from the times when workmen were a very different class of being to what they are now. At that time, colliers were sold in slavery in Scotland ... Since then, the workman has altered very much for the better.' Secondly, he suggested that, as the name of the acts implied, there was a basic lack of equality before the law: on the one side the exalted master, on the other his lowly servants. Naturally, when magistrates heard cases, 'they see the master in an elevated position; they see the workmen in a degraded position; and human nature is human nature.' Thirdly, he considered the essential function of these laws was punishment – what he termed 'the torturing process'. Faced with trouble from his servants, the master could say: 'I can send you to prison for three months with hard labour. Will you go back to your work?'[7]

Throughout his testimony to the select committee – Daphne Simon, the historical authority on the Master and Servant Acts, describes it as the most outstanding of those giving evidence – W. P. Roberts had been most trenchant in his denunciations. At one unguarded moment, he declared: 'There was as gross a failure of justice as could be. I do not believe that such a failure of justice could have occurred in any country but this.' But how, committee members asked, did he know? Was he acquainted with the various legal systems operating elsewhere? In reply, Roberts said that, if other countries' were more severe on their workers, 'it would have been published in this country, as showing the superior liberty enjoyed by Englishmen over other countries.'[8]

Generally, historians, even sympathetic ones like Daphne Simon, have tended not to appreciate the full force of Roberts' second objection; namely, that by the very nature of their title the Master and Servant Acts placed the employer in a vastly superior position *vis-à-vis* his employees. It should be remembered that, for most magistrates hearing such cases, the word 'servant' would be redolent with undertones of subordination and unquestioned obedience. Almost all of those sitting in judgement would have personal, daily experience of their own servants – domestic servants – who could be expected to do whatever they were told and to work whenever they were asked. Domestic servants had virtually no legal rights. In a notorious case a Devon farmer and his wife beat to death a fourteen-year-old servant, but were not found guilty of murder because it was impossible to prove which had been the fatal blow. This was simply a glaring example of the legal inequality: masters had all the rights, the domestic servants all the duties. However unreasonable an employer's conduct happened to be, domestic servants in practice had no redress through the courts.[9] W. P. Roberts wanted to see the abolition of the Master and Servant Acts because, among other things, he believed that they helped to extend a form of injustice from the cosy living-rooms of the employers to their factories.

But members of the select committee objected to Roberts' position, arguing that the retention of the Master and Servant Acts was vital. Without them, how could they deal, for instance, with a mine-engineman who absented himself from work without notice, with the result that the colliery flooded? Or a worker whose recklessness imperilled life? Surely, only a system of fines and imprisonment would meet the need? Answering these points, Roberts enunciated the principles that he thought should be applied. First, the contract between employer and worker should be the same as any other contract, with both parties operating on the basis of equality. Second, that the matter should be taken entirely away from the criminal law; disputes should be settled in civil courts. Admittedly, the conduct of workers could sometimes result in considerable mischief, but the same applied to other sections of society. Lapses by a lawyer, for instance, could be extremely costly for whoever engaged his services. 'But you cannot send him to prison,' said Roberts; 'Heaven forbid that you should have the power.' On the issue of industrial safety he also believed that equality was paramount: any regulations should equally apply to representatives of management and to workers – each should be liable to the same penalties. In this connection he cited the case of a vessel that had blown up in Liverpool harbour a few months earlier. Proper precautions had not been taken by the owner and many people had expected it to explode. Yet, Roberts added, 'there is no fine or imprisonment for him.'[10]

Naturally, when the select committee reported and Parliament eventually acted upon its recommendations, the new legislation did not contain the drastic changes Roberts had advocated. The Master and Servant Act (1867) introduced some modest amendments.[11] The power of a single magistrate to issue a warrant of arrest was abolished. Imprisonment, without the option of a fine or payment of damages, was restricted to cases where serious injury to persons or property had occurred. The hearings were to be conducted in open court, not in the magistrates' private rooms, as had often happened. But the ambiguous phraseology, providing ample scope for malicious interpretation, still left the master with considerable sway over 'his' servant. As well as the question of what constituted 'injury to person or property', the worker was threatened by section 14 of the act: aggravated 'misconduct, misdemeanour or ill-treatment', whatever that may mean, could still result in up to three months imprisonment with hard labour. The impact of the new legislation was marginal. In the ten years 1857–67, the average number of prosecutions in England and Wales was 9,900 a year, with 5,800 convictions. In the four years after the 1867 Act, this had fallen to an average of 8,800 prosecutions and 5,100 convictions. In 1872, however, a year of boom and militancy, the figures shot up to a record 17,100 prosecutions and 10,400 convictions. Three years later, however, the Master and Servant Act was finally abolished.[12]

In her article, Daphne Simon emphasises that the Master and Servant Acts had limited application. In many sectors of the British economy, employers never resorted to them. They were chiefly used, she suggests, by small employers. These were often operating precariously, on small profit margins, living on a hand-to-mouth basis. Large employers, able to take a long-term view, were less likely to initiate a prosecution, muddying industrial relations for years to come. She also argues that another factor was the declining utilization of yearly hirings. Short contracts gave employers greater flexibility, making it easier to react quickly to changing economic conditions, but they also lessened the need to go to court over contractual disputes. Conscious that growing anger was making the Master and Servant Act counter-productive, big employers saw no reason to use their considerable political clout, struggling to preserve legislation from which they derived little or no benefit.[13]

In periods of discontent, legal injustices can act as a catalyst, unwittingly fostering the growth of trade unionism. Daphne Simon acknowledges that this is exactly what happened in County Durham in 1869 with the Bond, a legally binding agreement of the same pedigree as the Master and Servant Acts. Reimposed with added harshness after the 1844 defeat, the Bond continued to function in the North-East coalfields for the next quarter of a century. Finally in 1869, the resistance of the pitmen of Wearmouth colliery at Sunderland, aided by W. P. Roberts, enabled the Bond to be smashed for all time. As a result of the struggle, the Durham Miners' Association was created. It became a much stronger and more enduring organization than all its predecessors, a trade union that continues to exist today.[14]

A trade depression, slackening demand for coal, provided the background to the Wearmouth colliery dispute. The coalowner decided to impose a pay cut. The precise amount was in dispute. Management claimed that it was only 8 per cent, made 17 per cent by the men's own actions; the pitmen alleged that in some instances the cut equalled a third. Nevertheless, they did not oppose it at the time, for in the prevailing conditions resistance seemed futile. The men feared it would simply result in management imposing further sackings, increasing the large ranks of the jobless without anything being accomplished. Two months later the mood had changed: unable to make a living wage, all the miners walked out on 18 May. They held a meeting on the green, opposite the colliery, and appointed six men to see Mr R. Heckles, the manager (previously of Thornley colliery). The deputation told him that the miners found it impossible to maintain themselves and their families on their present pay; they were determined not to resume work until the cuts were withdrawn.

Heckles, one of Durham's most well-known and astute managers, tried to break resistance, first with the carrot, then with the stick. After the stoppage had continued for a fortnight, he endeavoured to entice men back to work with promises of free beer. In reply, 250 of them met, reaffirmed their decision to stay out, and stated that 'the day had gone when the men were to be bought with beer.' Their letter to Heckles humorously added: 'Beef and bread would be better.' Failing with bribery, Heckles then turned to the law. On 21 June 1869, five men appeared before Sunderland magistrates' court, charged with breaking their Bonds.

W. P. Roberts, who had been kept briefed on developments, journeyed from London to conduct the defence. As he alighted from his carriage in Sunderland, he must have been acutely aware how closely his impending battle resembled the epic struggle at Thornley twenty-five years before. Then, as now, cheering crowds had greeted his arrival; both cases were *causes célèbres* in mining communities throughout the county; and, by a remarkable coincidence, his old adversary Heckles now managed Wearmouth colliery. After that long passage of time, the two men came face to face in the courtroom. As Heckles stood in the witness-box, the Miners' Attorney slowly stood and began his cross-examination with the inquiry: 'Mr Heckles, don't I know you?' The entire courtroom exploded with laughter.

In fact, Roberts' tactics closely resembled those used at the Thornley trial. He questioned the assumptions on which the prosecution's case rested. Where was the proof that miners had signed the Bond? Even when a mark had been made, had the document's content been carefully read over to them? Were they aware of the commitments they were entering into? The Miners' Attorney contended that the Bond was not a legally enforceable document: the prosecution had provided no evidence that many of the pitmen had signed it or knew its provisions. Yet, despite these grave – even insurmountable – objections to the prosecution's case, Roberts expressed pleasure that the court proceedings were taking place because he knew the future was on the miners' side: 'The magistrates might send the men to prison for violating a contract which there was no proof they had ever read, but one day they would not do so, though great changes might come before it.'[15]

Roberts recognized that improvements in the workers' legal position had occurred: 'Thank God, through the progress of public opinion, they were not quite so badly off as they were years ago, when the man was seized from his bed, tried within a few hours and sent to prison without the opportunity of any defence whatsoever.' Besides defending the prisoners in the dock, he saw himself speaking for posterity. He felt assured of final victory in the case; future generations of miners would benefit from the new freedom won. He contended that the men's only remedy was to strike. Their pay was so meagre that, like Oliver Twist, they had no alternative but to ask for more. This had been done in a perfectly peaceful and proper manner. Turning to the Bond, Roberts declared that, if the miners had merely 'the courage of mice', they still would resist 'the villainous and wicked Bond', devised with 'such disgraceful trickery'. Then began the long process of calling pitmen into the witness-box, each of whom declared that he would rather go to prison than work under the Bond. It demonstrated, the Miners' Attorney claimed, that 'these men believed they were in the right and were prepared to establish their conviction by martyrdom.'

In the face of this onslaught, the magistrates decided to have an adjournment. Roberts was amenable, as it gave time for informal negotiations, but he wanted it to be of short duration. When the magistrates announced it would be for a fortnight, he complained about the extra time and trouble involved in journeying to and fro from Heronsgate, quite a burden for an old man like himelf. But his appeal was unanswered and the two-week adjournment took place. During that period, the coalowners hardened their position, stating they would not grant a pay increase under any circumstances.

When the court reconvened on 6 July 1869, the magistrates pronounced the five-week strike to be illegal – with no effect, for the pitmen refused to return to work. Just as ineffective was the magistrates' rejection of Roberts' application to take the case to the Court of Queen's Bench – Roberts expressed his intention of making a personal application to it himself. Apparently, the magistrates feared an application on behalf of the five defendants. One of these was a marksman (that is, one who made his mark and could not sign his name), and they realized Roberts might establish that the Bond had never been read over to him.

Such legal issues became of little consequence in the light of subsequent events. Determined to display the strength of opposition to the Bond, the men decided to resign from their employment and vacate their tied cottages. A procession, each man carrying his lamp and copy of the colliery rules, marched to the manager's office and handed them in. The whole ceremony was so impressive that the deputies and supervisory staff, who until then had remained at work, came out in solidarity with the men. Heckles was faced with having Wearmouth colliery and no labour force whatsoever.

This was checkmate and the coalowners had no choice but capitulation. In court, they announced that they would be prepared to waive the Bond so long as the men went back to work. As for the issue of pay, the employers proposed the viewers should adjudicate on it. This suggestion brought from Roberts the tart riposte: 'I'd sooner send a question of sparrows to a jury of sparrow hawks.' After more wrangling, it was agreed to remit the wages issue to independent arbitration. The essential point, however, was that the Bond had been, finally and irrevocably, smashed. A triumphant Miners' Attorney, magnanimous in the victory that was the crowning

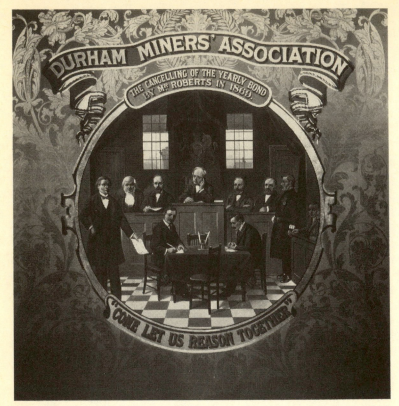

This is the banner at present used by the Monkwearmouth lodge of the NUM (John Gorman Collection)

laurel of his career, turned to address the magistrates. As at the Thornley trial, there had been many angry exchanges. Consequently, 'Mr Roberts begged to apologise for himself if, in the heat of the moment, he had said anything offensive to the Mayor of Sunderland or anyone else.'[16]

The death of the Bond transformed the industrial situation throughout County Durham. Workers, previously submissive, had a new feeling of hope. Whereas before they thought struggle was of no avail, they now began forming union lodges. The Durham Miners' Association soon sprang into life. Pitmen at Wearmouth colliery, proud of their achievement, had painted on their union banner – and it remains there today – the courtroom scene of W. P. Roberts breaking the Bond. As for the Miners' Attorney, he treasured this moment of glory. Annie Besant says in her autobiography that she learnt her radical principles from Roberts, and she remembers how he recalled his taming of King Coal tyranny:

> The old man's eye would begin to flash and his voice to rise as he told of these horrors, and his face would soften as he added that, after it was all over and the slavery was put an end to, as he went through a coal district the women standing at their doors would lift up their children to see 'Lawyer Roberts' go by and would bid 'God bless him' for what he has done.[17]

However, if the Wearmouth trial was his ultimate triumph, it was also his final tragedy. Never again would he appear in his beloved North East. His services were no longer wanted. Just as the coalowners dispensed with the Bond to minimize conflict, likewise the new union that he had helped to create sought to maintain industrial peace. A new breed of miners' leader had emerged, a moderate who strove for co-operation with the coalowners. The union boss, like any other boss, wanted the smooth, efficient operation of the organization he controlled, with the minimum of trouble. Whenever an industrial conflict flared up, he would run around as if he were a human fire-engine, trying to extinguish the flames. In contrast, W. P. Roberts was prepared to spread the fire, dousing the whole coalfield with paraffin, if he thought this could force his enemy to surrender. He regarded the courts as a battleground, where he used the law as a weapon, belabouring the coalowner until 'he bit the dust.' But to the new school of moderation, such an attitude was outdated and barbarous: the law should be used as a means of promoting employer–worker harmony, helping to resolve any conflicts that might arise.

In his history of the Durham miners, E. Welbourne adopted a highly critical attitude to Roberts – both his general attitude and his bombastic courtroom manner. Referring to the Wearmouth trial, Welbourne commented: 'After this case, the pitmen's attorney-general appeared no more in the North, and newspapers spoke the truth when they said no one was sorry. For, if he did not produce disturbance, his coming was always a sign of unrest.' Significantly, Welbourne was related to a leader of the Durham miners' union; his history reflects the abhorrence of class struggle which such individuals felt.[18]

An indication of the degree of estrangement existing between Roberts and the union leaders came a few months before his death. In March 1871, he wrote, and published at his own expense, a pamphlet criticizing their attitude towards the Trade Union Bill, then before Parliament. In the form of an open letter, addressed to Alexander MacDonald and his colleagues, it attacked them for giving the proposed legislation their support. In the long run, he was certain that workers would suffer as a result of its provisions, and the union leaders would be blamed for helping to gain its acceptance. Therefore, he urged them, even at that late stage – and even if they had no prospect of success – to mount a campaign against the proposed legislation. At least, such action would put the record straight and exonerate them from blame – otherwise they would be objects for execration when the day of reckoning arrived.[19]

These remarks proved to be prophetic. Almost before the ink was dry on the paper, extensive misgivings began to be expressed within the labour movement. Notably, the criminal clauses were regarded as highly objectionable. A campaign to secure changes was started, probably too late, and it was not successful. The one positive feature arising from the agitation was the formation of the TUC's Parliamentary Committee, its first permanent committee, the forerunner of the present-day TUC General Council.

Even though the Trade Union Act of 1871 did not embody the changes workers had called for, most trade unions considered it to be a positive assistance to labour. This view has been endorsed by historians, with the exception of A. E. Musson, who regarded the legislation in much the same light as did Roberts – 'fulfilling trade union fears and dashing most of their hopes'.[20] Those who thought the 1871 Act progressive at the time did so because they considered it had the effect of re-establishing protection for trade union funds as well as providing a legal framework within which they could successfully operate.[21] W. P. Roberts, however, disputed this, claiming theirs to be a hasty, panic reaction to an adverse legal judgement in the Hornby v Close case in 1867. If all that was required was to give security to union funds, then a much less far-reaching measure would have sufficed. In any case, he thought they had construed the Hornby v Close verdict too widely – and he had been the solicitor engaged by the Boilermakers' Society for the case. The verdict was not a *carte blanche* threat to all trade union funds for the reason that trade unions were considered to be a restraint on trade; it was only where trade union actions were regarded as 'unreasonable' that funds remained unprotected – and then only against prosecutions pressed under the Friendly Society Act (1855). W. P. Roberts maintained other legal remedies still remained open.[22]

In his open letter, Roberts did not go into the background of Hornby v Close. This arose because the treasurer of the Bradford branch of the Boilermakers' Society stole £24 from branch funds. When Roberts, prosecuting, appeared for the Boilermakers Society, he found the magistrates were both employers, staunchly anti-union and leading figures in a recent dispute in the iron industry. When the Boilermakers appealed to the Court of Queen's Bench against their adverse decision, Judge Bramwell delivered his verdict, not only upholding it but also giving the ruling that worried trade unionists so much. What has been overlooked by people commenting on Hornby v Close – including J. E. Mortimer in his recent book *The History of the Boilermakers' Society* – is that Roberts was successful with a very similar case which he was pursuing at the same time. The secretary of the Leeds branch of the Boilermakers' Society also absconded with union funds. Though Roberts did not succeed in making him repay what he stole, nevertheless he was sentenced to two years' imprisonment.[23]

Whether or not Roberts' opinion on the legal implications of Hornby v Close were valid, does not detract from the essential value of his open letter. An impressive document, the summation of his thoughts on industrial law, it not only deals in detail, clause by clause, with the proposed legislation, but also enunciates the principles which workers should strive to attain. First, he thought trade unions should fight to get the conspiracy law repealed. Until that happened, he argued, their position was more than unsatisfactory – it endangered their very existence. For almost every action taken by workers as a class, united in furtherance of their interests, could be defined in law as a conspiracy. Roberts considered that they should seek to establish that whatever one man alone can lawfully do, several men may lawfully do in combination. Second, he thought they should campaign to restrict the jurisdiction of magistrates. Over the years, persons appointed to the bench had increasingly been selected from the manufacturing and trading classes. These were less well educated than their predecessors, but more imbued with anti-working class prejudices. A grave defect of the proposed bill was to extend magistrates' jurisdiction. Third, he believed their interests would be best safeguarded if, in a greater proportion of cases, there was trial by jury, particularly when members were fairly selected. Another fault of the proposed bill was to restrict the use of juries – 'a heavy loss to a working man'.

Dealing with the clauses of the bill in detail, Roberts said trade unions would gain nothing from registering. But they would, under clause 2, have to adhere to observing certain rules, thereby limiting their autonomy. Moreover, they would have to furnish the Registrar with membership returns and regular financial statements. Such information would be exceedingly valuable to hostile employers and governments. Clause 3 made using violence, intimidation, molestation or obstruction criminal offences punishable with up to three months' imprisonment with hard labour. Here, Roberts objected to the vague terminology, which gave magistrates the opportunity to construe, for example, a stray oath as intimidation. (Though Roberts did not mention it, in R v Druitt (1868), Judge Bramwell had held that subjecting a blackleg to black looks or merely to place an advertisement in a newspaper, advising men not to seek employment at a given place, constituted intimidation.) Even where clear definitions were provided, Roberts objected to the proposed act because it could turn quite innocent behaviour into crimes. Molestation included following another person, a thing that might be done merely to peacefully persuade. Likewise, watching and besetting involved keeping a house or workplace under surveillance. Again, this could be quite legitimate activity Roberts argued: 'It is only by working men getting together and reasoning on the considerations which belong to their trade, its locality and special circumstances that they have a chance of persuading each other to act together for their mutual protection.' It is always in the interests of employers to restrict, or better still prevent, this from occurring, and they therefore seek to criminalize the activity. Roberts' solution to the problem was disarmingly simple. He felt that clause 3 should be expunged, that the offences it mentioned should not exist. Instead trade unionists should be treated like everybody else in society. There should be no specifically industrial offences that apply only to them. In other words, a crime – say, using violence – should be treated in the same way whether it happened in a park, a public house or on a picket line.

Many other criticisms were made. Under clause 5, trade agreements were 'not unlawful'. Yet, the authorities' anti-trade union malice made these legally unenforceable, thereby depriving workers of a weapon, admittedly rarely used, against recalcitrant employers. Clause 6 prevented trade unions from going to law to compel their members to observe democratically made decisions. Though unions were given no legal redress against disrupters or blacklegs, their enemies could turn to a string of clauses to arraign unions and their active members before the courts. Moreover, clause 21 increased magistrates' jurisdiction while clause 22 increased the sums of money required to obtain bail. Another clause placed general supervision of unions under the central control of the meddlesome Board of Trade.

W. P. Roberts contended that no private club, educational institution or other organization would agree to abide by the stringent conditions which this bill would impose. He warned, 'All this exposure and interference would be entirely destructive of the purposes of a trade union.' He urged them not to register and thus to avoid the attendant inconveniences and penalties. Throughout history, he declared, there had been 'the unceasing contention of our Parliament against the working man'. In 1351, it had passed the Statute of Labourers and from then onwards, 'It would seem that, as each law came into operation against the workman, a fresh attempt was made by him to preserve his power to act in combination with those who, like himself, were helpless when acting alone.' In the present circumstances, the People's Attorney advised them to repudiate the 1871 Trade Union Bill. They should 'insist upon it that workmen be not exceptionally treated; deny as loudly as you are permitted the assertion that working men require more than ordinary restraints from crime and wrong. Denounce to your fullest power the anomalies and iniquities of the present law. But don't commit the folly of accepting the proposed Bill as a substitute.'

The union leaders were not moved by his appeal and the misgivings he expressed in his pamphlet were soon justified. In 1872, Mr Justice Brett showed in the case R v Bunn how he defined 'improper molestation' in a dangerously wide manner. It was 'anything done with improper intent, which the jury should think was an unjustifiable annoyance and interference with the master's conduct of business, and which in any business would be such as to have a deterring effect on masters of ordinary nerve'. Trade unionists immediately responded to the Bunn decision with angry meetings and strikes, none of which prevented employers from continuing to use the act. For example, in 1873 sixteen women, the wives of agricultural labourers on strike, were imprisoned for intimidation of a blackleg.[24]

For unions, the 1871 Act represented a new departure. Admittedly, it furnished them with a means whereby they could recover funds from a defaulting official. Even so, to secure legal status was a two-edged weapon. Previously, they had no legal status; like a football crowd or a gang of hooligans, they could not be prosecuted as a collective entity, regardless of how violent or objectionable their conduct might have been. This immunity, especially in view of the judiciary's in-built hostility, had certain advantages for trade unions. Only as individuals could they be held legally liable. However, once they had acquired legal status, they had started along a new road. While they might be able to obtain the repossession of, say, £24 from an embezzling treasurer in Bradford, in return for this concession they left themselves dangerously vulnerable. Ahead of them lay the Taff Vale judgement, the loss of union funds because workers had taken industrial action, and, even more crippling, the sequestration of all union assets, as happened to the NUM during the miners' strike of 1984–5. Many workers today may consider W. P. Roberts was right: the price paid for legal recognition has been too high.

Similarly, there may be considerable agreement with Roberts on the threat posed to workers by the law of conspiracy. In 1973, three building workers – the Shrewsbury Three – were imprisoned for conspiracy. One of them, Des Warren, was designated a political prisoner by Amnesty International. This did not lead the Labour government, returned at the 1974 general election, to release them. Rather the Home Secretary, Roy Jenkins, permitted 'the liquid cosh' to be administered to Warren. As a result, his health has been damaged. Though not formally conceding liability, the Home Office has paid him compensation.

The fact that many of the issues raised by W. P. Roberts' open letter are still discussed today may indicate that many aspects of industrial relations have not fundamentally altered since it was written. Equally, it may be a sign that his proposals, however sound, were inherently controversial. Certainly, his speeches and writings isolated him from the union bureaucrats, the newly-emerging group who held the reins of power in the labour movement. To this group, his militancy seemed to be a relic from a bygone age.

In the last stage of his life, his services were less in demand. For some time he had settled in London, opening an office in Great Russell Street, and had hoped to be kept busy. He had also hoped to secure the parliamentary nomination for Thomas Duncombe's old constituency of Finsbury. In view of the deterioration in his health, he may not have been too disappointed that this did not happen. On one of his occasional visits to Manchester, he was taken ill, probably having suffered a stroke, and newspaper reports indicate he was not expected to live. Nevertheless, he made the train journey to London and then on home to Heronsgate.[25]

William Prowting Roberts died on 7 September 1871. He is buried with his wife in Chorleywood churchyard, just outside what had been the first Chartist Land Plan estate at Heronsgate.

17 The People's Attorney: a critical appraisal

W. P. Roberts was the English counterpart of Clarence Darrow, an American lawyer who was dubbed by one of his biographers 'the attorney for the damned'. Both men were quick to take up the cudgels on behalf of the poor, the underdog, the disadvantaged. Never did they reject a case because it would bring them hatred or contempt.

Obviously a controversial figure, widely divergent assessments can be made of Roberts' behaviour. What to one historian is a sign of stubbornness, an inability to see reason, would to another be an indication of his courage and adoption of a principled stand. His habit of arriving late at meetings, thereby disrupting proceedings, can be construed in different ways. On the one hand, it can be seen as a sign of his vanity, a means of drawing attention to himself, perhaps to get a standing ovation. On the other, it could be the result of his back-breaking work schedule, his constant struggle to cram more than possible into each day.

Roberts never expressed a sophisticated ideological position; rather his motivation arose out of strong personal experiences. He was very much a family man. The handful of his private letters that have survived reveal how attached he was to his wife and children, how he loved to be in their company. He believed that everybody else had the same right to this basic pleasure, but society denied it to the many. Poor pay, long hours of toil and oppression made a rich, fulfilling family life unattainable for most workers.

Although he rarely publicly expressed his religious views, Roberts remained throughout his life an ardent Christian. This strengthened his conviction in human fellowship and comradeship. All people were God's children and were entitled to be treated as such. Yet, many received only diabolical treatment, and Roberts regarded the individuals responsible for this as being diabolical themselves. Whether or not they hypocritically claimed to be Christian, they were really unchristian or, more accurately, anti-Christian. In court, he saw the struggle very much in the same light as Thomas Bunyan did in *Pilgrim's Progress*, as simply a battle between Good and Evil. It served to make his utterances still more outspoken.

From the beginning of his career, Roberts cherished a belief in the law. He considered that existing legal practice was a corruption; the underlying principles of the law, however, were sound. He strongly believed in the notion of equality before the law – not merely as a formal proposition, to be just mentioned in passing, but as an essential, integral part of the judicial process. The cynical manipulation of the courts – their use not as an instrument of justice but for maintenance of an unjust society – aroused his wrath.

Right to the end, Roberts remained the rumbustious rebel, fighting (as he saw it) the good fight. Others might capitulate or compromise; he did not. Addressing thousands of Durham pitmen at Pittington in his old age, he proudly boasted that he had stood in the same spot twenty-five years before and said the same things. This consistency was a source of his great strength – and weakness. It meant that he had failed to appreciate the dramatic transformation which was taking place in Victorian Britain. His message had not changed and taken account of changing circumstances. He failed to understand the social forces that were conspiring to marginalize him. While the workers' position in society had not fundamentally altered – they still did not control their own destiny – nevertheless their pay and conditions were improving. Growing affluence had a mellowing effect. Industrial strife became less frequent. The rhetoric of conflict was less frequently used. Insofar as workers turned to the law, they did so as a means of settling disputes rather than as a weapon to be used to win them. Both sides of industry wanted to create a legal framework to assist in the creation of greater amity.

A few illustrations, contrasting responses in early-Victorian and late-Victorian England, provide an inkling of the process taking place. In the 1844 dispute in the North-East coalfields, Lord Londonderry had instructed his agents to single out for victimization the union leaders at every colliery. They were to get the harshest treatment. Evicted along with their families, as they shivered in the roadside encampments, they ·could be certain in the knowledge that never again would they secure a job down the pit. What a contrast in 1889!

On 25 May of that year, the *Newcastle Weekly Chronicle* reported that Lord Londonderry, admittedly not the same one, had written to the North Seaham lodge of the Durham Miners' Association saying that 'nothing would give her Ladyship and himself greater pleasure' than to lay the cornerstone of the new miners' hall at Seaham.

In the 1844 dispute, when the press unfairly criticized W. P. Roberts, suggesting that he had deserted his post (whereas actually he had been rushing round the country, collecting money for the union's dwindling strike fund), he replied to the calumnies with a quotation from Shakespeare's *Macbeth* on the front page of his *Miners' Magazine*: First witch: 'Where hast thou been, sister?' Second witch: 'Killing swine.' To Roberts, the coalowners were swine, hated and detested swine. The best service they could perform would be to follow the example of their Gadarene counterparts in the Bible and drown themselves. The atmosphere in late-Victorian times had entirely altered; friendship and mutual understanding prevailed between coalowners and union leaders. At a public ceremony Lord Joicey, one of County Durham's largest colliery owners, made Thomas Wilson, general-secretary of the Durham Miners' Association, a personal gift of £250. He said that the union leader had been like a father to him; he could always go to him whenever problems arose. Thomas Burt, MP, of the Northumberland Miners', jocularly interjected that, if £250 was the going rate for bribes, he was quite amenable.

Since the 1840s trade unions had become more structured. A union bureaucracy, with interests distinct from the membership, had emerged. In various ways, this could help the employers, as they testified in their evidence to the Royal Commission on Trade Unions (1867–9). In times of economic crisis, a call from the coalowners for the pitmen to take a pay cut was liable to go unheeded. However, when the appeal came from the union leaders, then the same suspicion might not be there. Not only did people like Alexander MacDonald and Thomas Burt help, in a spirit of compromise, to smooth out problems, they also acted as a transmission belt, persuading colliers to accept new values and working practices that were helpful to the employers. Affluent and self-made men themselves, glowing examples of self-help, they could ask their members, quite sincerely, to eschew drunkenness and the taking of 'unauthorised Saints' days', i.e., absenteeism.

Whatever the accomplishment, there was of course a cost. A

fascinating insight into the changed relationship between union leaders and their members came at a ceremony in 1877. This was to unveil busts of Tommy Hepburn and Martin Jude, two pioneers of the movement, which still today adorn the union headquarters in Durham. Thomas Burt seized on the opportunity to compare the problems they faced in the 1830s and 1840s with those encountered then:

> At the period of Hepburn and Jude, it was more difficult than it has been since. The leaders had to face oppression and contumely, a hostile public opinion and a hostile press but perhaps Jude and Hepburn had one encouragement which the leaders of the working class did not possess in so great a degree, they had not the hostility of the men they took the lead of.

This period witnessed the emergence of the first rank-and-file movements. A feeling of hostility to union leaders, a belief that the leaders had 'sold out to the bosses' and a sense that the members no longer democratically controlled their own union structures would lead, from time to time, to grassroot rebellions. Usually they were quickly crushed. Both the employers and union leaders had a mutual interest in the maintenance of the status quo. Rank-and-file members, not possessing the financial resources or organizational strength, could rarely, if ever, withstand the combined onslaught of employers and union bureaucracy. Historically, as the shop stewards' movements in the First World War and in the 1960s and 1970s show, these provide the impetus that may create a move to the left politically, one that challenges the capitalist system.

In retrospect, the struggle against Alexander MacDonald in the 1860s which led to the attempt to build an alternative to the Miners' National Association, in the form of the Practical Miners, can be viewed as an early manifestation of this phenomenon. Marx and Engels never envisaged the possibility of reformism having an enduring impact. They thought that, as capitalism plunged deeper and deeper into crisis, working-class organizations would cast aside the cardboard characters of compromise. In the short run, however, Marx and Engels were determined to keep the goodwill of the junta, the key union leaders of the time, and completely disregarded this seething discontent from the lower depths. The union leaders' assistance was essential if the First International's British section was to have credibility. So, apparently, they did not utter a word of criticism. By contrast, W. P. Roberts, attuned to the day-to-day sufferings of pitmen, championed the anti-MacDonald cause. Workers had a right to control their own destiny. It was part of their struggle, which he always backed, to control democratically their own lives.

In terms of the duration and extent of his commitment to Chartism, W. P. Roberts had a record of activity that no one exceeded. Yet, he confined himself to addressing the demonstrations and fighting the court cases; he never became involved in the internal disputes about the movement's strategy. He appeared to have a naïve belief that, if the correct things were said sufficiently often, ultimately the cause would triumph.

Chartism did not triumph, of course, and the reasons for this can easily be given. Chartism did not represent the British working class fully mature, when it might have had the strength to enforce its will; rather its significance is that it represented the emergence, for the first time, of the working class as an important force in the political arena. Inevitably, it engendered hatred and suspicion in the middle and upper classes, who had no inclination whatsoever to indulge in a power-sharing arrangement. What they wanted was to keep the working class at arm's length. Moral force was therefore a non-starter; and the only alternative was physical force. For a revolution to succeed, three conditions are necessary: (i) society must be wracked by a crisis so profound that the ruling class, uncertain of the way forward, becomes divided and split; (ii) at the same time, the state's repressive forces no longer remain its loyal supporters, prepared to crush the opposition; (iii) conditions must be so intolerable that the mass of people are ready, if necessary, to sacrifice their lives to end them.

It can be seen, therefore, why physical force Chartism had to fail. On each occasion, the call to the barricades obtained enthusiastic, but localized, support. In 1839, South Wales, the West Country, and Northern England answered the call; London and the South, Scotland and North Wales remained largely quiescent. In 1842, the disturbances spread through the industrialized Midlands to Lancashire and Scotland; but most of the areas that had been rebellious in 1839 stayed calm. In 1848, London and the Irish immigrants raised the flag of revolt; Wales, Scotland and North-East England gave little or no trouble. This meant that the authorities had, on all three occasions, to deal with resistance of manageable proportions. This was particularly true because, while it was possible to point to isolated examples where the loyalty of troops was doubtful, there were no indications of serious disaffection. All this is related to the absence of the first two essential pre-conditions.

Disagreements may have existed in the upper echelons of society over the Corn Laws, but, generally, economic expansion, the rapid accretion of wealth and power, both at home and abroad, strengthened the British ruling class. A growing number of people looked to capitalism to provide a better tomorrow; they had no desire to take a revolutionary leap into the dark. For this reason, as Marx acknowledged in 1848, whatever happened in other countries, a successful revolution here in Britain was just not conceivable:

> Those who correctly assess England and the role she plays in modern history were not surprised that the continental revolutions passed over her without leaving a trace for the time being. England is a country which, through her industry and commerce, dominates all the revolutionary nations of the Continent and nevertheless remains relatively independent of her customers because she dominates the Asian, American and Australian markets (*Collected Works,* vol. viii, p. 101).

British working-class movements influenced the evolution of Marxism, then in its formative period. Initially, Marx and Engels merely reported events in Britain. As they grew in self-assurance and sharpened their analytical tools, critical comments started to appear. Also, enrichment of their theories came from the same source. In his *The Chartist Challenge*, A. R. Schoyen argues that the Marxist theory of the state as an organ of class rule came from studying the authorities' responses to the problems posed by the emergence of a working class. Hitherto, in a predominantly rural society, the authorities had to cope with disorders, usually local, sporadic and of short duration. Now, in an industrialized society, they faced a permanent threat of an entirely different magnitude. To cope with it, a new repressive apparatus needed to be built.

Constitutional authorities often talk about the liberties enjoyed by British subjects. They refer to the separation of powers, an elaborate system of checks and balances, that stops any individual or institution acquiring overweening power, and thereby being able to impose tyrannical rule upon the community. But such utterances are normally not put in a class context. In times of crises – for example, 1839, 1842 and 1848 – the authorities' conduct radically alters. These occasions were impressive illustrations of class consciousness and class solidarity, not of the workers but of their rulers. Sensing that their vested interests were under threat, the administration, government and judiciary, backed by those with wealth and privilege, acted as one in defence of the established order. Rules were bent, laws broken, violence used. Customarily, the defence of property remained paramount, a much more vital consideration than the rights of the individual. In his three books on popular protests, George Rudé shows that the impression conveyed by the press of mobs running amok, indulging in senseless killings and violence, was usually a figment of the imagination. Rather it was the authorities who displayed more brutality and violence than their opponents. This was manifested in the way demonstrations were crushed. Between the Porteous riots of 1736 and the Chartist disturbances of 1848, it was estimated by Professor Rudé that protesters were responsible for seven deaths while the forces of law and order killed 609. And it was not merely the scale of violence; it was also the judicial treatment of offenders. A *Punch* cartoon in 1848 showed a policeman talking to a Chartist demonstrator. He pointed out that the courts would adopt an entirely different response to the killing of a member of the Metropolitan constabulary and the killing of a demonstrator.

To the People's Attorney, that was wrong. As we have seen. Roberts struggled throughout his life to secure for everybody in society, even the most lowly, equal rights, including equality before the law. In the last analysis, he believed that this could be accomplished by the power of persuasion. The public had to be persuaded that the existing position was unjust and indefensible. Since government ultimately depended upon the consent of the governed, the withdrawal of consent was a very powerful weapon. Yet, this overlooked the vital question of how opposition is organized; merely having everybody, say, shaking their heads in the privacy of their homes about some iniquitous law would be quite useless.

In Roberts' lifetime, workers achieved some success with their attempts to repeal obnoxious legislation. The Combination Acts, the

Master and Servant Acts and the legally-enforceable Bond were removed from the statute book. How was this accomplished? Not on the basis, at least directly, of the strength of the workers' case. Rather it was on the strength of workers themselves, their ability to retaliate by punishing their masters. This made these laws counter-productive, acting as an incitement rather than a means to secure acquiescence. In these circumstances, the smooth running of the system demanded their removal. On the other hand, in a downturn in working-class activity, the ruling class seized the opportunity to introduce new repressive legislation as well as to interpret existing laws in a manner more hostile to workers' interests. Blaina provides a sad instance of this happening. In the wake of the Janet James case of 1864–5, when Roberts used the court for his ferocious denunciations of the truck system, his agitation helped pitmen to organize and build a union in South Wales. This, in turn, helped to force the coalowners to end the truck system. However, a few years later, resisting a pay cut in the economic depression, the pitmen's union was smashed and the coalowners returned to their old ways. In 1871, a royal commission reported that the truck system was operating again in South Wales, including Blaina.

In the last analysis, the relationship of class forces remained the determining factor. The judicial system, however, was not like the moon, passively reflecting the light-energy that came from elsewhere. Sometimes it had an important symbolic influence of its own. People's behaviour was altered not so much by what the law actually said as by their own perceptions of the law. That can be quite a different thing. The fate of the National Association of United Trades demonstrated this during a downswing in working-class activity. Short prison sentences for its three leaders, coupled with a few words of reproof from on high, and the organization ceased to function as a trade union. Were the price for smashing workers' organizations always as cheap, employers would be continually turning to the law. But the Monkwearmouth colliery dispute of 1869 illustrated that employers might find that to resort to litigation could have exactly the opposite of the desired effect. Far from smashing the local union, the fiery legal battles kindled the flames of militancy that spread throughout Durham, resulting in the creation of a powerful county association. Roberts realized this could happen, which is why he always spoke through the courtroom window. It helped reinforce the workers' conviction that they had justice on their side, making them still more determined to struggle. And, the Miners' Attorney-General was convinced, it was by struggle that progress was made.

It may be that this biography turns out to be of negligible historical interest. W. P. Roberts did not achieve his long-term ambition of creating a society where all people are treated equally, even before the law. Critics might rightly regard him as one of life's failures. They could, perhaps, quote W. H. Auden: 'For the defeated, history gives neither help nor pardon.' It could be argued, however, that parallels exist between the problems confronting workers in his day and today. As well as Victorian values, currently many Victorian legal practices are being reimposed. Increasingly, the law is used as a means of disciplining trade unionists, weakening their organization and sequestrating their funds. No equivalent sanctions are taken against employers. They can flout laws with virtual impunity, whether they relate to health, safety or workers' rights. Almost certainly, therefore, there is a need for greater interest to be taken in the legal system – the laws themselves, who operates them, and who benefits from their operation. When that happens, perhaps the spirit of W. P. Roberts will again stalk the land.

Notes

Chapter 1 The Making of a Chartist

1. *Dictionary of National Biography*, vol.xvii, p. 1284; J. H. Johnson, 'Chelmsford Grammar School', *Essex Review*, 1946, pp. 22–4; letter from Oliver van Oss, headmaster of Charterhouse, 20 January 1972.
2. *Bath & Cheltenham Gazette*, 2 October and 28 October 1832.
3. William Thomas, *The Philosophical Radicals* (Oxford, 1979), p. 212.
4. *Bath & Cheltenham Gazette*, 2 October 1832.
5. For R. B. Pugh's views see 'Chartism in Wiltshire', *Wiltshire Archaeological and National History Magazine*, no.54, 1951–2, pp. 169–84, and R. B. Pugh, 'Chartism in Somerset and Wiltshire', in Asa Briggs (ed.) *Chartist Studies* (London, 1959), pp. 174–219.
6. R. S. Neale, *Bath 1680–1850: a social history* (London, 1985), passim; R. S. Neale, 'Class and ideology in a nineteenth century provincial town: Bath 1800–1850', *Our History* no.42, Summer 1966, pp. 3–7.
7. E. Hobsbawm and G. Rudé, *Captain Swing* (London, 1968) pp. 308–358.
8. Joyce Marlow, *The Tolpuddle Martyrs* (London, 1985), p. 100.
9. Document written 11 September 1827, in the possession of Mr Charles Fitzgerald, of Tonbridge. Letter from C. Fitzgerald, 13 June 1984.
10. *Northern Star*, 8 December 1838.
11. For best account see David McNulty, 'Working Class Movements in Somerset and Wiltshire, 1837–1848' (unpublished Ph.D. thesis, Manchester University, 1981, pp. 21–25.
12. *Bath Guardian*, 20 February 1836.
13. Ibid., 19 November–3 December 1836.
14. David McNulty, 'Working Class Movements in Somerset and Wiltshire', pp. 39–40; *Bath Guardian*, 6 October 1838; *Bath Figaro*, 13 October 1838.
15. *Bath Figaro*, 2 February 1839.
16. *Bath Journal*, 28 August 1837.
17. *Bath Figaro*, 2 February 1839.
18. M. Hovell, *The Chartist Movement* (Manchester, 1970), p. 71.
19. R. S. Neale, *Class and Ideology in the Nineteenth Century* (London,

1972), p. 48, suggests that strong radical feelings had been increasing in Bath since 1812.

20. For Henry Vincent see R. G. Gammage, *History of the Chartist Movement* (London, 1854). p. 11; and Brian Harrison's entry, *Dictionary of Labour Biography*, vol. i, p. 326–34.

21. Letter of H. Vincent to John Minikin, 10 June 1839 (Vin.1/1/12); also H. Vincent to W. Lovett, 16 November 1838 (Lovett Collection, vol. i, 291a). In his letters Vincent refers to his triumphal arrival in Wiltshire, with meetings organized for him even in ladies' riding schools.

22. Albert Goodwin, *The Friends of Liberty* (London, 1979), pp. 56–7.

23. John A. Cannon, *The Chartists in Bristol* (London, 1964), p. 2.

24. H. Vincent letter to J. Minikin, 17 November 1838 (Vin.1/1/13).

25. *Bath Guardian*, 28 April and 12 May 1838; *Bath Chronicle*, 11 and 25 February 1839.

26. Lovett Collection, vol. 1, 259; H. A. Bruce, *Life of Sir William Napier* (London, 1864), vol. i,pp. 524–8; Priscilla Napier, *Revolution and the Napier Brothers, 1820–1840* (London, 1973), pp. 248–70.

Chapter 2   The Rise of Physical Force Toryism

1. 'The life and rambles of Henry Vincent', *Western Vindicator*, 4 April and 20 February 1839; also H. Vincent to W. Lovett, 10 November 1838 (Lovett Papers, vol. 1, 291a).

2. B. M. Place Collection, newspaper cuttings, vol. 56, Jan–May 1839. (Place Collection henceforth P.C.)

3. Public Records Office, Home Office papers 40/47, 25 March 1839. (Home Office henceforth H.O.)

4. *Devizes Gazette*. 2 July 1840; *Bristol Mercury*, 6 April 1839; *Northern Star*, 14 April 1939.

5. H.O.40/47, 21 March 1839; P.C., vol. 56, p. 184.

6. P.C., vol. 56, p. 209; H.O.40/48, 27 and 28 March 1839.

7. *Bath Journal*, 26 March 1838.

8. For the Battle of Devizes see *Bath & Cheltenham Gazette*, 9 April 1839; *Bath Journal*, 8 April 1839; *Weekly True Sun*, 4 April 1839; *The Charter*, 7 April 1839; B.M. Add MSS. 34,245 A, f.228; H.O.40/48. 21. For Roberts' personal account, *Western Vindicator*, 20 April 1839.

9. *Bath Journal*, 12 November 1839.

10. R. B. Pugh, 'Chartism in Somerset and Wiltshire' in Asa Briggs (ed.) *Chartist Studies*, pp. 183–4.

11. *Devizes Gazette*, 4 May 1839.

12. H.O. 40/48, 23 May 1839.

13. *Northern Star*, 12 May 1839; *Wiltshire Independent*, 9 May 1839; *Devizes Gazette*, 9 May 1839.

14. Roberts also complained to the Home Secretary that the authorities were preventing him from performing his professional duties (HO.40/48, 8 May 1839).

15. R. S. Neale, *Bath 1680–1850: a social history*, p. 373.
16. *The Charter* 26 July 1839.
17. *Northern Liberator*, 10 July 1839.
18. *Western Vindicator*, 20 July 1839.
19. Information from Canon Roberts, Charles Fitzgerald, Rosemary Tucker and other descendants of W. P. Roberts.
20. Wiltshire assizes, seven charges of conspiracy between June 1838 and July 1839, of armed assembly, advising arming and arson, as well as using seditious language and holding torchlight meetings (H.O.40/48).
21. J. R. Lewis, *The English Bar* (London, 1982), pp. 65–7.
22. *Northern Star*, 21 March 1839.
23. Full text of Roberts' letter published in *Bath and Cheltenham Gazette*, 30 June 1840.
24. Ibid., 13 June and 4 July 1840; *Bath Chronicle*, 9 July 1840.
25. Brian Abel-Smith and Robert Stevens, *Lawyers and the Courts* (London, 1983), p. 20; R. Robson, *The Attorney in Eighteenth Century England*, ch.x.
26. H.O. 46/56, 8 and 12 July 1840; *Wiltshire Independent*, 9 and 30 July 1840; *Bath Gazette*, 12 July 1840.
27. Edward Thompson, *The Making of the English Working Class* (London, 1962), p. 820.

Chapter 3 The Road to Newport

1. Leon Trotsky, *Writings on Britain*, vol. ii, pp. 93–4.
2. Reminiscences of G. J. Harney in *Newcastle Weekly Chronicle*, 5 January 1889.
3. W. E. Adams, *Memoirs of a Social Atom* (New York, 1968), p. 211.
4. W. Napier, *Life and Opinions of General Sir Charles Napier* (London, 1857), p. 42.
5. *Northern Liberator*, 18 November 1837. See H.O. 41/13 for Home Secretary's circular to Lord Lieutenants about forming armed associations.
6. F. C. Mather, *Chartism and Society* (London, 1980), pp. 150–2; J. Stevenson and R. Quinault, *Popular Protest and Public Order* (London, 1974), pp. 26–8; Robert K. Dent, *Old and New Birmingham* (Birmingham, 1880), p. 461; Conrad Gill, *A History of Birmingham* (Oxford, 1962), vol. i, p. 252.
7. *Northern Star*, 13 July 1839.
8. David Williams, *John Frost* (Cardiff, 1939), p. 122–3.
9. R. B. Pugh, 'Chartism in Somerset and Wiltshire', p. 194; *Monmouthshire Merlin*, 23 November 1839; David Williams, *John Frost*, p. 178.
10. *Western Vindicator*, 17 August 1839.
11. Dorothy Thompson, 'Chartism as an historical subject', *Labour History*, Bulletin 20, Spring 1970, for discussion of the new means of communication and organization.

12. R. v Vincent and others. Monmouth summer assizes, 2 August 1839. *Reports of State Trials*, vol. iii, pp. 1038–86; also *Northern Star*, 10 August 1839.
13. F. C. Mather, 'The Government and the Chartists', in Asa Briggs (ed.) *Chartist Studies*, p. 380.
14. *Naval and Military Gazette*, 5 January, 16 March, 23 March, 6 July and 17 August 1839.
15. W. Napier, *Life and Opinions of General Sir Charles Napier*, pp. 94–6.
16. Ivor Wilks, *South Wales and the Rising of 1839*, p. 253, names twenty while David Williams, *John Frost*, says there were twenty-two.
17. T. A. Devyr, *The Odd Book of the Nineteenth Century* (New York, 1882), pp. 194–5.
18. *Northern Star*, 30 November 1839.
19. Dorothy Thompson, *The Chartists* (London, 1984), p. 81.
20. Mrs Hardcastle (ed.), *Autobiography of John, Lord Campbell* (London, 1887), vol. ii, p. 127.
21. W. Napier, op. cit., vol. ii, p. 126.
22. David Jones, *The Last Rising: the Newport insurrection of 1839* (Oxford, 1985); Keith J. Thomas, *Chartism in Monmouthshire and the Newport Uprising*; Ivor Wilks, *South Wales and the Rising of 1839*.
23. *Monmouthshire Merlin*, 14 December 1839.
24. *Bath Herald*, 16 November 1839.
25. R v O'Connor, Yorkshire spring assizes, 17 March 1840. *Reports of State Trials*, vol. iii, pp. 1086–97, 5 QB 16. For W. P. Roberts' involvement see G. J. Holyoake, *The Reasoner*, 16 September 1855.
26. James Epstein, *Feargus O'Connor: The Lion of Freedom* (London, 1982), p. 211.

Chapter 4   The Years of Uncertainty

1. *Bath Herald*, 16 November 1839; Dorothy Thompson, *The Early Chartists* (London, 1971), pp. 241–63.
2. *Western Vindicator*, 16 November 1839.
3. Ibid.
4. *Northern Star*, 23 January 1841.
5. *Bristol Times*, 21 February 1839.
6. H.O. 40/53, 24 January 1840 and H.O. 40/56, 21 January 1840.
7. *Western Vindicator*, 14 December 1839; H.O. 40/45.
8. *The Chartist and Republican Journal*, 17 April 1841.
9. Mark Hovell, *The Chartist Movement*, p. 191.
10. David McNulty, 'Working Class Movements in Somerset and Wiltshire, 1837–1848', p. 378.
11. *Northern Star*, 16 January 1842.
12. Ibid., 1 September 1841.
13. *Northern Star*, 3 April 1841.
14. Ibid., 23 January 1841.

15. *Bath Journal*, 7 June 1841; *Bath Guardian*, 7 June 1841.
16. D. Thompson, *The Chartists*, pp. 262–3.
17. *Northern Star*, 24 December 1841.
18. *Bath Chronicle*, 2 September 1841.
19. *Northern Star*, 26 February 1842.
20. Ibid., 12 March 1842.
21. D. McNulty, op. cit., p. 430.
22. R. Welford, *Lore and Legend twixt Tyne and Tweed* (Newcastle, 1891), xlvii, pp. 12–15.

Chapter 5   The General Strike

1. H.O.45/262. Disturbances in Wiltshire 1842.
2. E. Hobsbawm, 'The British standard of living, 1790–1850' in *Labouring Men* (London, 1964),pp. 72–86; Mick Jenkins, *The General Strike of 1842* (London, 1980), pp. 41–5 passim; John Stevenson, *Popular Disturbances in England, 1700–1870* (London, 1979), pp. 262–6.
3. M. T. P. Pickard, 'Chartism and Trade Unionism', (unpublished Ph.D. thesis Sheffield University, 1986), pp. 135–8, emphasizes the interaction of Chartism and trade unionism in this period.
4. William Benbow, *Grand National Holiday and Congress of the Productive Classes* (1832), reprinted with introduction by A. J. C. Rutter in *International Review of Social History* (1936).
5. Rosa Luxemburg, *Ausgewahlte Reden und Schriften* (Berlin, 1955), p. 202.
6. Marx–Engels, *Collected Works*. vol. iii, pp. 204–5.
7. A. C. Bernson and Viscount Esher (eds), *The Letters of Queen Victoria* (London, 1907), vol. i, pp. 520–1.
8. Letter of Sir James Graham to Sir William Warre, 16 August 1842, quoted in F. C. Mather's essay in Asa Briggs (ed.) *Chartist Studies*, p. 389; Manchester chief constable's letter to Home Secretary, H.O.45/249.
9. Peel Papers, British Museum, quoted in F. C. Mather, *Public Order in the Age of the Chartists* (London, 1980), p. 53.
10. In the early 1950s, I edited a monthly journal called *Socialist Review* which was printed by Amey, of Lune Street, Preston. In the back wall of a bookshop in the street there were still the bullet-marks from 1842 when troops killed three demonstrators.
11. N. T. McLellan, 'Chartism and the Churches' (unpublished Ph.D. thesis, Edinburgh University, 1947), p. 66.
12. *The Life of Thomas Cooper*, written by himself, (London, 1872), pp. 271–2.
13. Bob Fyson, 'The crisis of 1842' in James Epstein and D. Thompson (eds), *The Chartist Experience* (London, 1982), p. 207.
14. *The Potters' Examiner and Workmen's Advocate* 22 March 1844.
15. George Rudé, *The Crowd in History* (New York, 1964), pp. 189–190.

16. Thomas Cooper, op. cit., p. 217.
17. *State Trials*, vol. iv, 1249. Stafford spring assizes, 29 March 1843.
18. A. P. Donajgrodzki, 'Sir James Graham at the Home Office', *Historical Journal*, 1979, pp. 111–2; Henry Pelling, *Popular Politics and Society in Late Victorian Britain* (London, 1968), pp. 63–4; Alan Harding, *A Social History of English Law* (London, 1973), p. 353; G. J. Holyoake, *Joseph Rayner Stephens* (London, 1881), pp. 131–2.
19. Leon Radzinowicz, 'Public order and Chartist disturbances', *Cambridge Law Journal*, 1960, pp. 53–67; also *History of English Criminal Law* (London, 1968), vol. iv, p. 250.
20. *Staffordshire Examiner*, 15 October 1842.
21. George Rudé, *Protest and Punishment* (Oxford, 1978), p. 131.
22. Robert F. Wearmouth, *Some Working-Class Movements of the Nineteenth Century* (London, 1948), p. 214.
23. George Rudé, *Protest and Punishment*, pp. 132–3.
24. H.O. 20/9.
25. William Brockie, *Sunderland Notables* (Sunderland, 1894), pp. 267–8.
26. *Newcastle Weekly Chronicle*, 11 October 1879; C. Godfrey and J. Epstein, 'Chartist prisoners', *Labour History Bulletin*, no. 34, spring 1977, p. 27; H.O.20/10.
27. John Vincent's letter to Minikin, 22 September 1840. VIN 1/1/35.
28. *Miners' Magazine*, June–July 1844.

Chapter 6   The Victorian Working Class and the Law

1. Brian Abel-Smith and Robert Stevens, *Lawyers and the Courts*, p. 12.
2. *Select Committee on Payment of Wages* (1842). Q.2090–2100.
3. J. U. Nef, *The Rise of the British Coal Industry* (London, 1932), vol. ii, pp. 157–64; R. Page Arnot, *The Scottish Miners* (London, 1955), pp. 3–13; Baron F. Duckham, *A History of the Scottish Coal Industry, 1700–1815* (Newton Abbot, 1975), vol. i, pp. 240–314; also see J. Barrowman, 'Slavery in the coal-mines of Scotland', *Trans. Mining Institute of Scotland*, xix (1897–8).
4. W. H. Fraser, *Labour Relations and the Courts of Scotland, 1707–1813*, [n.d.], pp. 1–3.
5. *Select Committee on Workmen* (1837–8). Q.1015–1025; William Napier, *The Life and Opinions of General Sir Charles Napier*, vol. ii, p. 142.
6. 39 & 40 Geo.III., c.38.
7. John W. Topping, 'The History, Law and Practice of Picketing in the United Kingdom' (unpublished Master of Law thesis, Belfast University, 1979), p. 5; Philip Bagwell, *Industrial Relations* (Dublin, 1974), p. 16.
8. Journeymen Tailors' case (1721) 8 Mod Rep.10; R v Eccles (1783) 1 Leach 274; Clifford v Bramlin (1801) 2 Camp. 369.
9. George Howell, *Labour Legislation, Labour Movements, Labour Leaders* (London, 1902), p. 84.

10. *Northern Star*, 25 July 1846, *Liverpool Mercury*, 19 August 1842.
11. S. and B. Webb, *The History of Trade Unionism*, p. 262; D. N. Pritt, *Law, Class and Society* (London, 1970), pp. 19–20.
12. 34 Ed.III. ci.
13. Patrick Quinlivan and Paul Rose, *The Fenians in England, 1865–1872* (London 1982), p. 125.
14. Daniel Duman, *The Judicial Bench in England, 1727–1875*, Royal Historical Society (1982), pp. 40–52.
15. J. A. G. Griffiths, *The Politics of the Judiciary* (London, 1978), p. 25.
16. Oliver Goldsmith, *The Traveller*, p. 386.
17. Burke's Speech, *Parliamentary History (1780–81)*, vol 21, col. 326; L. Radzinowicz, *A History of English Criminal Law*, vol. i, p. 4.
18. Edward Thompson, *Albion's Fatal Tree* (London, 1975), p. 18; Eric Partridge, *A Dictionary of Historical Slang*, p. 384.
19. Blake Odger, *Digest of the Law of Libel and Slander* (London, 1911), *5th ed.* p. 513; M. W. Patterson, *Sir Francis Burdett and his Times, 1770–1844* (London, 1931), vol. ii, pp. 490–9.
20. Brian Abel-Smith and Robert Stevens, op. cit., pp. 29–30.
21. William Napier, op. cit., vol. ii, p. 153.
22. John Foster, *Class Struggle and the Industrial Revolution* (London, 1974), pp. 64–8.
23. *Glasgow Sentinel*, 23 April 1864.
24. *Leeds Mercury*, 4 March 1864.
25. *Flint Glass Makers' Magazine*, October 1851.
26. *First Report Royal Commission on Constabulary*, pp. 70–6.
27. *Marx and Engels on Britain* (Moscow, 1962), p. 260.
28. W. L. Burn, *The Age of Equipoise* (London, 1964), pp. 153–4.
29. E. A. Antrobus, *London: its dangers and its safety* (London, 1848), p. 22; E. Chadwick's article in *Fraser's Magazine*, January 1868; E. C. Midwinter, *Law and Order in Early Victorian Lancashire* (York, 1968), p. 26.
30. John Stevenson, *Popular Disturbances in England, 1700–1870*, pp. 252–3; James Bent, *Criminal Life: 42 Years in the Lancashire Constabulary* (Manchester, 1891), pp. 25–35; T. A. Critchley, *A History of the Police in England and Wales, 900–1966* (London, 1967), p. 71.
31. E. C. Midwinter, op. cit., pp. 26–8.
32. Clive Emsley, *Policing and its Context, 1750–1870* (London, 1983), p. 74.
33. On Staffordshire, David Phillips, *Crime and Authority in Victorian England*, p. 272; F. C. Mather, *Public Order in the Age of the Chartists*, p. 128.
34. R. Challinor and B. Ripley, *The Miners' Association: a trade union in the age of the Chartists* (London, 1968), pp. 33–4.
35. William Napier, op. cit., vol. ii, p. 65.
36. George Rudé, *Criminal and Victim* (Oxford, 1984), p. 119.
37. Quoted Michael Ignatiev, *A Just Measure of Pain: the penitentiary in the industrial revolution, 1790–1850*, pp. 66–7.
38. W. Dixon's and J. Linney's remarks in *Northern Star*, 1 April 1848; David Jones, *Chartism and the Chartists* (London, 1975), p. 151.
39. Richard Fynes, *The Miners of Northumberland and Durham* (Sunderland, 1873), p. 13.

40. Bell Collection, North of England Mining Engineers' Library, Northumberland Records Office.

Chapter 7   The Battle Against the Bond

1. K. Marx and F. Engels, *Collected Works*, vol. iv, p. 542.
2. Letter quoted by R. Fynes, *The Miners of Northumberland and Durham*, p. 243.
3. *Miners' Magazine*, June–July 1844. Also George Howell, 'Ernest Jones, Chartist', (no pagination).
4. *Flint Glass Makers' Magazine*, October 1851.
5. *Northern Star*, 16 September 1843.
6. Ibid.
7. Ibid., 23 September 1843.
8. Ibid., also *Durham Chronicle*, 11 September 1843.
9. *Miners' Journal*, 21 October 1843.
10. *Northern Star*, 10 September 1843.
11. *Northern Liberator*, 3 July 1839.
12. *Gateshead Observer*, 31 August 1839.
13. *Northern Star*, 15 January 1842.
14. Thornley trial fully reported in Special Supplement to *Miners Advocate* (n.d.). Also in R. Fynes, op. cit., pp. 38–49, and R. Challinor and B. Ripley, *The Miner's Association*, pp. 99–106.
15. R. Fynes, op. cit., p. 243.
16. *Miners' Advocate*, 24 February and 10 March 1844; also Pitmen's Strike Collection, Wigan Public Library.
17. *Northern Star*, 5 August 1843; Frank Machin, *The Yorkshire Miners*, pp. 51–2.
18. *Miners' Magazine*, March–April 1844.
19. K. Marx and F. Engels, op. cit., vol. iv, p. 543.
20. Ibid., pp. 584–96.
21. C. Dickens, *Great Expectations*, chs 20 and 24; W. S. Holdsworth, *Dickens as a Legal Historian* (New York, 1972), p. 62.
22. Alan Anderson, 'The political symbolism of the labour laws', *Labour History*, no. 23, autumn 1971.
23. Pitmen's Strike Collection (no pagination); Robert Colls, *The Colliers' Rant* (London, 1977), p. 112.

Chapter 8   On the Eve of Battle

1. *Manchester Guardian*, 22 July 1843.
2. K. Marx and F. Engels, *Collected Works*, vol. iv, p. 541.
3. *Miners' Journal*, 21 October 1843.
4. *Miners' Magazine*, March 1844.
5. *The Inspector of Mines Report* (1844), p. 43.

6. *Miners' Advocate*, 13 January 1844.
7. *Flint Glass Makers' Magazine*, October 1851.
8. R. Challinor and B. Ripley, *The Miners' Association*, p. 8. S. and B. Webb, *The History of Trade Unionism*, p. 181; R. Fynes, *The Miners of Northumberland and Durham*, ch. viii.
9. *Northern Star*, 9 September 1843.
10. *Miners' Advocate*, 13 January 1844; R. Challinor, *The Lancashire and Cheshire Miners* (Newcastle, 1972), pp. 36–8.
11. *Miners' Magazine*, March 1844.
12. *Northern Star*, 24 February 1844; Executive Committee, Address to the Members, 6 March 1844.
13. Robert Colls, *The Great Northern Coalfield*, (Manchester, 1987), p. 284.
14. *Miners' Magazine*, March 1844.
15. A handbill signed 'A friend of the Coalowners and Pitmen', Pitmen's Strike Collection, North of England Mining Engineers' Library, Newcastle-upon-Tyne.
16. Matthias Dunn, *The Northern Coal Trade* (Newcastle, 1844), p. 203.
17. Dr Alan Heesom, of Durham University, has analysed Lord Londonderry's financial difficulties; D. J. Williams, *Capitalist Combinations in the Coal Industry* (London, 1924), p. 50; F. M. L. Thompson, *English Landed Society in the Nineteenth Century* (London, 1963), pp. 264–5.
18. George Hunter to Lord Londonderry, 21 December 1843, D.C.R.O. D/4/C149, Durham P.R.O.
19. P.R.O. 45/644 and 645; also H.O.45/644.
20. *Newcastle Journal*, 6 April 1844.
21. P.R.O. H.O.45/467. Letter of the Chief Constable of Staffordshire to Sir James Graham, 12 July 1844. Further report H.O.45/66.

Chapter 9   The Big Strike

1. P.R.O. H.O.45/644/75. Letter from Lord Londonderry to Home Secretary, 27 May 1844.
2. *Gateshead Observer*, 26 April 1844; *Newcastle Courant*, 19 April 1844.
3. *Durham Chronicle*, 20 May 1844; *Newcastle Chronicle*, 19 April 1844; *Newcastle Journal*, 13 April 1844.
4. P.R.O. H.O.45/349, 45/643–5.
5. *Newcastle Journal*, 13 April 1844.
6. The attitude of the *Durham Chronicle* drastically altered. As quoted in ch. 7, when Roberts was fighting his campaign against the Bond, the paper was laudatory, but a few months later, in the course of the strike, it published a lot of defamatory remarks and lies. See, for example, *Durham Chronicle* 11 September 1843 and 24 May 1844.
7. P.R.O. H.O.45/644/45. Letter from E. Dunelm to Home Secretary, 15 April 1844.
8. P.R.O. H.O.45/644/101 and 18/644. Letters from Lord Londonderry to Home Secretary, dated 1 June and 21 July 1844.

9. Pitmen's Strike Collection, Wigan Public Library.
10. H.O. 45/644/228, 236 and 239.
11. H.O. 45/644/261.
12. *Miners' Magazine*, June–July 1844; also reprinted in the *Miners' Advocate* and as a handbill.
13. R. Fynes, *The Miners of Northumberland and Durham*, p. 72.
14. H.O.45/ OS.650/104, 107, 110 and 112.
15. H.O.45/644/232.
16. H.O.45/644/56 and 57.
17. H.O.45/644/20. James Wemyss's letter to the Home Secretary, 12 April 1844.
18. H.O.45/644/52.
19. H.O.45/644/232.
20. R. Challinor and B. Ripley, *The Miners' Association*, ch. 10.
21. *Miners' Magazine*, June–July 1848; also handbill in Pitmen's Strike Collection (Newcastle upon Tyne Public Library) and Miners' Strike Collection (Wigan Public Library).
22. W. P. Roberts, *The Haswell Colliery Explosion* (Newcastle, 1845), p. 10.
23. B. Abel-Smith and R. Stevens, *Lawyers and the Courts*, p. 46.
24. *Miners' Advocate*, July 1844; also, Miners' Strike Collection, Wigan.
25. *Northern Star*, 8 November 1845; *Lloyd's Weekly Newspaper*, 1 November 1845.
26. Letter quoted in R. Fynes, op. cit., p. 239.
27. *Gateshead Observer*, 15 March 1845.
28. *Newcastle Journal*, 4 April 1845.
29. *Miners' Magazine*, March–April 1845.

Chapter 10 Uncle Bobby in Lancashire

1. *Northern Star*, 27 April 1844; *Manchester Chronicle and Salford Advertiser*, 27 April 1844.
2. *Bolton Free Press*, 31 January 1846.
3. *Northern Star*, 15 February 1845.
4. Ibid., 13 March 1847.
5. W. P. Roberts' letter to T. S. Duncombe, *Northern Star*, 8 February 1847.
6. Act 6 & 7 W. IV c114 stated that in cases of summary jurisdiction defendants have the right to the benefit of an advocate and 4 G. IV c34 made it absolutely essential for defendants to know the charges against them.
7. *Northern Star*, 26 April 1845.
8. R. Challinor and B. Ripley, *The Miners' Association*, pp. 214–5.
9. Ibid., pp. 196-200; P. W. Kingsford, 'Thomas Slingsby Duncombe', *Marx Memorial Library Bulletin*, no. 100, April 1982.
10. *Northern Star*, 29 March 1845.

11. *Preston Pilot*, 5 June 1847; *Bolton Free Press*, 31 January 1846.
12. *Northern Star*, 29 March 1845.
13. Ibid., 17 April 1848.
14. Ibid., 29 January 1848; also, R. Challinor and B. Ripley, *The Miners' Association* pp. 231–3.
15. *Northern Star*, 2 May 1846.
16. Ibid.
17. *Bolton Chronicle*, 31 January 1846.
18. *Northern Star*, 8 May 1847.
19. J. B. Jeffreys, *The Story of the Engineers* (London, 1946), pp. 26–7.
20. *Verbatim Report of the Trial for Conspiracy in R v Selsby and others* (Liverpool, 1847), p. iii.
21. *Northern Star*, 2 October 1847.
22. 5 Cox.497.
23. 5 Cox CC 495.
24. *Northern Star*, 17 July 1847.

Chapter 11   Politics, Parliamentary and Revolutionary

1. Letters to W. P. Roberts from John Edwards, 7 and 9 May 1847, and G. Chinnery, 10 May 1847.
2. *Blackburn Standard*, 28 June 1847.
3. R. S. Crossley, *Men of Note* (Accrington Public Library); W. R. Handle's Collection (Old Mill Museum, Accrington).
4. *Blackburn Standard*, 2 June 1847.
5. W. P. Roberts' election address published 5 July 1847, reprinted in *Miners' Advocate*, July 1847.
6. *Preston Chronicle*, 21 July 1847.
7. *Blackburn Standard*, 28 June 1847; *Preston Pilot*, 21 July 1847; *Gateshead Guardian*, 31 July 1847.
8. *Preston Chronicle*, 24 July 1847; Patrick Joyce, *Work, Society and Politics: the culture of the factory in late Victorian England* (Brighton, 1980), p. 212.
9. R. Challinor and B. Ripley, *The Miners' Association*, pp. 219–222.
10. Marx–Engels, *Collected Works*, vol. vi, p. 285.
11. *Liverpool Mercury*, 3 December 1847; *Bolton Free Press*, 10 December 1847.
12. *Northern Star*, 25 March 1848.
13. D. Williams, *John Frost*, p. 240; also, Rachel O'Higgins, 'Ireland and Chartism' (unpublished M.A. thesis, Dublin University, 1959), p. 195.
14. John Saville, *1848: The British State and the Chartist Movement* (Cambridge, 1987), passim.
15. *Newcastle Weekly Chronicle*, 13 August 1898.
16. George Howell, *Ernest Jones, Chartist*, no pagination; The Marquis of Normandy, *A Year of Revolution* (London, 1857), vol. i, p. 315; David Goodway, *London Chartism* (Cambridge, 1982), p. 143.

17. H.O.45 2410 re electric telegraph.
18. J. W. Campbell, 'The Influence of the Revolutions of 1848 on Great Britain' (unpublished Ph.D. thesis, Georgia University, 1960), p. 236; *Hansard*, xcvii, pp. 136–7; Henry Weisser, *British Working Class Movement and Europe*, pp. 164–5.
19. *State Trials*, vol. vi, p. 1127. Liverpool assizes, 28 August 1848; *The Trial of Peter Murray McDouall*, published by W. P. Roberts; H.O.45 O.S.2410 A.225; R. Challinor, 'P. M. McDouall, Physical Force Chartist', *International Socialism* (1981), no. 12, pp. 77–80; *English Patriot and Irish Repealer*, 22 July 1848.
20. *The Trial of Peter Murray McDouall*, p. 2.
21. *Northern Star*, 30 September, 1848.
22. J. R. Lewis, *The Victorian Bar*, pp. 88–91, gives a fuller account of the problems of Sir John Jervis.
23. *Daily News*, 11 September 1848; *The Times*, 9 October 1848.
24. *The Reasoner*, 26 December 1849; *Reynolds' Poliical Instructor*, 12 March 1850.
25. F. C. Mather, *Public Order in the Age of the Chartists*, p.210, argues Powell committed deliberately provocative acts but questions whether the letter to O'Connor was authentic.
26. *Northern Star*, 20 January 1849.
27. A. J. Peacock, *Bradford Chartism* (York, 1969), p. 25; *The Times*, 31 May 1848; J. C. Belchem, 'The spy system in 1848: Chartists and informers – an Australian connection', *Labour History*, 39 (1980), pp. 15–27.
28. J. C. Belchem, op. cit., pp. 22–3.
29. T. Frost, *Forty Years Recollections* (London, 1880), pp. 167–8.

Chapter 12   Mid-century Malaise

1. *Reynolds Weekly Newspaper*, 5 May 1950; *Staffordshire Advertiser*, 4 May 1850.
2. *Northern Star*, 21 July 1850; *Reynolds' Weekly Newspaper*, 21 July 1850.
3. R. W. Proctor, *The Barber's Shop* (Manchester, 1856), p. 92; J. B. Leno, *The Aftermath* (London, 1892), pp. 54–5.
4. *Northern Star*, 1 October 1851.
5. *The Reasoner*, 16 September 1855.
6. *Notes to the People*, vol. ii, p. 923.
7. D. Read and E. Glasgow, *Feargus O'Conner, Irishman and Chartist* (London, 1961), pp. 139–43; D. Thompson, *The Chartists*, p. 389.
8. *Northern Star*, 3 February 1849 and 6 September 1851.
9. Ibid., 15 November 1851.
10. Ibid., 4 October 1851.
11. *People's Paper*, 6 August 1853; Alice M. Hatfield, *The Chartist Land Plan Company*, p. 54; *Dictionary of National Biography*, p. 1284; letter of Mr C. Fitzgerald, 10 November 1985; J. T. Ward, *Chartism* (London, 1973), p. 217; Dorothy Haigh, 'Heronsgate and the Chartist Land Scheme',

Hertfordshire Past and Present (1967), no. 7, pp. 19–26. Neither Hatfield nor Ward confront the testimony of W. H. Grey, the government's own accountant. In 1851, when he examined the Land Company's books, he pronounced them to be correct and in order.
12. *People's Paper*, 4 April 1857; J. T. Ward, *Chartism*, p. 271.
13. A letter from Martin Jude to T. W. Wheeler, 13 May 1851, quoted in *A Memoir of Thomas Martin Wheeler* (London, 1862), p. 57; *People's Paper*, 3 July 1852.
14. *People's Paper*, 9 May 1857.
15. *Northern Star*, 5 July 1851.
16. *People's Paper*, 4 April 1857 and 26 July 1858.
17. John Vincent (ed.), *The Political Diaries of Lord Stanley*, p. 79; Disraeli's aid quoted in David Jones, *Chartism and Chartists*, p. 122; George Howell, *Ernest Jones*, no pagination; B. Dawson, *Newcastle Weekly Chronicle*, 25 July 1891.
18. *People's Paper*, 4 February 1854.
19. J. Saville, *Ernest Jones: Chartist* (London, 1952), p. 40; Marx–Engels, *Collected Works*, vol. 18, p. 352.
20. *Bath Chronicle*, 6 August 1838.
21. Marx–Engels, *Collected Works*, vol. 27, p. 144.
22. Ibid., p. 533, note b; also Ernest Jones' letter to Karl Marx, 10 February 1860, ME.D2498 Amsterdam.
23. A recent example is David McLellan's biography of Marx, p. 312.
24. *Select Committee on Masters and Operatives*, 1860, App.3, p. 105.
25. *Manchester Times*, 9 June 1851.
26. *Manchester Guardian*, 5 October 1851.
27. *Select Committee on Masters and Operatives*, 1856, Q.23–26. Evidence of Thomas Winters.
28. *The Labour League*, 2 and 9 September 1848.
29. R. v Duffield and R. v Rowlands (1851), 5 Cox 404,436.
30. *Reynolds' Weekly Newspaper*, 3 August and 30 November 1851.
31. *People's Paper*, 22 May 1852; *Northern Star*, 4 October 1851; *Glasgow Sentinel*, 21 August 1851.
32. *Reynolds' Weekly Newspaper*, 3 November 1861; F. E. Gillespie, *Labour and Politics in England, 1850–1867*, p. 50.
33. *Select Committee on Masters and Operatives*, 1860, Q.29 Evidence of Edward Humphries.
34. Alan Anderson, 'The political symbolism of the labour laws', *Labour History Bulletin*, no. 23, autumn 1971.
35. R. Y. Hedges and Alan Winterbottom, *The Legal History of Trade Unions* (London, 1930), p. 59; R. v Druitt (10 Cox CC 592).
36. *Reynolds' Weekly Newspaper*, 30 November 1851; D. N. Pritt, *Law, Class and Society*, pp. 29–30.
37. J. R. Lewis, *The Victorian Bar*, p. 40.
38. C. Dickens, 'On strike', *Household Words*, 11 February 1854; also, *Miscellaneous Papers*, p. 431.
39. H. I. Dutton and J. E. King, *Ten Per Cent and No Surrender*, (Cambridge, 1981) for an account of the Preston lock-out.

40. *Reynolds Weekly Newspaper*, 2 April 1854.
41. R. Challinor, *The Lancashire & Cheshire Miners*, pp. 46–8, for an account of the Wigan strike.
42. *Wigan Observer*, 12 August 1854.
43. *People's Paper*, 12 November 1853.
44. *Preston Guardian*, 13 May 1854; *Preston Pilot*, 14 May 1854.

Chapter 13   The Collapse of Chartism

1. *People's Paper*, 12 November 1853. Full article reprinted in John Saville, *Ernest Jones: Chartist* (London, 1952), pp. 202–4.
2. *Manchester Guardian*, 11 March 1854; R. Challinor, *The Lancashire and Cheshire Miners*, p. 48.
3. *People's Paper*, 15 July 1854.
4. *Blackburn Standard*, 26 May and 16 June 1847.
5. *The British Miner*, 31 January 1863.
6. *Reynolds' Newspaper*, 4 June 1853.
7. *People's Paper*, 13 May 1854.
8. Friendly Society Act (18 & 19 Vict.c.63); George Howell, *Conflict of Capital and Labour* (London, 1890), pp. 473–4; *Lloyds Weekly Newspapers*, 1 January 1860.
9. Finlen quoted by Marx–Engels, *Collected Works*, vol. 14, p. 303.
10. *The Times*, 2 July 1855; also, Thomas Frost, 'An old man's recollections', *Newcastle Weekly Chronicle*, 8 October 1887, for participant's personal viewpoint.
11. Marx–Engels, *Collected Works*, vol. 14, pp. 302–7;, also p. 734, n.227.
12. Brian Harrison, 'The Sunday trading riots of 1855', *Historical Journal*, vol. viii (1965), pp. 222–6; and Brian Harrison, *Drink and the Victorians* (London, 1971) p. 390 for the long-term effects of the 1855 rioting.
13. Owen Jones' comments, Manchester Reference Library, MS F 923/2/J5.
14. John Frost, *The Horrors of Convict Life* (London and Manchester, 1856), pp. 11, 13–6.
15. Ibid., pp. 8–9.
16. *People's Paper*, 14 November 1857.
17. Ibid., 9 January 1853.
18. *Northern Star*, 6 January 1839; T. A. Devyr, *The Odd Book of the Nineteenth Century*, pp. 177–8.
19. See my article in *North East Labour History*, no. 16 (1982), pp. 28–32, for examples of Chartist upward mobility on Tyneside; P. W. Slossom, *The Decline of the Chartist Movement* (London, 1967), pp. 188–99; John Benson, *The Penny Capitalists*, p. 140.
20. *People's Paper*, 2 July 1853: 'Thomas Livesey, Esq., Chief Constable, in the chair. The chairman impressed on the meeting the truth and justice of The Charter and the necessity of re-organising the Movement.' John Elliott, former doorman of the Newcastle Chartist Club, was Chief Constable of Gateshead for many years. In 1886, when he received a

presentation for 30 years in that office, he thanked everyone present for the honour they had accorded him. But the greatest honour he had ever received was being introduced, many years before, to those magnificent revolutionaries, Garibaldi and Kossuth.

21. *The Weekly Times*, 13 February 1858.
22. *Wigan Observer*, 21 January 1859 and *Manchester Guardian*, 17 January 1859; Kate Tiller, 'Working Class Attitudes and Organisation in Three Industrial Towns', (unpublished Ph.D. thesis, Birmingham University, 1975), pp. 369–71, deals with the Wigan dispute in detail.
23. *Manchester Guardian*, 13 April, 16 April, 22 April and 27 April 1859. F. E. Gillespie, *Labour and Politicis in England, 1850–1867*, p. 167.
24. *Manchester Guardian*, 10 December 1859.
25. *The Cabinet Newspaper*, 10 January 1860.

Chapter 14   Back to the Coalfields

1. *Newcastle Weekly Chronicle*, 1 February 1850.
2. *People's Paper*, 13 April 1854; *Newcastle Weekly Chronicle*, 2 March 1882. It is indicative of the importance of the victory that it was recalled twenty-seven years later.
3. *Reynolds' Newspaper*, 4 September 1858.
4. Ibid., 25 September 1858.
5. *Newcastle Weekly Chronicle*, 24 September 1858; *Glasgow Herald*, 24 September 1858; *Gateshead Observer*, 24 September 1858.
6. National Association for the Promotion of Social Science, *Report on Trades Societies and Strikes* (published 1860, reprinted New York, 1968), pp. 34–5. The *Colliery Guardian*, of 21 August 1858, suggests that Roberts may first have come to an arrangement with the pitmen of Northumberland and Durham to be their legal adviser.
7. S. and B. Webb, *The History of Trade Unionism*, pp. 304–6; R. Page Arnot, *The Miners*, vol. i, p. 46.
8. *Glasgow Sentinel*, 19 March 1859; Gordon M. Wilson, *Alexander MacDonald: Leader of the Miners* (Aberdeen, 1982), p. 98.
9. *Newcastle Weekly Chronicle*, 19 March 1859.
10. *The Cabinet Newspaper*, 9 July 1859.
11. *Report on Trade Societies and Strikes*, p. 41; Gordon M. Wilson, *Alexander MacDonald*, p. 98.
12. Walsby v Auley, e E1 & E1 516, 517 (1861).
13. R. Postgate, *The Builders' History* (London, 1923), p. 160.
14. C. W. Sutton entry on W. P. Roberts (Manchester Reference Library).
15. H.O. O.S.3272; John Benson, *British Coalminers in the Nineteenth Century* (Dublin, 1980), pp. 74–5.
16. Mrs Roberts kept a personal account of their journey, which Mr C. Fitzgerald has in his possession.
17. Gordon M. Wilson, *Alexander MacDonald*, pp. 53–7; Royden Harrison, *Before the Socialists* (London, 1965), pp. 292–7; R. Challinor, *Alexander*

MacDonald and the Miners, 1969, passim; John Benson, op. cit., pp. 18–19.

18. *Miners' & Workmen's Advocate,* 10 October 1863.
19. Ibid., 27 February 1864.
20. Ibid.
21. Ibid., 5 March 1864; G. W. Hilton, *The Truck System* (Cambridge, 1964), pp. 121–3 details the crippling costs confronting workers contemplating taking any action.
22. *Miners & Workmen's Advocate,* 5 March 1864.
23. Ibid., 27 February 1864; George Howell, *Labour Legislation, Labour Movements, Labour Leaders,* p. 151.
24. *Miners' & Workmen's Advocate,* 27 February 1864.
25. Ibid., 5 March 1864.
26. Ibid., 12 March 1864.
27. *The Beehive,* 30 July 1864.
28. *Miners' & Workmen's Advocate,* 20 February 1864.
29. *The Beehive,* 14 January 1865.
30. R. Fynes, *The Miners of Northumberland and Durham,* p. 239.
31. Ibid., p. 239; R. Challinor, *Alexander MacDonald and the Miners,* p. 13.
32. *Miners' & Workmen's Advocate,* 16 July 1864.
33. William Smith, *Old Yorkshire* (Leeds, 1894), vol. iii, pp. 57–9; *Leeds Mercury,* 9 June 1894; *Miners' & Workmen's Advocate,* 18 March 1865; *The Beehive,* 18 March 1865.
34. *Report on Trades Societies and Strikes* (1860), op. cit., p. 37n and p. 41; George Howell, op. cit., p. 138.
35. *Miners' & Workmen's Advocate,* 20 and 27 August 1864.
36. *The Beehive,* 12 November 1864.
37. *Miners' & Workmen's Advocate,* 11 March 1865, and *The Beehive,* 18 March 1965. Gordon M. Wilson, op. cit., p. 209, criticizes my booklet *Alexander MacDonald and the Miners.*
38. *The Beehive,* 12 November 1864.
39. Ibid., 26 November 1864.
40. R. Fynes, op. cit., pp. 241–2; Chris Fisher and Patrick Spaven, 'Edward Rymer and "the moral worker"' in Royden Harrison (ed.), *Independent Collier* (Brighton, 1978), pp. 238–9.

Chapter 15   The Manchester Martyrs

1. *Reynold's Newspaper,* 6 October 1867.
2. Antony Glyn, *High on the Gallows Tree* (Tralee, Co. Kerry), p. 60.
3. *Manchester Guardian* 5 October 1867.
4. Henry Mayhew, *London Labour and the London Poor,* vol. iv, p. 32.
5. The account was given me by the late Canon Roberts and Mr C. Fitzgerald, descendants of W. P. Roberts.
6. *The Times,* 25 October 1867.
7. *Our Corner,* 1 May 1884.

8. Ibid.
9. See *The Murder of Sergeant Brett: a full report* (Manchester, 1867). For more general background see Kevin B. Nowlan, 'The Fenian uprising of 1867' in T. W. Moody (ed.) *The Fenian Movement* (Cork, 1968), pp. 23–37.
10. Paul Rose, *The Manchester Martyrs* (London, 1970), pp. 65–7.
11. *The Murder of Sergeant Brett*, pp. 45–50.
12. *Manchester Guardian*, 17 November 1867.
13. Patrick Quinlivan and Paul Rose, *The Fenians in England*, pp. 57–8.
14. *Our Corner*, 1 May 1884.
15. Marx–Engels, *Selected Correspondence*, p. 195.
16. *Marx–Engels on Ireland*, p. 145.
17. Patrick Quinlivan and Paul Rose, *The Fenians in England*, p. 142; K. R. M. Short, *The Dynamite War* (Dublin, 1979), pp. 8–10; Douglas D. G. Browne, *The Rise of Scotland Yard* (London, 1964), p. 142. Bernard Porter shows in his book, *The Origins of the Vigilant State* (London, 1987), p. 8 that the Clerkenwell fiasco hastened the formation of the Special Branch.
18. David Ascoli, *The Queen's Peace* (London, 1956), p. 134.
19. *Reynolds' Newspaper*, 28 January 1868; *The Beehive*, 30 January 1868.
20. West Middlesex Coroner's Court Register. 1867; Patrick Quinlivan and Paul Rose, *The Fenians in England*, p. 105; *Reynolds' Newspaper*, 1 March 1868; *Islington Gazette*, 29 December 1867.
21. Patrick Quinlivan and Paul Rose, op. cit., p. 115.
22. *New Law Journal*, vol. 13, p. 270, 17 April 1868.
23. A. H. Manchester, *Modern Legal History*, p. 200.
24. Patrick Quinlivan and Paul Rose, op. cit., pp. 119–120.
25. F. Sheeny-Skeffington, *Michael Davitt: revolutionary agitator and labour leader* (London, 1908), p. 37.
26. Interestingly, R. M. Pankhurst came from a family with strong radical-democratic sympathies. His mother's family had attended the Peterloo demonstration. He had been christened Richard Marsden after the delegate for Preston and Chorley to the first Chartist convention. Sylvia Pankhurst named her son Richard Marsden Pankhurst, who later wrote a biography of William Thompson (1775–1833), a pioneer socialist, feminist and co-operator. So remarkably, for almost 200 years, but spanning only four generations, the Pankhursts have struggled in the people's interests, for greater public accountability and democracy.

Chapter 16   The Final Tragedy and Ultimate Triumph

1. George Howell, *Labour Legislation, Labour Movements, Labour Leaders*, p. 151 and Harry McShane, *Glasgow Trades Council: 100 years of progress* (Glasgow, 1958), pp. 9–10.
2. Christopher J. Kauffman, 'Lord Elcho, trade unionism and democracy' in Kenneth Brown (ed.), *Essays in Anti-Labour History*, pp. 198–207.
3. *Wigan Observer*, 13 January 1865; Raymond Challinor, *Lancashire and Cheshire Miners*, p. 69.

4. *Select Committee on the Master and Servant Acts* (1866), W. P. Roberts gave evidence on 12 June 1866. Q.1662–4.

5. Ibid., Q.1665.

6. Ibid., Q.1667 and 1774–8.

7. Ibid., Q.1651, 1681, 1659.

8. Daphne Simon, 'Master and Servant' in John Saville (ed.), *Democracy and the Labour Movement* (London, 1954), p. 184.

9. Theresa M. McBride, *The Domestic Revolution* (London, 1976), pp. 26–7.

10. Daphne Simon, 'Master and Servant', Q.1650–1.

11. *Master and Servant Act, 1867* (30 & 31 Vict, c 141).

12. It was superseded by legislation with a more even-handed title: *Employer and Workers Act, 1875* (38 & 39 Vict, c 90).

13. Daphne Simon, op. cit., pp. 190–2.

14. John Wilson, *A History of the Durham Miners' Association* (Durham, 1907), pp. 3–9, for an account of the Wearmouth strike; also, Sidney Webb, *The Story of the Durham Miners* (London, 1921). pp. 59–60.

15. *Newcastle Chronicle*, 22 June 1869.

16. Ibid., 10 July 1869.

17. *Our Corner*, 1 May 1884, p. 263. Part of Annie Besant's serialized autobiography; also, David Tribe, *President Charles Bradlaugh, MP*, (London, 1971), p. 157.

18. E. Welbourne, *The Miners of Northumberland and Durham* (Cambridge, 1923), p. 145.

19. The open letter to George Potter, William Allan, Alexander MacDonald and others interested in trade societies, published 18 March 1871.

20. A. E. Musson, *Trade Unions and Social History* (London, 1974), pp. 55–6; H. Samuel, *Trade Union Law* (London, 1966), p. 2; N. A. Citrine, *Trade Union Law* (London, 1950), pp. 11–12.

21. Hornby v Close (1867) L R 2 Q.B., 153; also Farrar v Close. In his essay 'The law of strikes, 1847–1871', p. 140, John V. Orth says he thinks that these decisions may properly be described as judicial aggression.

22. Open letter, p. 15. Roberts claimed successful action had been taken at the assizes, under Common and Statute Law, against defaulters.

23. Boilermakers' Society Monthly Reports, 30 December 1865 and 31 January 1866.

24. R v Bunn (12 Cox CC 316); H. Pelling, *A History of British Trade Unionism* (Harmondsworth, 1976), p. 74.

25. *Manchester Evening News*, 9 September 1871, referred to him 'lying dangerously ill in the city'. *Manchester Examiner and Times*, 12 September 1871 and *Manchester City News*, 16 September 1871.

Selected Bibliography

PRIMARY SOURCES

Collections of Documents

Bell and Buddle Collections, Northumberland Public Records Office.
Cowen Collection, Tyne and Wear Public Records Office.
History of the Coal Trade (12 vols.), Picton Library, Liverpool.
Howell Collection, Bishopsgate Institute, London.
Lovett Collection, Birmingham Central Library.
Jones, Ernest: correspondence, International Institute of Social History, Amsterdam; legal papers and scrapbook, Manchester Central Library; prison letters and appeal for funds, Chetham's Library, Manchester.
Londonderry. Third Marquis of, Papers, Durham Public Records Office.
Lovett Collection, Birmingham Central Library.
Minikin–Vincent papers, Labour Party headquarters, London.
North-East Strike of 1844 Collection, Newcastle-upon-Tyne Public Library.
Pitmen's Strike Collection, Wigan Public Library.
Place Collection, British Library.
Official Papers, Public Records Office:–
Disturbance Books, H.O.40,41,45,46.
Law and Order, H.O.43,44,48,50,51,79.
Social Papers relating to the Chartist Land Plan, Board of Trade 41 and Chancery Records C.101, C.121 and C.36.
State Trials, T.S.11.
Prison Correspondence and Papers, H.O.20,21.
Taylor, Dr John, Papers relating to the authorities' surveillance of him in the Gray Collection, Priors Kitchen, Durham Cathedral and Tyne and Wear Public Records Office.
Trade Societies and Strikes, National Association for the Promotion of Social Science (1860), reprinted New York 1968.

Newspapers and Periodicals

Newspapers: *Bath Chronicle, Bath & Cheltenham Gazette, Bath Figaro, Bath*

Guardian, Bath Herald, Bath Journal, Birmingham Journal, Blackburn Standard, Bolton Chronicle, Bolton Free Press, Bradford Observer, Bristol Mercury, Bristol Times, Derbyshire Courier, Devizes Gazette, Durham Chronicle, Durham Gazette, Gateshead Observer, Glasgow Sentinel, Islington Gazette, Leeds Times, Leeds Mercury, Lloyds' Weekly Newspaper, Manchester Chronicle & Salford Advertiser, Manchester City News, Manchester Evening News, Manchester Examiner & Times, Manchester Guardian, Monmouth Merlin, Newcastle Courant, Newcastle Journal, Newcastle Weekly Chronicle, North Staffordshire Mercury, Preston Chronicle, Preston Guardian, Preston Pilot, Reynolds' Weekly Newspaper, Sheffield Independent, Sheffield Iris, Staffordshire Advertiser, Staffordshire Mercury, The Times, Tyne Mercury, Weekly Times, Wigan Observer, Wiltshire Independent

Journals and Periodicals: *The Beehive, The British Miner, The Cabinet Newspaper, The Chainmakers' Journal, The Charter, Chartist Circular, Colliery Guardian, Cooper's Journal, Democratic Review, Flint Glass Makers' Magazine, Fraser's Magazine, Illustrated London News, The Labourer, The Labour League, Miners' Advocate, Miners' & Workmen's Advocate, Miners' Journal, Miners' Magazine, New Law Journal, Northern Democrat, Northern Liberator, Northern Star, Northern Tribune, Notes to the People, The People, People's Paper, The Potters' Examiner and Workmen's Advocate, Punch, The Reasoner, Red Republican, Reynolds Political Instructor, Weekly True Sun, Western Vindicator*

Parliamentary Papers and other Official Publications

Select Committee on the Combination of Workmen, 1837–8.
Children's Employment Commission, 1842.
Select Committee on the Payment of Wages, 1842.
The Midlands Mining Commission, 1843.
Reports of H.M. Inspector Mines and Quarries, 1844–71.
Parliamentary Report on Accidents in Coal Mines, 1849.
Select Committee on the Stoppage of Wages, 1854–5.
Select Committee on Masters and Operatives, 1856.
Select Committee on Masters and Operatives, 1860.
Royal Commission on the Master and Servants Act, 1867.
Royal Commission on Trade Unions, 1867–9.

SECONDARY SOURCES

Abel-Smith, Brian and Stevens, Robert, *Lawyers and the Courts*, London, 1973.
Abraham, Gerald, *Trade Unions and the Law*, London, 1968.
Antrobus, E. A., *London: its dangers and its safety*, London, 1848.

Ascoli, *The Queen's Peace*, London, 1956.
Bagwell, Phillip, *Industrial Relations*, Dublin, 1974.
Briggs, Asa (ed.), *Chartist Studies*, London, 1959.
Brockie, William, *Sunderland Notables*, Sunderland, 1894.
Browne, Douglas G., *The Rise of Scotland Yard*, London, 1964.
Burn, W. L., *The Age of Equipoise*, London, 1964.
Bythell, Duncan, *The Handloom Weavers*, Cambridge, 1969.
Cannon, John A., *The Chartists in Bristol*, London, 1964.
Challinor, Raymond, *Alexander MacDonald and the Miners*, 1969.
    The Lancashire and Cheshire Miners, Newcastle, 1972.
Challinor, R and Ripley, B., *The Miners' Association: A Trade Union in the Age of the Chartists*, London, 1968.
Colls, Robert, *The Collier's Rant*, London, 1977.
    The Great Northern Coalfield, Manchester, 1987.
Dent, Robert K., *Old and New Birmingham*, Birmingham, 1880.
Duckham, F. Baron, *A History of the Scottish Coal Industry, 1700–1815*, Newton Abbot, 1975.
Duffy, C. G., *Young Ireland*, Shannon, 1969.
Dunn, Matthias, *The Northern Coal Trade*, Newcastle, 1844.
Dutton, H. I. and King, J. E., *Ten Per Cent and No Surrender*, Cambridge, 1981.
Emsley, Clive, *Policing and its Context, 1750–1870*, London, 1983.
Faulkner, H. U., *Chartism and the Churches*, London, 1970.
Foster, John, *Class Struggles and the Industrial Revolution*, London, 1974.
Fraser, W. H. *Labour Relations and the Courts of Scotland*, n.d.
    Trade Unions and Society, London, 1974.
Fynes, Richard, *The Miners of Northumberland and Durham*, Sunderland, 1873.
Gammage, Richard G., *History of the Chartist Movement*, London, 1854.
Gill, Conrad, *A History of Birmingham*, Oxford, 1962.
Glyn, Antony, *High on the Gallows Tree*, Tralee, Co.Kerry.
Goodway, David, *London Chartism*, Cambridge, 1982.
Goodwin, Albert, *The Friends of Liberty*, London, 1979.
Griffiths, J. A. G., *The Politics of the Judiciary*, London, 1978.
Harding, Alan, *A Social History of English Law*, London, 1973.
Harrison, Brian, *Drink and the Victorians*, London, 1971.
Harrison, Royden, *Before the Socialists*, London, 1965.
Harrison, Royden (ed.), *Independent Collier*, Brighton, 1978.
Hilton, G. W., *The Truck System*, Cambridge, 1964.
Hobsbawm, Eric, *Labouring Men*, London, 1964.
Hobsbawm, Eric, and George Rudé, *Captain Swing*, London, 1968.
Hodges, R. Y., and Winterbottom, Allan, *The Legal History of Trade Unions*, London, 1930.
Holdsworth, W. S., *Dickens as a Legal Historian*, New York, 1972.
Hollis, Patricia, *The Pauper Press: a study of working class radicalism in the 1830s*, Oxford, 1970.
Hovell, Mark, *The Chartist Movment*, Manchester, 1970.

Howell, George, *Labour Legislation, Labour Movements, Labour Leaders*, London, 1902.

Jeffreys, J. B., *The Story of the Engineers*, London, 1946.

Jenkins, Mick, *The General Strike of 1842*, London, 1980.

Jones, David, *The Last Rising: the Newport insurrection of 1839*, Oxford, 1985.

    Chartism and the Chartists, London, 1975.

Jones, G. Stedman, *Language of Class: studies in working class history, 1832–1982*, Cambridge, 1983.

Joyce, Patrick, *Work, Society and Politics: the culture of the factory in late Victorian England*, Brighton, 1980.

Leno, J. B., *The Aftermath*, London, 1892.

Lewis, J. R. *The Victorian Bar*, London, 1982.

Keith-Lucas, Bryan, *The Unreformed Local Government System*, London, 1980.

Kirk, Nevill, *The Growth of Working-Class Reformism in Mid-Victorian England*, London, 1985.

McBride, Theresa M., *The Domestic Revolution*, London, 1976.

McLellan, David, *Karl Marx: his Life and his Thoughts*, London, 1973.

McShane, Harry, *Glasgow Trade Council: 100 years of progress*, Glasgow, 1958.

Manchester, A. H., *The Modern Legal System*, London, 1980.

Marlow, Joyce, *The Tolpuddle Martyrs*, London, 1985.

Mather, F. C., *Chartism and Society*, London, 1980.

    Public Order in the Age of the Chartists, London, 1980.

Napier, Priscilla, *Revolution and the Napier Brothers*, London, 1973.

Neale, R. S., *Bath 1680–1850: a social history*, London, 1985.

    Class and Ideology in the Nineteenth Century, London, 1972.

    Class and Ideology in a Provincial City: Bath, 1800–1850, London, 1966.

Odger, Blake, *Digest of the Law of Libel and Slander*, London, 1892.

Page Arnot, R., *The Miners: Years of Struggle*, London, 1959.

    The Scottish Miners, From the Earliest Times, London, 1955.

    South Welsh Miners: Glowry De Cymru, London, 1967.

Peacock, A. J., *Bradford Chartism*, York, 1969.

Pelling, Henry, *A History of British Trade Unionism*, Harmondsworth, 1976.

    Popular Politics and Society in late Victorian Britain, London, 1968.

Porter, Bernard, *The Origins of the Vigilant State*, London, 1987.

Postgate, Raymond, *The Builders' History*, London, 1923.

Pritt, D. N., *Law, Class and Society*, London, 1970.

Quinlivan, Patrick and Rose, Paul, *The Fenians in England, 1865–1872*, London, 1982.

Radzinowicz, Leon, *A History of English Criminal Law*, London, 1968.

Rose, Paul, *The Manchester Martyrs*, London, 1970.

Rosenblatt, Frank F., *The Chartist Movement in its Social and Political Aspects*, London, 1967.

Rudé, George, *Criminal and Victim*, Oxford, 1984.

    The Crowd in History, 1730–1848, New York, 1964.

The Crowd in London and Paris, London, 1975.

Protest and Punishment, Oxford, 1978.

Saville, John, *1848: The British State and the Chartist Movement*, Cambridge, 1987.

Scott, Hylton, *The Miners' Bond in Northumberland and Durham*, Newcastle, 1947.

Shelton, W. J., *English Hunger and Industrial Disorders*, London, 1973.

Short, K. R. M., *The Dynamite War*, Dublin, 1979.

Slosson, Preston William, *The Decline of the Chartist Movement*, London, 1967.

Smith, C. Woodham, *The Great Hunger: Ireland, 1945–9*, London, 1962.

Smith, William, *Old Yorkshire*, Leeds, 1894.

Stevenson, John, *Popular Disturbances in England, 1700–1870*, London, 1979.

Stevenson, John, and Quinault, R., *Popular Protest and Public Order*, London, 1974.

Sweezy, P., *Monopoly and Competition in the English Coal Trade, 1550–1850*, Harvard, 1938.

Tholfsen, T. R., *Working-Class Radicalism in Mid-Victorian England*, London, 1976.

Thomas, William, *The Philosophical Radicals*, Oxford, 1979.

Thomis, M. I. and Holt, P., *Threats of Revolution in England, 1789–1848*, London, 1977.

Thompson, Dorothy, *The Early Chartists*, London, 1971.

The Chartists, London, 1984.

Thompson, Edward, *The Making of the English Working Class*, London, 1962.

Tobias, J. J., *Crime and Industrial Society in the Nineteenth Century*, Newton Abbot, 1972.

Ward, J. T., *The Factory Movement, 1830–55*, London, 1962.

Chartism, London, 1973.

Wearmouth, Robert, *Some Working Class Movements of the Nineteenth Century*, London, 1948.

Methodism and the Struggle of the Working Classes, 1850–1900, Leicester, 1954.

Webb, Sidney, *The Story of the Durham Miners*, London, 1921.

Wedderburn, K. W., *Cases and Materials in Labour Law*, Cambridge, 1967.

Welbourne, E., *The Miners' Unions of Northumberland and Durham*, Cambridge, 1923.

Williams, D. J., *Capitalist Combinations in the Coal Industry*, London, 1924.

Williams, J. E., *The Derbyshire Miners*, London, 1962.

Wilson, John, *A History of the Durham Miners*, Durham, 1907.

Biographies, Autobiographies and Memoirs

Adams, W. E., *Memoirs of a Social Atom*, London, 1903 and New York, 1968.

Armytage, W. H. G., *A. J. Mundella, 1825–97: the Liberal background to the labour movement*, London, 1951.

Bent, James, *Criminal Life: 42 years in the Lancashire Constabulary*, Manchester, 1891.

Belchem, John, *'Orator' Hunt*, Oxford, 1985.

Bernson, A. C., and Viscount Esher (eds), *The Letters of Queen Victoria*, London, 1907.

Bruce, H. A., *Life of Sir William Napier*, London, 1864.

Burt, Thomas, *From Pitman to Privy Councillor*, London, 1924.

Cole, G. D. H., *Chartist Portraits*, London, 1965.

Cooper, Thomas, *Life of Thomas Cooper*, London, 1872.

Devyr, Thomas Ainge, *The Odd Book of the Nineteenth Century*, New York, 1881.

Driver, C., *Tory Radical: the life of Robert Oastler*, Oxford, 1946.

Epstein, James, *Feargus O'Connor: The Lion of Freedom*, London, 1982.

Frost, John, *The Horrors of Convict Life*, London and Manchester, 1856.

Frost, Thomas, *Forty Years Recollections*, London, 1880.

Hallam, William, *Miners' Leaders: thirty portraits and biographical sketches*, London, 1894.

Hardcastle, Mrs (ed.), *Autobiography of Lord Campbell*, London, 1887.

Harrison, J. F. C., *Robert Owen and the Owenites in Britain and America*, London, 1969.

Howell, George, *Ernest Jones: Chartist*, Weekly Chronicle, Newcastle, 1889.

Holyoake, G. J., *Joseph Rayner Stephens*, London, 1881.

Kirby, R. G., and Musson, A. E., *The Voice of the People: John Doherty, 1798–1854*, Manchester, 1975.

Lovett, William, *Life and Struggles of William Lovett*, London, 1967.

Miller, Henry (ed.), *Memoirs of Dr Robert Blakey*, London, 1879.

Napier, Priscilla, *Revolution and the Napier brothers, 1820–1840*, London, 1973.

Napier, William, *Life and Opinions of General Sir Charles Napier*, London, 1857.

Patterson, H. W., *Sir Francis Burdett and his Times, 1770–1844*, London, 1931.

Read, Donald, and Glasgow, Eric, *Feargus O'Connor, Irishman and Chartist*, London, 1961.

Saville, John, *Ernest Jones, Chartist*, London, 1952.

Schoyen, A. R., *G. J. Harney: the Chartist challenge*, London, 1958.

Williams, David, *John Frost*, Cardiff, 1939.

Articles

Belchem, John, '1848, Feargus O'Connor and the collapse of the mass platform' in J. Epstein and D. Thompson (eds), *The Chartist Experience*, London, 1982.

Epstein, John, 'Feargus O'Connor and the Northern Star', *International Review of Social History*, xxxi, 1976.

Field, John, 'Police, power and community in a provincial English town: Portsmouth 1815–1875' in V. Bailey (ed.), *Policing and Punishment in the Nineteenth Century*, London, 1971.

Fyson, Bob, 'The crisis of 1842', in J. Epstein and D. Thompson (eds), *The Chartist Experience*, London, 1982.

Godfrey, C., 'The Chartist prisoners, 1840–41', *International Review of Social History*, xxiv, 1979.

Godfrey, C., and Epstein, J., 'Interviews of Chartist prisoners, 1840–41', *Labour History Bulletin*, Spring, 1977.

Hobsbawm, Eric, 'The British standard of living, 1790–1850', *Economic History Review*, 2nd series, August 1957.

Johnson, Carol, 'The problems of reformism and Marx's theory of fetishism', *New Left Review*, no. 119, Jan–Feb.1980.

Jones, G. Stedman, 'Class struggle and the Industrial Revolution', *New Left Review*, no. 90, March-April 1975.

Mather, F. C., 'The government and the Chartists', in Asa Briggs (ed.), *Chartist Studies*, London, 1959.

O'Higgins, Rachel, 'The Irish influence in the Chartist movement', *Past and Present*, no. 20, 1961.

Phillips, David, 'Riots and public order in the Black Country' in R. Quinault and J. Stevenson (eds), *Popular Protest and Public Order*, London, 1974.

Pugh, R. B., 'Chartism in Somerset and Wiltshire', in Asa Briggs (ed.), *Chartist Studies*, London, 1959.

Radzinowicz, Leon, 'New departures in maintaining public order in the face of Chartist disturbances', *Cambridge Law Journal*, 1960.

Samuels, Ralph, 'The workshop of the world: steam power and hand technology in mid-Victorian Britain', *History Workshop*, no. 3, 1977.

Saville, John, 'Chartism and the year of revolution, 1848', *Modern Quarterly*, viii, winter 1951–2.

'The Christian Socialists of 1848', in J. Saville (ed.), *Democracy and the Labour Movement*, London, 1954.

Simon, Daphne, 'Master and Servant', in J. Saville (ed.), *Democracy and the Labour Movement*, London, 1954.

Storch, R. D., 'The policeman as a domestic missionary: urban discipline and popular culture in Northern England, 1850–1880', *Journal of Social History*, ix, Summer 1967.

Tholfsen, 'The Chartist crisis in Birmingham', *International Review of Social History*, 1958.

Thompson, Dorothy, 'Ireland and the Irish in English radicalism before 1850', in J. Epstein and D. Thompson (eds), *The Chartist Experience*, London, 1982.

Wilson, A., 'Chartism in Glasgow', in Asa Briggs (ed.), *Chartist Studies*, London, 1959.

Weisser, Henry, 'Chartism in 1848: reflections on a non-revolution', *Albion*, xiii, Spring 1981.

Index